# THE MAKING OF
# AN ASSASSIN

# THE MAKING OF AN ASSASSIN:

*The Life of James Earl Ray*

by George McMillan

**LITTLE, BROWN AND COMPANY**
**BOSTON — TORONTO**

FIRST EDITION

T10/76


The author acknowledges Delacorte Press
for the permission to reprint excerpts from
*He Slew the Dreamer* by William Bradford Huie.
Copyright © 1968, 1969, 1970 by William
Bradford Huie.


LIBRARY OF CONGRESS CATALOGING IN PUBLICATION DATA

McMillan, George.
    The making of an assassin.

    Includes index.
    1. Ray, James Earl, 1928–     I. Title.
HV6248.R39M33   364.15′24′0924 [B]   76–18685
ISBN 0–316–56241–6


Designed by Janis Capone

*Published simultaneously in Canada
by Little, Brown & Company (Canada) Limited*

PRINTED IN THE UNITED STATES OF AMERICA

For Scilla

# Preface

This is the biography of an American, an American assassin. He hated passionately, hated enough to kill, to kill without help someone he did not know, to slay an abstraction.

The geography of that hatred is domestic. We cannot deny to James Earl Ray his American heritage. The roots of his crime were seeded in our native soil and nourished within our familiar landscape. He shared our common life and *he* believed he shared our common ideals. Our national history, our politics, our economics, our traditions and our uniquely American social systems and social classes — *these* are the elements that conspired to produce his murderous act.

This is an American story.

# Chapter 1

In the fall of 1926 George and Lucille Ray set out on a honeymoon — and to make a new life if they could — in Florida. They were operating on a characteristic American assumption: that the grass is greener someplace else, greener than it was where they had come from: Soulard, a white slum behind the breweries in St. Louis.

His name was Ray — and it wasn't. He went by a dozen names; usually a variation with the letter "n" in it, like Rayns or Raynes, and very often he preferred, perhaps as more lilting, the name Jerry over George.

His nickname was Speedy, a joke. He spoke so slowly that he seemed to have an impediment; this often led people to think that he was a Southerner. His physical movements were not so much deliberate as wary, measured out by his suspicion of almost everything in the world around him.

He was a small fellow, a belligerent little bantam whose approach to people was that of the folk song:

> *I'm lookin' for the bully,*
> *The bully of the town.*
> *I'm lookin' for the bully,*
> *I'm gonna knock him down!*

He wasn't looking for trouble . . . oh, no, not Speedy! . . . but in fact he saw trouble everywhere. Of all the things Speedy was suspicious of one of the most was women. He had put off marrying and now that he had married he was not at all sure that he had done the right thing. Women were emotional, and it was emotions that Ray seemed to live in deepest apprehension of.

Perhaps that was the reason that he had gone ahead and married Lucille Maher. He had no language, at best only an inarticulate impulse with which to signal any emotion he may have felt for his bride, and "Ceal" was one of the few women he had ever met who did not seem to need that reassurance. She was almost mute, an indistinct, quiet, broad-cheeked, raw-boned woman, with deep-sunk enigmatic, almost expressionless eyes.

Speedy and Ceal were equipped in their fashion for travel and for settlement in the new land to which they were journeying. They possessed a Sterno stove on which to heat up the new husband's favorite dish, a bowl of chili beans. And they owned two World War I surplus tents, one a wall tent in which they intended to make their new home, the other a pup tent under which they slept along the side of the road, wherever they pulled up for the night. As a means of transportation they had a 1922 Studebaker touring car with isinglass windows that could be mounted in the doors in case of rain. The car had cost $24.

It was a jalopy, and the hope that it would carry them the distance they wished to travel lay not in its intrinsic quality but in Speedy's ingrained and typically American ability to fix it, to improvise its repair, to keep it on the road moving. In fact, Speedy loved cars and had made a kind of living in St. Louis running what might be called, by stretching the words, a used car business. Not that he had a *place* of business. He was a street corner trader. He would buy himself an old car or two, or haul in one he might find abandoned on the street. He would sell you parts off a car, sell you a car as is, or fix it up and sell it to you. You might, in those days, get a car off him for as little as $15. He had reduced the style of auto merchandising to the level of the bazaar, and he loved to trade. "When I was in the car business," Ray remembers, "I bought cars for two dollars and a half apiece, drove them home, see? One time I bought a Dodge and a Willys for a five dollar bill. Drove 'em home and sold the Willys for fifteen dollars. They were damned good cars, too. I used to wreck 'em too, trucks and stuff like that there. Any way to make money."

In 1926 everybody who could put wheels under him was heading for Florida. One of those characteristic American happenings was going on: a boom, the hope of something for nothing, the chance to make a fast buck. Florida had become something more than merely sand: it was "running feet" of beach frontage, "gold coasts" made from pink stucco mirages. Speedy's father had bought a tract of that Florida land and Speedy was going down to see what he could make of the situation. The couple chugged south in their Studebaker more or less following the course of the Mississippi, down through Memphis and Jackson and then southwestward to their destination which was not Miami, not Palm Beach, but a town called Wewahitchka. The thirty acres of land there had cost his father $10 an acre, a purchase to be found on the records of Gulf County, Florida, as a parcel in "the northwest corner of Section 36, Township 3, Range 10 West."

Wewahitchka is in the Florida panhandle on the Gulf Coast — nearer Mississippi than Miami. There were no running feet of beach in Wewahitchka; the frontage was swamp made unsatisfactory for swimming or sunbathing by the knees of cypress trees and the unwelcoming stares of water moccasins. Wewahitchka was famous for these black water "dead lakes" into which the Apalachicola River flowed as it passed to the Gulf. Once an Indian trading post, Wewahitchka had a brief history before the Civil War as a sanctuary for runaway slaves. But after the Civil War the place took on a definitely "southern" character when Confederate veterans from Georgia settled there, drawn by the easy subtropical life and the good fishing. Somebody once planted an orange grove, but Wewahitchka was really too far north for citrus-growing, and the people had resigned themselves to live on what little money they could make out of turpentine and tupelo honey. Such were the states of the unpaved sand roads at the time the Rays went south that the easiest line of communication was still the river. Two riverboats, *The Little Belle* and the *Calhoun,* plied from the Gulf up to Columbus, Georgia.

The only improvement on the Ray land was an abandoned,

rotting one-room building known as the old Buckhorn School, and it is difficult to figure out what Ray hoped to do with his thirty acres and old schoolhouse.

"I had two tents, pup tent and this big tent — we stretched that down there on this land I had," Speedy has said. "We were gonna clean it off. They had a big schoolhouse on the corner there. What I should have done was move in there. It was *mine,* you know. But I never thought about that. I ought to have cleaned that up and made a house out of it. That's what I was going to do, build a new house on there."

But he did nothing with the land, and he did not build a house. It was not that he was lazy. His life had brought about in him a distrust of the commonly accepted values about work; he did not have the kind of confidence in the supposed rewards for work that would cause him to make a sustained vocational commitment. Thus the Florida land project was like other projects Ray undertook which called for long-range effort. It was doomed at the outset; its failure was built into its very concept.

Nor did he find his new wife quite the helper he had thought she might be. "I got some ham down there," he has recalled. "Fresh meat, they had to cook it and sell it 'cause it got full of worms. They didn't have any refrigeration down there in Florida. But everything Ceal cooked, she burned up. But she couldn't cook much, I guess, on a can [Sterno burner]."

And Ceal did have expectations. She wanted *things.* "She wanted to get some clothes. So I said, go down and get you a couple of *house* dresses. It wasn't no place for dress dresses. But she went out and got a voile dress and gave 'em fourteen dollars for it. She had to have them silk stockings all the time out there in them goddam weeds. Every day she'd tear up a pair of them stockings and they cost two and a half or three dollars a pair down there. I didn't *go* with that kind of shit, see."

The fact is that neither of them was *practical*, and Ceal was not, in her way, any more capable of sustained, directed effort than he was. Yet he had a certain admiration for Ceal, for women, for their absurdity, for their very inconsequentiality. "Hell," he said, with obvious pleasure at the recollection, "one night she put on that goddamned dress . . . wasn't nothing to it. Women *like* them things, see."

What Speedy did, instead of doing all the things he told himself, and Ceal, that he meant to do, was get into what he calls "the whiskey business." There is simply no telling — he will not tell — what this meant. There was rum-running in the Gulf; William Faulkner, the writer, was in that kind of whiskey business for a while. And Ray already had experience in making whiskey at a still, in selling it by the drink in piccolo joints in the dark alleys and back streets of a dozen southern and middle western towns.

This went on for some time, this work in the whiskey business, until, says Ray, "Ceal got to where she couldn't get her breath." That may have happened. The gap between the organic and the functional medical distress is often almost indistinguishable with people like the Rays, and they seldom go to doctors. However, one medical fact was incontestable. Ceal was going to have a child. When she told Speedy, he did not welcome the news. He did not like it. One of the reasons he hadn't married was that he didn't "want to bring any children into the world." The world was a wicked place, no fit place for children. It certainly had not been a fit place for *him* when he was a child.

Whatever his pleasure in the matter, Ceal and Speedy conceived their first child in Florida; that was Speedy's achievement there.

# Chapter 2

Sometime during the year 1865 a man of "considerable personal address" named Henry Plummer turned up in the Montana gold mining town of Bannack.

In 1865 Bannack was full of "vile men and women," says a history of the West. "Not a day or night passed which did not yield its full fruition of vice, quarrels, wounds or murders. The crack of the revolver was often heard above the merry notes of the violin. Street fights were frequent. Pistols flashed, bowie knives flourished, and braggart oaths filled the air."

"The voices of auctioneers on the street corners, the shouts of horsemen as they rode up and down the streets, the rattle of vehicles arriving and departing — Indians, gamblers, the unmeaning babble of numerous drunken men, the tawdrily apparelled dancing women of the hurdy-gurdys. There is no vice unrepresented," says another history.

The job of imposing some law and order was given to Plummer; because of the favorable impression he had made he was named sheriff. Bannack was isolated; it was four hundred miles from civilization (it took a year for word of the Civil War battles and who won them to reach Bannack), so it is not surprising that the people of Bannack did not know that Henry Plummer was one of the fastest men in the West with a Colt revolver. He had already murdered an unspecified number of men before he came to Bannack. No sooner was Plummer given his badge than a new and much worse reign of terror set in. Something more than a mere boisterous and random lawlessness was wrong with Bannack. It got so a man couldn't get his gold out of Bannack; solitary riders, wagon trains, even guarded express coaches were held up, and guards, anybody who raised a voice, were ruthlessly cut down with shotgun, rifle or pistol. "Such a light valuing of human life has seldom been found in any other time or place," says one report.

A feeling of uneasiness turned to anger and outrage. The decent citizens formed up into one of the first vigilante groups in the West. They soon put nooses on two men. One of them, Red Yager, unfolded just before he died the perfidious story of what Plummer had done. He had organized while he was sheriff one of the largest and most ruthless gangs of ruffians and cutthroats ever to operate in the West then or later, putting to shame Dead Wood Dick's gang and the James brothers. Plummer, as sheriff, knew when the gold was leaving Bannack, so he posted his men in huts (they called these "she-bangs") along the trails to waylay the gold-laden traffic. Before Plummer's men were through, they had killed 102 men.

One by one, Plummer's men were caught — Bill Bunton, his second in command; Sam Bunton, "roadster"; George Shears, horse thief and roadster; and finally Plummer and one of his deputies, a man named Ned *Ray*.

Ray was caught asleep on a gambling table and was taken, along with Plummer and a man named Buck Stinson, to the gallows. "Terrible must have been its appearance as it loomed up in the bright starlight, the only object visible to the gaze of the guilty men on that long waste of ghastly snow," says an account. As he was led to the gallows Ray filled the air with curses, and as they put the noose around his neck, he "got his fingers between the rope and his neck to thus prolong his misery." The bodies of Plummer, Stinson and Ray were left to stiffen in an icy breeze. No one grieved for Ray except Madam Hall, his mistress. When they told her he was dead, she blasphemed everyone in Bannack.

It seems probable that this Ned Ray was James Earl Ray's great-grandfather. People like the Rays don't keep family trees, perhaps for the very reason that they might find nooses on them. But there is a strong oral tradition in the family; the keeper of this spoken archive is Speedy. He is not a bad keeper, either. He is a surprisingly truthful man for, struggle as he might, as he most often does, to conceal the truth, he just as often unwittingly reveals it. Speedy sees life so differently, his values are so opposite. He is proud of things that others would deplore.

Most of us would not brag that we had a grandfather who "sold liquor to the Indians off the back of a wagon," or who "gunned down six men." These are the clues that led me to search histories of the West in the 1860's and 1870's, and to Ned Ray. When I told Speedy about the Plummer gang and

Ned Ray, he did not seem surprised. "That sure sounds *right*, just like what my Old Man used to tell me about his father." Ned Ray's dates fit themselves into the Ray genealogy.

Violence in the Ray family began more than a hundred years ago, and has been passed down from one generation to the next ever since. It is an unbroken family tradition extending over ten decades. Nor did they ever fail during those hundred years to find in the United States an appropriate environment for their vocational specialty. The Rays are comfortably embedded in American history. Their family history proves that violence is an enduring quality of American life.

Trying to get the *facts* of his life out of Speedy Ray is like fishing for coins with chewing gum. Speedy has told many stories about his birth. When he applied for a marriage license, for example, Speedy told the clerk that he had been born at Carthage, Illinois. One day, talking with him in his small clapboard "rabbit box" house "just past the garbage dump," as he tells people, outside the small town of Center, Missouri, I asked him where he was born.

A. In the back of a wagon.
Q. Well, where was the wagon?
A. Out west. . . .
Q. Well, where out west was the wagon?
A. (Impatiently) Why, Needles!

Needles, California, rings true. "I once crossed the Mojave Desert on a doughnut," he has said.

The Mojave Desert begins on the outskirts of Needles or, to be more exact, Needles is a Mojave oasis, and it is a fair guess that Speedy was born in Needles somewhere around the turn of the century. He spent his early childhood there.

Needles was a blisteringly hot, rough place. The thermometer sometimes reached 112 degrees *at night* and the Mojave was "a black plateau furrowed by scores of untillable valleys, shimmering in the fierce sunlight and unrelieved in their desolation," according to the California WPA *Guide*. Lawlessness reached the point where the best known figure in town was a judge called "Ninety-day Root" because he handed down that sentence to almost everyone brought before him. Every third building along its muddy streets was a bar — which is perhaps what attracted Speedy's father there in the first place.

Speedy's father was an itinerant bartender known as Jim Ray, a logical son to the infamous Ned Ray of the Plummer gang. Speedy remembers being told that Ned, before he joined the Plummer gang, had run a "barrel house," which a dictionary defines as "a low drinking place, with racked barrels of whiskey along the walls," and the spiritual birthplace of "barrel house music" and its low-down songs. It followed that Ned Ray's son might come to a place like Needles — itself a mining and railroad town, a division stop on the Santa Fe and the terminal of two mining railroads, the Mojave and Milltown Express and the Tonopah and Tidewater Railroad.

There wasn't much love being passed around in the Ray home, which, if it had ceased to be a wagon, was nothing more than a crowded room in a ramshackle boardinghouse in Needles. Jim Ray was a hard man and a callous father. Speedy was afraid of him. "My father," Speedy has said, "didn't think a boy was something worth *looking* at. I once got it into my head that I wanted to be a lawyer. If I had told my father *that*, he would have run me off."

To make matters worse for Speedy, his mother (he was a child of her second marriage) favored his younger brother, Earl, and some idea of how harsh and loveless the Ray home life was can be deduced from what quickly happened to Earl. By the time he was ten Earl was in trouble, had been brought into court for stealing and "associating with immoral persons." Nor did he improve; when he was eleven, Earl was declared a delinquent and sent off to an institution.

No love was lost between Speedy and Earl. Speedy was jealous of Earl. "About all I remember my mother ever doing," Speedy has said with bitterness, "is running out to raise money to get Earl out of jail when he would only be back in the next day." The sibling rivalry was open, often bloody. The brothers fought brutally. "You couldn't hurt Earl," Speedy recalls. "He didn't have no feeling. But I never did care enough about him to *kill* him."

Speedy had no vocational training and a profession only in a very special sense. In Needles, one of the bars, run by a man named Schotmiller, featured boxing as entertainment. The ring was behind the saloon, enclosed with mesquite and willow tree trunks. You had to go through the saloon, and buy a drink, to get to it. Order was preserved by a deputy marshal named Frank Porter who "could roll a Bull Durham cigarette with one hand," according to the memory of an old timer. The crowd was never satisfied till blood had been let. The bouts were in the tradition of boxing at smokers, of battle royals, with the Queensberry rules out the window.

"They hurt each other so bad," remembers a witness of the fights at Schotmiller's, "it looked as if their gloves was made of muleskin."

Speedy and Earl were spectators at this carnage and began, when still boys, to fight in the Needles rings themselves. They had become "ham and egg fighters" by the time they were in their early teens, Earl fighting as "Johnny Malone," and Speedy as "Speedy Stillwell." They drifted up to Selma, California, the "raisin capital," and there are still boxing cards with their names on them at Fresno, California.

Earl began to travel with carnivals as a boxer; he was the man the barker said "can whip anybody in this crowd," and Earl did, by fair means and sometimes foul — kicking, biting, gouging his way past a thousand small town roughnecks. At some point, when the boys were still young, their father moved across the country to Quincy, Illinois, a wide-open, vice- and gambling-ridden Mississippi river town. That became the boys' orbit.

Speedy traveled too. The annals of his youth make an odyssey of transcontinental scuffling — spending the night in a boxcar in Nebraska at forty degrees below zero, running a moonshine whiskey still in Greenville, South Carolina, and celebrating his coming of age by being arrested at twenty-one in Keokuk, Iowa, for Breaking and Entering. For this, Speedy was sentenced to ten years in the Iowa State Penitentiary at Fort Madison, a sentence of which he served only two years. Prison records show that he was giving his name as George Ray, the son (correctly) of Mrs. James Ray of 300 Maple Street, Quincy. Speedy then weighed 123 pounds, was five feet seven inches tall; his hair was dark brown. He went in in May, 1921, and was paroled in June, 1923.

Speedy had, in the chapters of his life that are known, and obviously in some chapters that are unknown, earned himself a reputation as a man who could handle himself in the crack, when the going got tough. He brags that he was invited to join "The Egan Rats" of St. Louis. "That was a good bunch," he has said. "They divided everything. Whether you were on that particular job or not, you got your share." He didn't join, he says, "because when they told you to put a gun on somebody, you had to put a gun on somebody." He would leave you to infer that he did not wish to put a gun on anybody, or at least that he insisted on the right to choose his victims for himself.

---

It was from these beginnings, from the agony of his childhood and from the sordid, violent world of his youth and young manhood, that Speedy developed his view of the world. He converted the episodes of his life into moral tales, and the kind of lessons he drew, considering the kind of life he was born into and had led by the time he was married, are not as unexpected as they are unconventional. He remembers his first day as a young prisoner in the New Orleans workhouse, the first time he was, he says, ever "inside."

"All I had when I went in that day was an extra pair of overalls. I hadn't been inside ten minutes when I got up to get a drink of water out of the bucket, walked twenty feet away. Why, goddamit, when I got back those overalls were *gone!*

"Now, if there's anything I hate it's *petty* larceny. I can't stand the fella that will steal just this and that. Now, when a man holds up a bank, that's a *different* thing. The fella that holds up a bank is trying to make good, he's trying to *make something of himself*."

In Ray's view little people like him are pawns to be exploited and brutalized. His experiences as a club boxer strengthened him in this view. "They want you to get in there and beat one another's head all to pieces," he has said. "They don't care what happens, whether you get crippled up or what. It looks to me like people got *sadist* in them or something.

"Oh," he said, reflecting on the bitterness of it, "it looks like so many people have got to take so much *punishment* in life."

It is not surprising that Speedy does not believe in God, at least not a benevolent one. When a Catholic priest once asked him to come to church, Speedy replied: "If I came, I'd be a *hypocrite*." Speedy emphasizes words like that as his way of defining the moral issues that underlie commonplace events.

"If I'd gone to church that time, that would have been hypocrisy, but I'll tell you something that *isn't*. If a man came to buy a cow from me and I saw that to sell that cow I would have to say she was calving when she wasn't, then I would *say* she was calving. If a man has a family to support he has a right to do that. Now that isn't hypocrisy."

But for all his rough life, Speedy is not the kind of figure that "tough guy" evokes.

Speedy may have had his greatest, if least conscious, misgivings about himself when he seemed to be the "toughest," the most belligerent, the most violent. One of the clues to a deeper understanding of him is in his attitude toward his own body. When he was sixteen, he became intensely interested in physical culture, in "building his muscles," and has exercised almost every day of his life. His love of his body, his self-preening, was almost childlike in the same way that a child is fascinated with its body. For an adult to be preoccupied this way with his body suggests an arrested emotional development: he has stopped growing emotionally at the point where he loves himself but has not yet learned to love others. It is narcissism, on the surface, and the currents that flow beneath it probably carry unconscious, perhaps at times conscious, fear of attack by another person, sometimes of the same sex: the world is a hostile place; assault and attack are to be expected, and the attack you fear most is an attack by a man on your body, so you keep in trim to repel the attack.

Speedy's attitudes toward women are simply other colors in the same prism of his sense of his own manhood. For all his tough talk, Speedy feared women and mostly kept them at a distance. He attributes some of his feelings about women to an incident that happened to him when he was thirteen years old. He says that he was seduced by a young girl and that he did not like it.

Somebody once, when Speedy was an older man, pointed out to him the presence of a well-to-do widow in his neighborhood. "You marry her for *her* money," he replied, "and she'll just make a slave of *you*. You couldn't get to her money anyway."

There was something about cleanliness, or what he thought of as cleanliness, in his attitudes toward women: "I don't understand women. They keep a house spotless and then turn around and wash their goddamned *underwear* in the dishpan. I don't *go* for that kind of shit. Cut up the potatoes in a dishpan, wash the potatoes in the same goddamned dishpan. Damn! What I eat I want *clean*."

Like all of us, Speedy is a man of contradictions. He disliked women as a class but he loved his wife Ceal with all the capacity for love that he possessed. She made few demands on him. She was quiet, self-contained. He came to the conclusion that she did not like men any more than he liked women. It was his assurance that she did not care for men that gave him, he says, his confidence that she would not "run around." "You could trust Ceal," he has said.

The one thing that is certain about a man like Speedy is that, with all his fears and preoccupations, he does not have much warmth left over to invest in anybody else — not in his wife or, for that matter, his children.

---

It does not matter whether everything Speedy said was true. If Speedy lied a little bit in fact, most of us are liars in far more subtle things. Which of us is not doing exactly what Speedy was doing? Which of us is not rendering, coloring, fleshing out his own life story with tints and hues from what he wishes his life might have been? Like Ray, most of us are living two lives: a life of hard event and actuality on the one hand, and on the other the myth we are creating out of that real life almost at the time we are living it so that reality and myth become inextricably mixed in our minds, in our vision of ourselves and, quite unavoidably, in the picture of ourselves we present to others.

What does matter is that Speedy *steeped* his children in the mythical story of his life, and in the parables he drew from it, the myth of Speedy's birth, his childhood, his young manhood was the version he laid before his children over and over again, day in and day out.

Especially to his oldest child, that first child conceived in Wewahitchka. To that child, Speedy's myth became *life*, the only explanation he had for a long time of what life is, how it works, what its real goals are, how you get what you want.

# Chapter 3

In the first week of March, 1928, Mrs. Mary Maher, a poor, hard-working but tireless woman, rented two damp basement rooms in a run-down house in Alton, Illinois.

She took the rooms as an *accouchement* for her daughter who was about to have a baby by a man Mary Maher had never liked or approved of. A bustling, somewhat managing blue-eyed child of Irish immigrants, Mary Maher had by no means used up her resources for protecting, sheltering and guiding the lives of others merely in raising her own two children. One of them was Willie, ten years old in 1928, and the other was Lucille, whose husband had put her down in a slum room in St. Louis. Mary's impulse, of wanting to make sure that her first grandchild was not born in a slum, was to commit her to a lifelong struggle.

This was the struggle to keep her head up, the struggle to stay on the upper side of that border of social class that separates the *respectable* people from the *trash*. In America we assume that everyone is going up the social ladder. We hear less about those who are desperately trying to hold their own, or to keep from dropping *down* the social ladder. The struggle at the bottom (where Mary Maher was) is the bitterest, if the least acknowledged, of all the social class struggles in American life.

To fall there is to become faceless, to descend into social obloquy, into the world that society disowns, of the lower-lower class, the poverty-stricken and their miserable periphery, the criminals, the deviants. From there it is hard ever to rise again. For Mary Maher to lose the struggle meant that Lucille and her husband and that child Lucille was about to give birth to would remain *trash* forever, locked into poverty and disreputability.

Not much is known about the origins of the Maher family. One of the few clues is a listing in the 1910–1911 Alton city directory: "Maher, John T., husband of Mary, glass blower, r 1015 East 3rd Street." About John T. Maher only this much more is known: that he worked at the grimy old Owens, Illinois, glass factory that still sits, a monument to industrial ugliness, along the banks of the Mississippi in southern Alton, and, according to family legend, he "drank." Whether for this reason or some other, he and Mary Maher separated, and he disappeared from her life.

Mary Maher's maiden name was Fitzsimmons and she was a Roman Catholic descended from Irish immigrants. Americans insist on thinking of immigration as "the starting point of the great American success story . . . a kind of *rite de passage* to an American identity." But all this is being questioned in the 1970's.

The job ahead for the historians is to "disentangle immigration from the encompassing legend. The second wave of immigrants, the Irish, the German, coincided with the growth of industrialization in the U.S. and, so far from providing a class that was upwardly mobile, instead gave the U.S. its working class," took up their lives in "the standardized, mechanized life of the industrial city." This is an outline history of the Mahers.

Mary Fitzsimmons Maher was barely maintaining herself in a low-paid job. All day she wrestled with a hot steam pressing machine at Sadie's Cleaners in Alton — "Sadie" was Mary's sister, Sadie Fitzsimmons, who ran it. Sadie was a source of strength to Mary, a maiden lady who had found a more fulfilling outlet for her Irish gregariousness and expansiveness than had Mary. Sadie made her living in two ways. She ran Sadie's Cleaners but Sadie's other life, the life that she loved, was her life as a politician.

Sadie was a political canvasser in Alton's Fourth Ward. Nobody knew the Fourth like Sadie: "If you wanted to carry the Fourth in those days," an Alton politician has reminisced, "you would be wise to hire Sadie." Sadie would work for anybody. She was indifferent to party labels and to issues. The value of a professional canvasser like Sadie is that she can dependably deliver a certain number of votes for whichever side she is working for, perhaps only two hundred votes in a ward where two thousand votes are cast, but those two hundred votes often make the margin of victory. The professional politician does not so much depend on a voter's interest in an election as he does on the voter's lassitude and inertia; the fewer the votes cast, the larger loom the votes that the Sadies deliver.

Sadie was tireless. She was a thin woman, kinetic, walked with quick steps, and it was her whimsy to wear heavy rouge on her cheeks. When she wasn't behind the counter at her cleaning establishment, she was somewhere "in the Fourth," up and down the streets, in and out of its modest, blue collar homes, mostly two-story red brick row houses, which sat on a bluff overlooking the muddy Mississippi, talking with people about their ailments, helping them find jobs or get their old age benefits, laughing as she lifted their babies in the air.

---

As Mary Maher saw it, her daughter Lucille had made a bad marriage, married a fellow who had come to Alton with a banjo, sideburns, no money and an uncertain reputation. As he himself often said, he did not give a *hotdamn* for respectability. They had no sooner met than they had run over to Edwardsville (on April 26, 1926) the county seat and got married by the clerk, and that itself was a wrong thing for a good Catholic girl like Lucille to have done. Then he had taken Lucille to Florida on a foolish honeymoon and brought her back, not to Alton, but to a furnished room in a slum over in St. Louis. Brought her back pregnant.

Mary Maher was determined that her first grandchild was not going to be born in a slum. Her own solution, those two furnished rooms on Ninth Street, was not a solution she would have chosen if she had had much choice. But she had had so little money that she had actually taken money out of her son Willie's (Lucille's younger brother) piggy bank, from his savings as a newspaper carrier boy, to put a deposit on those rooms.

The neighborhood around that house on Ninth Street was not itself too wholesome. Not many doors away, down the hill on Rock Street, sat one of Alton's most popular whorehouses, the Nehi Valley Hotel, named with some whimsy for a then popular carbonated drink. The nearest intersection to the house was Belle and Ninth; Belle Street, an avenue of taverns and turmoil, was the artery of Alton's ghetto of vice, and the corner of Belle and Ninth was the hub of the district.

It was not a nice neighborhood, but Lucille Ray bore her child there at three o'clock on Saturday afternoon, March 10, 1928. The attending physician, the aging Dr. D. F. Duggan (Alton's public health officer) brought along another doctor for help. There was a certain difficulty in the delivery. In the end, with the two doctors working together, things turned out all right and a healthy baby entered the world. Dr. Duggan wrote the child's name on the birth certificate in his labored scrawl: James Earl Ray.

As for the new father, he was as much at home around Belle Street as a worn dime in a Coke machine. He had friends there. The same night the child was born, two of the men who had gone with Speedy and Lucille to Edwardsville, to stand up with them, Dan Berberich and Bert Waggoner, were arrested on the corner of Belle and Ninth for holding up a store.

And the man who gave part of his name to the child, the child's uncle Earl Ray, was, on the day of the child's birth, locked up in Menard State Prison for his felonious ways.

# Chapter 4

It is almost certain that nobody had ever prospered on the old Adams place. The house had long ago been breached by the extremes of the northern Missouri winters and summers. The edges of its tin roof, red with rust, curled up to let the rain in. The boards on the sides of the house were warped open to the wind. It didn't matter. There was nothing inside the house that could be hurt by the weather. It was not furnished with any of the amenities, no electricity, no running water, no plumbing.

The sixty acres that went with it were gullied, in an infertile section of Lewis County called Grub Prairie on a dirt road just outside the little country town of Ewing, an unprosperous, mean-spirited place of about 350 people.

Standing there on the brow of a low hill, encrusted with a century's accumulation of Missouri mud and dust, the old

Adams place gave off an air of hopelessness and despair. It dictated its own terms for living: a *hard* life.

In the second week of August, 1935, a family whose luck had been unfailingly rotten everyplace else turned up to take a chance on the old Adams place. It was the Rays, or as they now called themselves, the Rayneses. It was Speedy and Ceal, Speedy in his mid-thirties, Ceal in her late twenties. And four children. In addition to James Earl, the first child born in Alton, there were Marjorie, born June 8, 1930, John Larry, born June 19, 1931, and Gerald, born July 16, 1935.

If Speedy was an older man he was not a more trusting one. After nine years of marriage, Speedy found himself more beset than he had ever been with his suspicions of the world around him. That is why he had moved to the country, to the old Adams place. Many of the sources of his fears were concentrated in cities. He *detested* cities.

Just before he moved to Ewing, someone had tried to get Speedy to eat in a Chinese restaurant in Quincy. "I'd never come out of there *alive!*" he said with alarm. "Those people will *poison* you." He had this same fear of doctors: "If you go to 'em, they'll just poison you so you have to go back to 'em." He also hated lawyers. "They're in cahoots with the politicians," and the politicians are "every damned one of 'em just *gangsters.*" His philosophical position was: "The little fellow can't beat the government." He not only hated the Chinese but he also hated anyone who was to him strange. About Negroes, he would say with a mixture of contempt and distrust, "They just lay around and fuck all the time."

"I never did like cities," he has said. "I don't like the idea of when you got to piss you got to run up and down alleys seven or eight blocks hunting *a place* to piss. I just like to go outside and *piss*. I get so I can't stand to be in a town. A lot of people they just thrive on that, you know. But I don't like artificial stuff. There just ain't no use trying to stay in the city and make money. You just can't *beat* the city.

"You wouldn't believe what goes on down there in St. Louis. There's girls eleven and twelve years old hustling on the streets. And there's old *perverts* down there, some of them so old they can't hardly get around but right after these young girls giving them candy and money for *it*.

"That's *shit*. I never did ... couldn't stand that shit. That turns my *stomach*."

"All those women are diseased," Speedy believed. "If a man hangs around 'em, he'll get diseased. A woman can throw off her diseases but a man can't." He once warned someone: "You're a young fellow and your teeth are dropping out because you hang around all those old whores. Next thing you know, your arm will drop off."

The city is no place to raise a family: "These guys get married and then get out here and taking jobs and stuff. First thing you know they got four or five kids and they don't know what the hell to do with them. They can't feed them. Then they go out stealing and all kinds of trouble, in the *city*, you know. You take kids in the city and hell, they go up and down the street, in pool rooms and stuff. Now in the country it ain't so bad."

---

It was Earl who forced Speedy to choose. Earl was out of Menard — it was one of those rare times that he was free — and he could not seem to leave Speedy alone. "It was because I was having so much trouble with Earl that I moved to Ewing," Speedy has recalled.

Earl was always at Speedy. He would look Speedy up, and the visit as often as not ended in a fight, in bloody knuckles and shirttails. Earl was kind in a way. He seemed to like the children, and they liked him. And Speedy was drawn to Earl; Speedy trusted him in their world where trust was crucial. But he was also afraid of Earl.

Earl was *mean*. He was unpredictable. He had never stopped fighting, professionally or otherwise. When Earl was out of prison he was either in Quincy or traveling with a carnival as a boxer, the kind who would take on anybody in the crowd.

"Children are always born to their families' position," says Warner in his *Social Class in America,* and Speedy and Earl were both born *below* the lower-lower class, into the world of crime and violence. It was a world of cops and whores, robbers and bartenders, pimps and tavern keepers, gamblers and drug pushers, numbers runners and bail bondsmen, clerks in all-night drugstores, peddlers of dirty literature, sheriffs and their deputies, of blackmailers, counterfeiters and forgers, of bad check artists, of madams and keepers of cheap, seedy hotels — a world of soiled sheets, cracked linoleum, unshaded light bulbs, towels that would never again be white, of musty uric odors, of bedbugs, lice and body crabs, and clap, and the syph, and always the jail door ahead. It was a life of being either behind bars, just out, or just about to pull a job that would get you back in. The criminal's world is a world of despair. He lives in a world of unreal hopes and expectations, of shallow self-knowledge. He has given up all hope for making it within society. Its rewards seem too remote; nobody he knows within his world has ever really received them. He comes to think only a fool would try. Crime is the only vocation open to the criminal, and he begins to treat it as if it were one.

Prison is the only world of *order* that he knows. When he is outside the world is fragile and chaotic; when he is inside, his world is stabilized into a hierarchy he understands and can place himself within. In the outside world he sees his failures as the result of bad breaks: if *that* cop had not turned *that* corner at *that* moment . . .

If Earl was resigned to all this, Speedy was not. Speedy, born into it though he was, somehow was never wholly at home within it.

He was afraid of prisons, for one thing. One of the Ray children has said: "The old man was 'broken' at Fort Madison. Prisons were worse in those days. They strung him up by his thumbs for a while. He's had kidney trouble off and on ever since."

For all his bragging, Speedy was afraid of Earl and Speedy was really afraid of the underworld: afraid of it and temperamentally unsuited for it in many ways. Speedy was puritanical. He drank, but sparingly and never so much as to lose control of himself. He had known women before he was married, but since he had married Ceal he had been faithful to her.

And Speedy could not bring himself to the state of utter despair and self-hatred it took to lapse into the world of crime. Speedy kept trying to make it in the straight world. Referring to the period between the time he was married (1926) and the time he moved to Ewing (1935), he has said with pride: "I never used no other names all that time, just my own right name," his way of confirming that he had been trying to live a straight life. For a while in 1931, for instance, he lived in the little town of Winchester, Illinois, where he had a job wrecking cars. As was always the case when he was working around automobiles, he was happy.

"There was a time there when I thought I was going to be President," he has said, meaning of the United States.

This was part of the trouble. His vocational commitment was not only shallow but his vocational sense was also unreal. He either believed he was going to be President, when he had a job, or that nobody could be who wasn't a gangster, when he got fired. His career was the story of a series of failed possibilities.

He and Ceal needed help to get along in those years from 1926 to 1935, before he moved to Ewing. Speedy's family in Quincy had helped some. Speedy's mother and father, Lillian and Jim Ray, his sister Mabel (Mrs. Frank Fuller), and Earl (when he was out) all lived in Quincy.

Jim Ray ran a tavern on Fifth Street in the heart of Quincy. "My people had their own ideas," Speedy has recalled, in evaluating their help. "They didn't live for their kids. My mother was sick practically all her life. My Old Man drank but he drank it *all*. He never did give none to nobody else."

Mom Maher — they were now calling her that — had helped too. Another eye-witness to those days in the Ray marriage, William Maher, Mom Maher's son and Ceal's brother, a painting contractor in Alton, Illinois, is bitter about Speedy and the way Speedy treated Ceal and Mom Maher.

According to Maher, Speedy began to sponge off his mother almost from the minute he married Ceal. In 1930, according to Maher, "he talked my Mother into quitting her job and moving her four rooms of furniture into a shack perched on a clay hill several miles southeast of Bowling Green, Missouri. Tobacco Road would have been paradise compared to that clay hill. Not only was my Mother's furniture needed to fill the shack, but her limited finances and her willingness to work was also needed. Mom cashed in a couple of small life insurance policies right off the bat so we could exist. My mother finally found a job in Louisiana, Missouri. Two days a week, $3.50 per week. Later I found a job at a nursery pulling weeds, 10 hours for $1.00 a day. Mom and I both walked a distance of 22 miles a day, coming and going. Meanwhile, all old Jeeter [his name for Speedy] would do was whine that times were terrible."

Whatever effect these times may have had on anyone else, they almost certainly deeply affected James Earl Ray, then in his infancy.

The price for Mom's help was her almost daily noodling (as Speedy saw it) into Speedy's family affairs. She would have been insufferable if it had not been for Ceal. Whenever there was an argument, whenever Speedy blew up at Mom, Ceal stood by him, took his side. After all, she had married him to get away from Mom's managing ways. Ceal had, in her way, become a source of strength to Speedy. She almost never bothered him. She was quiet, sometimes wistful, sometimes, he noticed, quite sad. She almost never laughed but, as he often thought, what was there in life to laugh about? When they had courted, Speedy had told Ceal he was in "show business." He was then, or seemed to be, light-hearted. Once they were married, especially once they had a child, Speedy lost even the appearance of his carefree ways, turned more and more inward.

--------

If he was trying to move out of the criminal world, when he took his family to Ewing, he was not moving upward very far, only into the world of the lower-lower class, into the subculture of poverty, which has its own class characteristics.

Speedy would boil with frustration at his failures in the straight world, and, like most poor people, he would be mad at the wrong people. The poor man "does not grasp the structure of the world he lives in, cannot understand his place in it, and never knows what to expect from it." In the world of the poor, "People alternate between being hostile and aggressive, and then apathetic, withdrawn and isolated," and there are "extreme states of anxiety and depression as well as hostility and paranoid thinking."

On January 5, 1935, Speedy was arrested in Alton for forgery, but the grand jury in Edwardsville, Illinois, the county seat, did not indict him and the charges were dropped. This was a narrow squeak with the law. It was the thing that caused Speedy and Mom at last to agree on something, that he should move with Ceal and the children to the country. And the move did settle one thing: Speedy was never again to be arrested, indicted or convicted of a crime.

On August 2, 1935, Mom bought the old Adams place in Ewing, a sixty-three-acre tract, for less than $1,000 with little or no cash down, from Nettie Uhlein, and Speedy and Ceal immediately went there.

--------

There may have once been a time when small town life was cozy, when people felt secure and content in the American rural setting. But the one feeling that was common to the people of Ewing was insecurity. Speedy couldn't have chosen a community better suited to his suspicious, bigoted temperament. Ewing was not so much a community as it was an emotion, and the emotion was fear. The folks in Ewing could not precisely describe their fear, and the fact that they could not made them defensive and angry in their insularity. They acted as if they were under siege, surrounded by evil threatening forces. They did know that they didn't like cities, or city life, or city people, or their seemingly overpowering weight, and, most of all, their menacing ethnic collections. One thing they did know in Ewing, there was one enemy they recognized.

"No nigger's ever spent the night in Ewing," they proudly told visitors to the town.

The trouble with Ewing was that it was not a country town so much as it was a backwash from the city. The kind of man who lived in Ewing could not quite adjust himself to urban life; and, though he said he liked the "outdoors," he did not like the hard physical tasks in wresting a living from the soil. He would rather have worked in the city at a low-paid, even seasonal job and didn't get too upset when he was laid off for a few weeks.

There never was an "old" (gracious) Ewing. The earliest settlers, who came to Lewis County in the 1830's, were "poor and never became wealthy," says the local history. "They were rough, uncouth, unpolished. . . ."

And those who came to Lewis County were Southerners,

from Kentucky, from Virginia, from Tennessee. Some of them brought slaves and the emotional baggage that went with the peculiar institution, the encompassing set of defenses it called for — slavery was like a dye that stained the smallest thread of common life. By 1845 it was obvious that Lewis County had cast its lot with the South; its churches began to leave the "northern" branches and affiliate with "southern" branches.

The men without slaves, the poorer men, moved inland from the Mississippi river bottom, up the branches of the Fabius River (the Fabby, local people call it) to the less desirable rolling land, land more difficult to farm and not as fertile, and, in the tradition of poor whites, accepted the political imperatives of slavery without gaining its economic benefits. From the beginning Ewing was inhabited by people living a marginal economic, social and cultural life, getting little out of life and resenting their pinched deprivation.

They fit the description that General Ulysses S. Grant, who raised troops in this part of Missouri, gave them: "The great bulk were men who owned no slaves; their homes were generally in the hills and poor country; they too needed emancipation . . . they were looked down upon as poor white trash."

It is not surprising that there was a strong Klan in Lewis County in the 1920's, and that the people there spoke with a drawl. To them, "fire" often becomes "far" and sometimes "fawr," and Missouri is "Miz-sour-a." It was the country hill people, like those around Ewing, who were still in the 1930's saying things like, ". . . making mo' racket 'n a jackass in a tin barn."

There never was a period of prosperity in the little town, but there was a time when life was so very, very hard that the town's mean fears and narrow prejudices were *transfixed.* This time was the 1930's. The Depression is a vivid, indelible memory in Ewing, and nothing that happened before it, nothing that has happened since then, raises so high a pitch of feeling. Speedy could not have chosen a worse time or place to try to make a living as a farmer. Everybody was failing, even people who knew how to farm.

"Them was son-of-a-bitchin' hard times around here," a Ewing resident has said.

"There wasn't enough lard to fry an egg," said another.

A young researcher who went to Ewing to find out something about life there ran into physical threats.

"Scat! Get out of here," a store owner said, charging at the young researcher, "you're not even old enough to *remember* the Depression!"

At the moment Speedy started to farm, the trend in Lewis County was to give up on agriculture. In 1925 there were 163,397 acres in cultivation in the county, but one-third of them, or 52,396 acres, had been abandoned by 1930.

"When I became county supervisor in December, 1935," recalls Charles H. Baldwin, who was in Lewis County for the federal Farmers' Home Administration, "my first job was to go around to the WPA projects and try to talk the men into the notion of going back to farming. Many did, but we had a severe drought in 1936, and in the fall and winter of 1937 we had to advance folks money to feed their livestock.

"I recall one family of four in Ewing had a gross income

of a hundred ninety-eight dollars in 1938. If the homemaker had not canned enough food during the summer of 1938 to carry them over to 1939, this family would have starved."

A killing economic blight had fallen on the whole country, and in March, 1933, 14,762,000 Americans were out of jobs. "Americans experienced a tremendous loss of income *to the vanishing point in millions of cases,*" said a government report. "In 1935–36, over 6.7 million families had incomes of less than $500 (a year); more than 18.3 million families had less than $1,000; almost 32.3 million (or 82 percent of all American families) had incomes below $2,000."

Farm living was hard for *most* farm families. The old Adams place wasn't that different. Only 16 percent of American farm families lived in homes with running water. Only 10 percent of all farm dwellings had an indoor toilet.

Most families who stayed on in Lewis County and Ewing continued to live on farms. A Department of Agriculture study of farm family income in the 1940 *Yearbook of Agriculture* showed that the national median cash income was less than $500. A family with $250–$499 annual income (half cash), a category that would have included most of the farm families in Lewis County in the 1930's, would spend:

$31 a year for clothes;
$12 for medical care;
$1 for recreation;
$3 a year for formal education and reading;
$3 a year for "personal care";
$52 a year for household operation;
$5 a year on gifts, family welfare and taxes;
$293 annually on food, but cash purchases came to only $49.

To dress the entire family on $31.00 meant that the husband got only $11.00 for the entire year — about $3.60 of which went for shoes and about $4.00 for shirts, overalls, trousers and suits, leaving only $3.40 for hats, coats, sweaters, underwear. Wives spent $9.21 a year, one-third of which went for shoes; hats took only fifty cents.

A family at this income level spent $12.00 on medical care. The number of visits to physicians averaged 0.41! "Routine dental care must have been almost unknown," the report says, and "self-medication must have been common."

There weren't any factory jobs to speak of in Lewis County. An industrial directory showed only two installations in Ewing, a chicken feed mill with one employee and the farmer's elevator and exchange with four employees. Wages for such jobs as there were were low — $2.50 a day for a road worker, $1.50 for wood cutting; farm laborers were getting seventy-five cents a day.

In 1933 only thirty-eight people in Lewis County made enough money to cause them to file income tax returns.

Relief didn't amount to a hill of beans, or in 1933, precisely $450.99 for *all* of Lewis County with only seventy persons on the rolls out of the population of nearly twelve thousand people, almost all of whom might have qualified. The average grant was $13.51 for those who did get relief.

There was a county almshouse with forty-one inmates — twelve of them were feebleminded, nine were insane, five were crippled and fifteen were listed simply as "old age."

---

The best way to put an estimate on the sophistication and style of life in Ewing in the thirties is to say that only two houses in town had flush toilets. The same two were the only two that had electricity — for anything, not to say for lights. There were people in Ewing who were still lighting their houses with candles, and the common source of illumination was the glass lantern with its wick saturated with coal oil giving off plenty of soot and a certain amount of dim light.

"Ewing was behind the moon, that's all there is to it," remembers an expatriate now living in Quincy, Illinois.

It was just about as isolated, spiritually and geographically, as an American small town can be. "At that time people in Ewing even felt that Lewistown and La Belle were sophisticated places," recalls a Ewing woman. The two towns are near Ewing and about the same size.

Ewing was behind the moon and there wasn't too much chance to get out. The roads were bad, very few people had cars, those who did couldn't afford gas (not even the fifteen-cent "green gas"), and a trip to Quincy, the nearest city, had the then formidable handicap of a fifty-cent toll on the Mississippi River bridge.

Ewing was on the Cannonball Trail, the highway that ran from the Mississippi west to Kansas City, but one good rain or a winter snow turned it to mud and the motorists who dared its hazards often got stuck and had to spend the night. One Ewing man remembers these exotic strangers and their unexpected visits as the most exciting events in his boyhood.

There certainly wasn't much else, no movie house, no library, only a handful of social organizations: a Masonic Lodge, four chapters of the Grange, a 4-H Club, and that was all. Sometimes in the summer a local man would rig up a sheet behind the market and show movies. Once a year a traveling show came to town; it was the "Toby and Susie Camp Show," a well-known small town institution featuring homespun humor. Sometimes a medicine show would come to town — that is, some man and his wife driving a beat-up truck with a back platform from which they would do an act with a dog and sell snake oil.

Of course there was Cason's, the barber shop with a pool table in the back, and in the front a checkerboard. Cason's was *the* place for a man to spend some idle time in Ewing.

There were three churches: the Baptist church with 118 members; the Queen of Peace Roman Catholic with 81 members; and the "evangelical" Assembly of God Pentecostal church whose membership is unrecorded. Somehow the churches do not seem to have played in Ewing their usual, or what is thought to be their usual, role in small towns. Attendance was not good, even at the Catholic church. When Ewing people think of the Depression, they do not spontaneously mention the church as a factor in their lives then.

There was an astonishing lack of community facilities. There was no public water or sewage system, not one doctor, no bank, no paved streets.

You could make quilts from cotton scraps, and quilt-making was popular, especially the making of "friendship quilts." Each of the women who worked on one of these collective sewing efforts embroidered her name on one of the pieces. The quilts were needed, used. One of the principal feminine activities in Ewing during the Depression was not social at all; the women canned, preserved, often fruits and vegetables they had grown themselves in kitchen gardens. "Ninety-five percent of the women in Ewing canned," one woman remembers. "If we hadn't, we wouldn't have made it." One of the dietary standbys was a meal of navy beans and ham hocks.

A teacher in the Ewing school remembers how one mother kept saying that she wanted the teacher to come for Sunday dinner but "wasn't ready yet." It was a year before the invitation came. As it turned out, it had taken that long for the mother to accumulate enough glasses to go around, at least by the process by which she was getting them, by buying a brand of peanut butter which came in drinking glasses.

One popular form of social activity was the Charivari. "When I was at Ewing," says a woman who left there in the 1930's, "the young people had begun to charivari just any couple who married. After the marriage the kids would wait several days (keeping the couple in hot water) before they would surprise them. They usually took something to beat on or firecrackers to set off. Sometimes the kids would get pretty excited and talk rough and even do damage to property. The couple was supposed to invite everyone in and serve refreshments. Most of the time these affairs were like parties and games were played. Sometimes they would take the groom for a ride in a wheelbarrow...."

It was a time when people were thrown on their own for recreation. The main resource around Ewing was the "Fabby," the muddy, twisting Fabius River. What was probably the most popular single pleasure spot in Ewing during the Depression was Hall's Mill, a site on a low bluff that rose above the Fabby just outside town

There was really nothing there, not even a picnic table, nothing except the remains of an old limestone fireplace. Before the mill, where the river took a turn, there was a sandbar which made a beach and swimming hole, muddy much of the year, but sometimes in the summer it would run clear. To swim there was one of the delights of being a boy in Ewing. Church suppers, school "weenie" roasts, informal social affairs of all kinds were held at Hall's Mill.

# Chapter 5

There was a brief moment of hope in Ewing, when it seemed Speedy might actually work, maybe even make, despite the hard times, a living. Somehow Speedy came by an old truck, a 1931 Chevrolet 1-ton, dual-wheel. He painted his name on the door and proclaimed himself in the "hauling business." He took a new name for Ewing, Jerry Raynes, sometimes "Rains."

There was hauling to be done even in those poor times. There was livestock to be hauled to and from the sales at nearby Palmyra and Lewistown, for very few farmers in those days owned trucks. Speedy and two or three others who did hauling got a dollar, more or less, for a cow or a horse or three hogs. Some hauled cows to bulls and mares to stallions. One of the things people did in those days to relieve the hopelessness of their lives was to move, even if it was only over the hill, and their limp mattresses and rusting iron bedsteads were often lifted onto the old stake body of Speedy's rattling Chevy. Two years' tenure on a farm was common then.

There was so little actual money around, bartering was big. People used to stand around, or squat on their heels, swapping — for the fun of it if nothing else. A man could pass a morning "talking around a little," parleying over nothing more valuable than, say, a Barlow knife. Merle Wenneker, who still lives around that part of Missouri and who was a boy in Ewing in the thirties, remembers an extended negotiation between his father and Speedy over two trucks.

The Wennekers still believe they got the best of Speedy. "We gave Raynes a Ford Model A 1-ton for his Chevy," Wenneker recalls, savoring the memory. "We had lots of mud in Lewis County in those days. When we bought this Ford it had been running on mud roads and we thought it was OK. But when we began to use it we found out it wouldn't track and we traded it off on Raynes."

Speedy's version of his career as a hauler is marked by the usual mixture of defensive and belligerent bragging, frustration and anger, and actual or fantasied violence.

"I done a lot of trucking there in Ewing," he has asserted. "I had three trucks. I had a Nash and two different Chevrolets. [He seems to have forgotten the Wenneker Ford.] Hell, it never got *too* cold or *too* late for me to haul. I'd a hauled all night. I worked the *shit* out of those trucks of mine.

"Sometimes people won't pay you," he continued, his dander rising as his memory played over the period. "I trucked for one guy I never did get anything out of. He burned himself up after that in that house I moved him into. That fixed *him.*"

He did at least one piece of hauling he has never spoken of outside the family. Once when Earl — Speedy called him "Gimp," and he called Speedy "Pity'Wit" — came over from Quincy to visit at the old Adams place, Speedy and Earl together planned a cattle rustling job. They went out with the old truck (whichever one it was Speedy was driving then), and stole some cows, and got away with it.

But eventually the truck came to a more or less permanent resting place behind the house, and sat there helplessly suffering the ravages of the weather.

Speedy insists that when he was not hauling he was trying to farm: "I like to raise things, like to see things grow, corn. I like to stock, cattle and stuff like that. I like to improve things. I kept one milkcow, you know. We had a brindle cow I bought for twenty-eight dollars. Everybody would milk her. We had a hog so friendly he would come into the house. Got to be three hundred pounds."

People in Ewing defend Speedy. He shared the hardships of the Depression with them. If he wasn't much of a farmer, well, "the old Adams place was quite brushy and timbered, also thin soil," Wenneker remembers. "Fertilizer was expensive and land had to be cleared by hand," something Speedy was certainly not likely to do.

There was some day labor but the amount was "variable" according to Wenneker. "Cutting wood and sawing it, cutting wheat, shucking corn, pitching hay, unloading feed and fertilizer cars — all hard work and I don't remember just how much of this Raynes did." He apparently did none.

Speedy was on WPA for a while, a rock crushing and gravel project on the Keller farm, but to remind him of this is to provoke a cry of outrage.

"Relief? Hell, I wasn't on relief! Why I was hiring *them people* to work."

The truth is that Speedy seldom got up in time to be picked up by the truck which rounded up the WPA crews.

"Jerry didn't work, that's true, but it's also true that there just wasn't much work to be found," says another Ewing resident, Jerry Ball, the mailman who served the old Adams place. "As for that old truck, it wouldn't do much more than pull itself. To get right down to it I never saw Raynes do much of anything." "It was my impression," says Wenneker, "that he wasn't well, asthma or something of that type."

As had happened so often in the past, Speedy was caught between a dream and his crippling distortions. His dream of farming was something that hung about in the American atmosphere, "the myth of the garden and the ideal figure of the yeoman." But it was a reality Speedy never gripped. He thought he had left his phobias behind in the city, but he was as unable to rid himself of them as he was his old boxing scars. That "city shit" turned out to be stuff that was in his head, a mental hand luggage he had to carry with him wherever he went.

A man like him, he believed with ever greater passion as the years passed, didn't stand a chance in a world that was everywhere crooked:

"I told the kids they wasn't no use working. I told 'em they'd never have anything if they worked. That was what

I told them: get out and around people who've got money, people in show business . . ."

He began to accept defeat, to change his daily routine so that he no longer made any particular pretense of working. He began to spend more and more time in Cason's pool room — behind the barber shop.

He got so he would go to bed almost at dark, never later than 9:00 P.M., then insist that the house be quiet, the children still. He stayed in bed until noon the next day.

"I'd drop into Cason's in the later afternoon," Speedy says. "Just drop in there. Sometimes there wouldn't be anybody in there for three or four days. ·

"I never did go too much on playing pool. But that's all the recreation they had over there. We used to play for a quarter a game and stuff like that there."

Even in Cason's his anger bubbled up. "Playing pool I'd usually wind up arguing. I'd get mad and there was something I *hate* to do, get mad." The "noise" in Cason's got on his nerves. "There wasn't no fighting in there but there was so much goddamned *racket.*"

Things were beginning to get to him. "I began to have severe headaches all the time in Ewing, every single afternoon. I went down to about 112 pounds. One afternoon I was over in Quincy and I went in a drugstore and I got a shot of Bromo. It killed my headaches just like *that.*" Whatever powers Bromo has, it is not magical; the "cure" itself was a symptom, only confirmed what his headaches hinted at: his mind had become rigid in its preoccupation with his trusted ideas.

He was now turning helplessly within a vicious circle, a

victim of his splintering emotions. His lower-than-dirt view of himself, carried forward from childhood, was deepened by his adult failure to provide for his wife and children.

---

They had a rather unpleasant way of referring to Ceal in Ewing. They spoke of her as "that Raynes woman," in the way people used to speak of women in frontier towns, the ultimate masculine view of woman, as if she were more an object with specific functions than a person. But it spoke their sense of her remoteness from them. In Ewing they seldom saw her in the flesh. Although the old Adams place was within walking distance of town, she seldom went there. Almost nobody ever came to see her at the farm. People in Ewing were not that friendly, not even the womenfolk. There was nothing in the parched and barren life of the little town to which she could turn for comfort or for help. There was a Roman Catholic church and priest in Ewing. They sent food on occasion, but Ceal never went to church or talked with the priest.

Those who caught a glimpse of her remember her vividly.

"I saw her one day standing outside the grocery," remembers one man. "Her head was bowed, her hair all messed up, her children hanging about her feet, and *all* of them were in rags. She looked up as I passed. She had the saddest most woebegone look in her eyes."

"I remember going out to their house when I was just a boy," says another Ewing resident. "She came to the door and the sight of her scared me so much I just turned and ran, halfway back to town."

---

Ceal's looks only spoke the despair she felt. She was desolate. She was deeply ashamed of the circumstances in which she found herself, and she had no way in which to change them. Even Speedy has admitted: "Ceal *hated* the farm."

Speedy wasn't much help. When Ceal first married him she put some of her difficulties with Speedy down to the fact that he was a *man*, for she expected men to be different, unpredictable, inconsiderate, insensitive. It was true that she had married Speedy partly to get away from Mom, but also partly because, in her world of class and social values, to marry was to become *someone*. It was the same with having children; to become a Mother was to *avoid* becoming all the things you might become if you didn't have children. Ceal's predicament was like Mom's: the distance between being respectable and being trash was not that wide. Marriage and children helped to bridge it. In the only style of marriage Ceal knew anything about the man is dominant, controlling; the woman feels inferior and must resign herself to it.

Ceal's view of marriage left her with no leverage, and with Speedy give-and-take was impossible. He never had been good at sharing his feelings with women. He had said a hundred times and would say again that he did not believe there was any such thing as love between a man and a woman, only between a man and his children. But underneath the bluster with which he kept Ceal at a distance, Speedy had his own yearnings.

This was a sad irony: both Ceal and Speedy wanted the same thing, love. But they had started out without a common language of emotion and they had never been able to learn one.

Even if Ceal had been the most inventive and energetic

woman in the world, seven years of marriage to Speedy would have drained her of energy and hope. Hope was not something, anyway, that she had had much traffic in; with Ceal the present was everything, and she turned with what intensity of feeling she had toward her children. Caring for the children became the central physical and emotional activity of her life.

And always in the back of her mind was the fear that Speedy might abandon her, that he might "go off." For in Ceal's and Speedy's world, marriage was not the same kind of contract it was in the middle class world, where the penalties for breaking it were high. In their world a man could leave a woman with no more than carfare and start "staying with" a new woman who would become his wife by the simple fact that he called her his missus.

There was underneath these sharply differing views of marriage a shared nostalgia for a kind of love both of them had missed. Speedy missed the love he failed to get from his mother. When he saw Ceal cuddling the kids, it irritated him; he could not figure how to get such love from Ceal.

Ceal kept with her wherever she went a thumbed photograph of her father. This was her one personal possession and it hinted at the difficulties Ceal brought to her marriage from *her* family. Ceal's eagerness to get away from her mother was heightened by her affection for her father, who had also found her mother difficult, and had left them when Ceal was approaching her teens. When Ceal came to look for a husband, she chose one who was nine years older than she was.

It was the fact of her having been abandoned by her father that more than anything else colored her human encounters, made her seem to lack warmth. One of her children, offering what he thought was a compliment to his mother, said that she "never had any favorites. She treated every one of us the same." But that may have been only a measure of her incapacity for affection.

All of us have a tendency to repeat the most significant patterns of feeling in our lives and it might be possible, it is certainly plausible, that Ceal unconsciously picked Speedy as a mate because she sensed he would disappoint her, too. But aren't we all, like uninspired scenario writers, reworking over and over again the same tired plot, our own psychologically predestined autobiographical tragedies?

---

Late one afternoon, as the shadows were lengthening around the old Adams place, at about the time country people call "first dark," Speedy arrived home. He put a poke of groceries down on the back porch, and went off to the wood pile. Ceal was in the kitchen, busy at the stove. Marjorie was playing on the back porch and looked in the bag and, as children will, she found a box of matches. The next thing anyone knew she was running into the house screaming, her dress afire, the flames covering her face.

By first light the next morning the child was dead. Speedy went for Mr. Ball, the undertaker. Ceal wept in stunned bewilderment as they took Marjorie away. She put a yellow dress on the little body.

A child's death is a somber thing in a small town, an unseasonable event in a setting where everything, even death, has its seasons. Marjorie's death cast a chill over Ewing, and the town responded by elevating for a few hours the Rayneses' family tragedy, and the Rayneses themselves, into the town's ritual life. School was let out, and the student body walked the short distance to the Queen of Peace cemetery for the burial. The Catholic priest conducted the ceremony although the Rayneses had never been to the Catholic church in Ewing.

The Wennekers came with their truck and winch to lower the small casket into the grave.

# Chapter 6

When James Earl Ray turned up at the Ewing elementary school in the fall of 1935 to begin his education, his very presence embodied a rude repudiation of the American dream. It was Ray's destiny that day (and would be later) to show the distance that stretches between our mythic image of American life and the actual life most of us live.

Ray reported for school with his hair tousled, uncombed; barefoot, but with ragged pants, torn, dirty shirt, a man's suit coat over that, its sleeves threadbare and greasy. And he smelled of urine.

His preparation for school was the kind that would only help the boy to make the worst, not the best, of the social experience that was in front of him. It was obvious, from a moment's encounter with him, that he did not trust anybody.

He was his father's son; he looked warily, suspiciously, at everything that presented itself to his gaze. He was quiet, and if you looked directly at him, he would turn away, or cast his eyes downward on his feet; perhaps, if he thought you had turned away from him, he would cock his head to the side and steal a glance at you, as if measuring you. He smiled sometimes, but only laughed as if he were experimenting with the gesture.

By the time the family got to Ewing and the boy entered school, they were calling him "Jimmy," and treating him in a way that showed they knew he was *different*. Already (he was seven) the family was taking his temper for granted. Speedy and Ceal had learned not to argue in front of Jimmy. He would fly into a rage if they did.

"You'd go along with Jimmy and everything would seem OK and then — WHAM!" says Speedy.

Speedy and Ceal viewed Jimmy with a mixture of awe and pride. They did not see his "differences" as flaws; they took them as virtues. Jimmy's violent feelings they took as an omen of masculinity, of courage.

Besides, the boy was "smart," the family was convinced of that. He was the quickest of all the children. Both Speedy and Ceal acknowledged that he was smarter than either of them. But whether this was intelligence or just a crude system of psychic semaphores to warn him of danger — only time would tell. If he seemed old for his age, it was because he had devised out of an instinct for survival a kind of deceptive and misleading *intactness*. It was only a child's improvisation. Jimmy had spliced it together, out of fragments of experience he could not quite give meaning to, some dark, under-exposed, some over-exposed, bright, too vivid, night-marish, as if he had constructed a life story from discarded film off the cutting room floor.

---

The Ewing school was the most impressive building in the little town. It was brick, one of the few brick buildings in Ewing, and it was nearly new, having been built in 1926. Its eight grades were housed in three rooms, taught by three teachers. All students in the first, second and third grades were in Room 1; Room 2 had the fourth, fifth and sixth grades; and Room 3 had the seventh and eighth. The total attendance in the grade school varied between thirty-five and fifty during the 1930's. This meant that a student entering school would have the same teacher for three years in a class-room where he got the benefit of her virtues, if she was a good teacher, or the uninsulated shock of her vices, if she was a bad one. When James Earl Ray entered the school, he was one of only three students in the first grade, and he felt the full force of Miss Madeline "Tots" McGhee's pedagogical deficiencies. The dislike between teacher and student was mutual, and instant.

Tots was a small woman, strict, a spinster, and her family was "prominent" in Ewing. As local girls did in those days in small towns (perhaps they still do), Tots tended to look down on the teachers who were not local girls. She treated these colleagues as if they were guilty of some unspecified form of vagrancy. The out-of-town girls often found them-selves lonely at night ... "looking out the bedroom window, after spending the evening grading papers, to find that every light in town was out," as one of them remembers her life in Ewing in the 1930's.

Tots had no warmth. "She was stand-offish," a colleague recalls. "She never quite understood or liked children. There was one quite nervous little girl in her class who needed a little extra kindness. Tots didn't want to give her that. The child's parents took her out of school a year until she could get another teacher." "Just her voice scared me," says a former student.

Tots was not popular even with children who came to school clean, and James Earl Ray's appearance etched him in her mind and fixed him at the bottom of her snobbish social scale. It is an illusion that there are no social classes in small towns. There are, and there was no doubt about where the Rayneses stood — they were the town's "white trash."

Tots was the last person to help James Earl Ray out of his troubles, to give him the warmth he wasn't getting at home or even sympathetic help with his studies.

And it wasn't altogether Tots's fault. She stands as a symbol of what was to be understood three or four decades later as a crucial problem in public education — the problem of social class. "The lower the position the child's family occupies, the less his chances are of being helped by a teacher." A lower class student soon finds that his social position isolates him in the school: "he is made to feel unwanted," he is "channelized into associations with others of like social class," until his "escape from his low position becomes well-nigh impossible." A student's grades often depend more on his social class than on his ability, and lower class children like Ray are expected to be "dumb," to make bad grades.

There wasn't any help for James Earl Ray in the school *system*, backing Tots up, not in the Missouri school system in the 1930's, where on a twelve-month basis the median salary for rural schoolteachers was $36.05 a month, or about $9.00 *a week.*

The Lewis County schools were absurdly disastrously decentralized into (in 1931) *sixty-two separate* administrative units for 2,765 students, or a school district for every 46 students. Of the seventy-two schools in the county then, sixty-two were one-room, one-teacher schools. When it was built in 1926, the Ewing school had just two classrooms, two rest rooms and a long "playroom" ·with low ceilings that later, nevertheless, was divided into two classrooms. There were two outdoor toilets, privies, actually used more than the indoor ones because of water shortages. The boys' privy was in its way a recreation room, the place where boys "sneaked a smoke," cubebs if nothing else, where they told dirty jokes, and where they pulled that rural prank, of "de-panting." "A group of us boys would gang up on a boy and remove his pants and hang them up high so he couldn't get them, or someplace where he would have to go out in the open to retrieve them. Anybody might get that treatment — new boys, tough boys, sissies, anybody. I guess it was something to do for excitement. I know they still do it today on school buses when they take long trips."

Something of the uncharitable temper of the little town of Ewing showed through — and could because decisions were so decentralized — when the federal school lunch program was offered to Ewing. There was obviously hunger and malnutrition among the students but the Ewing school board "didn't want anything to do with the government," and turned the lunches down at first. "Several children obviously hadn't had enough to eat," a teacher there says, "because their grades went up significantly as soon as they began to have hot lunches." The board finally, then, gave in and some mothers started a garden around the school, planted and harvested turnips and other vegetables, made biscuits, and stretched the meat that was furnished by making stews. The board OKed the lunch program with beadlelike stinginess; they made the students bring their own bowls and spoons.

Yet, when a state board of health team of doctors looked at 2,000 Lewis County students (including Ewing) in 1934 it found: 181 were seriously underfed; 288 had imperfect vision; 1,165, or more than half, had decayed teeth; 641 had throat infections; and 306 had nose infections.

It could not have been a worse time for James Earl Ray to enter school. "We permitted school terms to decrease in length," is the indictment handed down by an investigative report. "We reduced the number of school services to the child by: reducing programs of studies, curtailing extracurricular activities, eliminating instructional aids, dispensing with medical examinations and physical education courses, and we permitted deterioration in buildings and grounds. We are not yet prepared," the report prophetically concluded, "to save fellow citizens from ignorance or ourselves from the consequences of it. . . ."

There was something else wrong with the Ewing school. It was bad enough that there was snobbery between teacher and student there in the little town where everybody was broke. Social distinctions of the kind Tots brought down on

James Earl Ray were obscenely inappropriate in that setting at that time. But even worse was the objective training the school gave in racial bigotry. The taboo that kept any Negroes from living in Ewing was strictly applied in the Ewing school; the students were not even allowed the momentary association with Negroes on visiting athletic squads. When the Quincy basketball team came to Ewing to play it was warned to leave its Negro players at home and it did so. No, there wasn't any social training in the Ewing school that would contradict the kind of twisted racial education the boy was getting from Speedy; what he learned in the Ewing school reinforced Speedy's racial apartheid.

James Earl Ray, in his first encounter with an American institution in a "typical" small American town, at once became the victim of class distinction and had racial hatred ingrained in him; in other words, he learned in his most formative years the lower class white American's response to being discriminated against; you turn on, not the upper class, not the oppressors, not on those who are stronger, but on those weaker than you, the Negroes.

---

It should have surprised no one that Jimmy flunked the first grade, although it was discovered later that he had an IQ of 108. He was absent 48 of the 190 school days. He went back the second year to repeat the first grade, was absent 47 times, but passed. He was absent one-third of the time through the third grade. By then, Tots's contempt for the boy was open. In the space on his report card where the teacher recorded her judgment of the child's "Attitude toward regulations," Tots wrote, "violates all of them." Was the child honest? Tots warned, "needs watching." Was he courteous? "Seldom if ever polite," she wrote. His appearance? "Repulsive," was her hateful answer.

There were clues that his social adjustment was as poor as his academic record. His flawed appearance caused the boy to be teased on the school playground at recess, and the *way* he fought back is the most vivid memory his former schoolmates retain of him. "He fought as if he would never stop, flailing away at whoever was around him, tears streaming down his cheeks."

When a photographer came to take a school picture, Jimmy, at the last minute, just when the photographer put the black cloth over his head, ducked down behind the boy in front of him. All that the photo shows of Jimmy is his black crop of hair, the upper part of his face — one eye closed tight, the other half-open, squinting suspiciously at the camera.

# Chapter 7

When Jimmy was eleven or twelve he began to be seen around Ewing with three other boys. Two of them were Peacock boys, Charles and Robey. The other was Gerald Hobbs. They were all about the same age, give a year, take a year. Robey Peacock was the oldest. Hobbs had the muscles; he was the strongest. Charles was the closest to Jimmy Raynes. Charles Peacock was the picture of a country boy — snaggle-toothed, string blond hair down in his eyes, round-faced, blue-eyed, and wearing faded, patched bib overalls.

The Peacocks were not as poor as the Rayneses: nobody in Ewing was *that* poor. But they were poor, poor but carrying on, the boys taking it for granted that they would work all hours around the place, staying home from school if necessary. The same was true of Gerald Hobbs. He did chores around Ewing, stoking the furnace at the Catholic rectory.

Standing at a distance in time away from the boys, their pleasures seem almost demure — hunting rabbits and squirrels, fishing in the Fabby or simply playing in a ditch on the way home from school.

But to some of the older students these four were the toughest boys in school. "I gave them plenty of room!" says one who took the same route home. "I either let them go ahead or went ahead of them. They'd be going along the road and all of a sudden they'd break out fighting amongst themselves."

Yet another sees the boys, or at least Charles Peacock, more temperately. "Charles Henry was not tough — poor, yes! And he had a narrow-minded-mean-bullying father, but Charles was shy and he didn't talk plain."

There is evidence that Jimmy wasn't that tough either. He may have even joined forces with the other boys because he was being picked on. "If Jimmy was by himself, he was OK. He didn't have the push."

Anyway, Jimmy Raynes was never quite wholly within the group. He never went hunting with them. Gerald Hobbs, now (1972) a factory worker in Peoria, Illinois, remembers: "We used to catch catfish with worms, and go hunting and trapping. But Raynes never did go trapping, he never fished, and he never went hunting with us at night. Mostly when I saw him it was going back and forth to school. Or in the school yard. We used to shoot marbles for keeps. He was better at marbles than I was. We played with steelies, and when we'd get a pocketful, we'd shoot them away in slingshots."

Jimmy had something to gain from being a member of the group. A boy needs friendships with boys his own age. It gives him some distance from and perspective on his parents to be able to talk with, compare notes with, his contemporaries. Just as certainly, the gang didn't give him a completely detached view of his family. That world out there on the old Adams place, that was the world that claimed Jimmy's first loyalty.

"Jimmy wasn't the kind to be telling his troubles to anybody, especially outside the family," insists Jerry Ray, his brother. "Anyway, he was much closer to us at home than he was to those boys."

But Jimmy did make a friend in the group. It was Charles Peacock, and their relationship was one of the few friendships Jimmy was ever to form. From town you had to pass the Peacock house to get to the Raynes house. The two boys began to play in the afternoons around the Peacock house, and sometimes, but not often, Charles would go over to the Rayneses'. Apparently Charles felt a little more sure of himself in the ordinary life in Ewing than Jimmy. For one thing, Charles was a Boy Scout. Charles is remembered by Jerry Ball, the Scoutmaster, as being especially good at tying knots. Charles once asked Ball for permission to bring Jimmy on a Scout field trip. Ball said OK, but Jimmy did not show up. When the troop was going to Hall's Mill to cook weenies, Ball asked Charles to bring Jimmy along. Charles said Jimmy didn't have the dime each boy was supposed to chip in, but Ball went by and got him anyway, and took him. Finally, Ball asked Charles to bring Jimmy around to join the troop. "But Charles said Jimmy couldn't afford the fifty-cent manual," Ball recalls. "I sent mine to Jimmy by Charles, and Jimmy did come a few times and then dropped out." And so, after a while, did Charles.

Scouting is another of those cherished American images which is a cruel and humiliating delusion to boys like Jimmy Raynes and Charles Peacock. Millions of American dollars have been poured into Community Chests, United Funds, United Ways by middle-class families to support Scouting — under the guise of charity and with a charitable tax deduction and a salving of conscience — when in fact Scouting is an activity for middle-class boys whose parents can afford Scouting anyway. With its expensive uniforms, its manuals, its "official" gear, compasses, knives, cooking kits, for the poor boy it only underlines the inferiority and social isolation he feels.

About Jimmy, Ball noticed: "He wasn't the kind of boy to be forward. He was kind of withdrawn. He stayed in the back row."

It was not clear how close Jimmy and Charles Peacock* were, and it is very unlikely that Jimmy Raynes could, even with the help of a friend his own age, look objectively at his family, at Ceal and at Speedy. Nobody could challenge Speedy's high claim to Jimmy's emotional engagement.

There was proof of this in an episode that happened when Jimmy was about twelve. It took place, where so much of Ewing life took place, at Hall's Mill. It happened on what they called in Ewing, "Flunk Day." This was that glorious day that school let out, Graduation Day for some, but as those local wits had it in Ewing, flunk day for others. It was the custom for all the boys in the school, a couple of dozen, to stream off to Hall's Mill the minute the ceremonies at

* Peacock wrote the author on February 22, 1971, that he was the only person alive who could give a complete story on James Earl Ray and asked $3,000 for an interview.

school were over. The odds were that for Jimmy Raynes it was flunk day; he failed as often as he passed in the Ewing school. But that would not have seemed to matter to him; he wasn't the kind to show his disappointment. When the barefoot brigade moved off down the dusty country road toward the muddy swimming hole in the bend of the Fabby, Jimmy joined them.

Something happened after they had been swimming for a while.

Somebody tried to take Jimmy's pants off, and they all started teasing him. He squirmed around in the muddy shallows of the slow-flowing river until he was covered with mud. And then he fled down along the bank, holding his pants up as best he could, around the bend in the river.

Gerald Hobbs followed him. "You can't go home like that," Gerald said. But Jimmy would not move. He huddled there within his coat of slime. In disgust, Hobbs threw Jimmy back into the river and strode away.

What was in Jimmy's mind that day? Of what was he ashamed? Of what was he frightened?*

---

\* In adult life, Ray has often refused to let doctors examine his anal area, his medical records show.

---

# Chapter 8

Nothing, they say, ever happens in a small town. Of course that only seems to be true: a great deal happens. It is only that small town life is made up of things that are familiar, of accustomed events, and one of these in Ewing, Missouri, in the mid-1930's, was the arrival in town almost every day of Jerry Raynes and his old truck with his boy Jimmy bouncing along in the seat beside him.

It was their custom to pull up at Terrell's gas station. There Raynes would get down slowly, hitch up his pants with his elbows, as if to take the slack out of his pride, and ask Terrell if he could spare some oil. Terrell kept a drum of black, grimy used oil around the side of his station, and it was one of Terrell's accustomed events to let Raynes have some of the oil for nothing. Raynes might, or he might not, buy one or two gallons of fifteen-cent green gas.

What they had really come to town for was to go to Cason's. Everybody knew that. Nobody cared that the boy wasn't in school. Who cared whether or not boys like the Raynes boy got an education? Those people were just white trash, living out there in squalor on the old Adams place. It was said that things were awful out there, and nobody wanted to go see just how bad they, in fact, were. Besides, a man had a right to have his son around, beside him, to help. It was nobody's business if the boy's help seemed to amount to nothing more than watching his old man shoot pool. As for hanging out in a pool room with his boy, Speedy said: "You *know* I wouldn't let Jimmy go in there and play unless I was with him." And then: "Oh, yeah, we'd go in there and play. Jimmy *loved* pool. He used to blow up because he couldn't beat me. I don't believe he *ever* beat me."

---

There in the back of the Ewing barbershop, in that man's world of bib overalls, chewing tobacco, and two-bit bets, the boy and his father grasped for each other.

From the time he was seven or eight until he was in his early teens, Jimmy worshiped his father. "Well, he was close to both of us," Speedy has said, "to me and to Ceal. Now of course he ran around with me *more*. He was always running around with me. Yeah, Jimmy was with me just about all the time in those days."

Jimmy was already a boy who watched intently everything going on around him and he now turned his attention narrowly onto his father. Men who played pool in Cason's then remember the boy well. "He was so quiet, not like any boy I ever saw before," one of them said. "He made so little rumpus, I thought he must have a complex or something. He just sat there watching." What he was watching was his father.

---

In the country, silence is the reference of the night. It is not at all like the city, where every sound is lost in the general cacophony. In the country the smallest audible stirring makes its own unique ping, twang, against the silence. It was on the floor of the old Adams house in Ewing, in the silence of the prairie night, where a dog's bark sounded like an exploding shell, where he slept on the floor alone, unlike the other Raynes children who huddled together, it was there Jimmy had nightmares. He himself is the witness that he had them. He later told a prison psychiatrist he had become "quite fearful" (in the doctor's words) over a particular nightmare he had in Ewing when he was ten years old.

All children have nightmares, but that doesn't make a nightmare any the less frightening to the child who is having one. "The archaic fears, conflicts . . . the nameless terror, the sense of helplessness, the violence, the persecution by monstrous forces . . ." are the things that make a nightmare a nightmare, says a study.

The helplessness . . . that is the worst thing of all for a child. He cannot hope to defend himself against these monstrous shapes which are not the less fearsome because some of them stand for his own strong, powerful wishes and desires. A child may be small but his instinctual drives are man-sized.

---

Jimmy may all day have seemed to be idolizing his father, to be following the movement of those billiard balls around the table as Speedy skillfully pocketed them. But in the night, his feelings sprang loose from their conscious censorship, and other kinds of feelings came out.

It is not surprising that Jimmy's dreams had to do with the other side of his admiration, with his fear and his Oedipal feelings toward Speedy. In fact, his nightmares were pointed directly at the Oedipal dilemma.

That prison psychiatrist, the one Jimmy had told about his nightmares, learned that Jimmy "at the age of ten awoke one night and thought he had lost his eyesight." This is what happened to King Oedipus in the myth on which the psychological insight is based: King Oedipus blinded himself in self-punishment for murdering his father to wed his mother.

The emotion that set Jimmy apart from his brothers and sisters, from others for the rest of his life, was the quality of his *anger*.

The source of some of but not all of this anger in Jimmy was in his feelings about Speedy, that were lodged in the deepest recesses of his being, ready to produce anger, deep, sullen, hateful, even murderous anger.

Most of us defiantly refuse to acknowledge such explanations of our behavior. We find them offensive, sinister in their implications and, though we seldom admit it even to ourselves, quite unsettling. But just when we have safely put these "theories" behind us, they pop up in front of us, they find their *substance* in some vagrant, unexpected piece of evidence like James Earl Ray's dream.

*He* remembered the nightmare for thirty years.

_____

It was Speedy's chance, here in this boy, a pair of virgin ears to whom he could recite those twisted alibis for his failures. Here was someone who had to listen to Speedy's philosophy of what made the world go around — in such a *crooked* way.

Speedy laid his message on the boy with all the pressure of a man himself dragged down by cares. It was a time when Speedy was being asked to husband an ever-growing family — and not doing it. He resented his own failure with the fret of a man who had failed to get love and affection from *his* father and mother. It only seemed to bring out in Speedy his own conflicts, old feelings he had never been able to put in their place. He was asking Jimmy to grow up through him when he had never finished growing up himself.

The boy, a famous psychoanalyst has said, can do the father's work, and Speedy was now ready to give Jimmy the assignment: to be powerful where Speedy had been powerless, to right the wrongs Speedy had suffered, to change society.

Jimmy was quiet and a good listener. "He was such a good boy," Speedy has said. "He always minded everything I told him." Jimmy seemed old in understanding for his age. "He was just a man when he was a kid, you might say," said Speedy.

The idea that Jimmy might want to be like him perplexed Speedy. "I couldn't understand him wanting to be like *me*. That boy's *ahead of me!* I couldn't have been like him 'cause he was so witty." Mother-wit is what Speedy means.

"Hell, he learns so fast!" is Speedy's belief. "He's awful

intelligent. Well, he could accomplish things! If anything happened or anything, it looked like he could solve it right there." And Speedy remembers an example of the boy's aptitude.

"One time I was out with a disc harrow, and the goddamned disc jumped out of the thing. And I was working in the hot sun out there sweating and trying to get that damned bolt back in. And Jimmy was sitting there looking at me and he said if you raise that up there and put that bolt in the other way why it'll go right in. And I said, well, hell, if you know so much about it you do it. I raised it up and he put the bolt right back in there and that was all there was to it."

---

There is something about those two figures, something else, some other way of seeing them, as they rattle back and forth across the lean landscape of the American 1930's. It was not just the shadow of a Greek myth that shaped their actions. They were products of their native culture.

The native culture defined their vision of the world, gave them their linguistic materials and the dramatic style in which they expressed that vision. They both had the quality of absorbing, of incorporating within themselves, some *essence* of the environment, interacting with it without perhaps being aware that they were doing so, with the folk nature of that world of the Mississippi River basin, its lore and legends, its tales and songs, its oral tradition — "the great flood of the Mississippi and its elementary place in the American experience."

And their lives were lived within the magnetic field of a powerful American legend. Just a few miles away right there in that neck of Missouri, in another town, one on the banks of the river, had once lived a family named Blankenship who were, in their way, to become folk figures, and who were much like the Rayneses — a no-account, good-for-nothing father, a weak mother, a passel of smelly, damp children, one of whom was something like Jimmy Raynes. That boy's name was Tom Blankenship.

Old Man Woodson Blankenship sounded just like Speedy. "A man can't get his rights in a govment like this," Blankenship would say, as often in his cups as out of them. "The law jams a man into an old trap of a cabin, and lets him go round in clothes that ain't fittin' for a hog. Sometimes I've a mighty notion to just leave the country for good and all." In other words, a slightly paranoid blowhard.

His ethics were Speedy's ethics, and he passed them on to his children, especially to Tom. "Always take a chicken when you get a chance," the elder Blankenship instructed. "It warn't no harm to borrow things if you was meaning to pay them back," was his excuse, as if he ever paid anything back.

The Blankenship family had just about as much — and as little — standing in their community as the Rayneses did in Ewing. They were snug within what was already a well-established American tradition of "dirt eaters, tobacco-chewing, yellow-faced squatters." He did apparently own a piece of land, for the county levied on it once for back taxes: the bill was twenty-nine *cents*.

Both old man Blankenship and Speedy were violent, bigoted men, and it is not surprising that their boys, Tom and Jimmy, ended up with some of the same feelings about their fathers. Or seemed to. For more is known about Tom under another name he came to bear than is known about the real Tom Blankenship. Tom grew up in Hannibal, sixteen miles away from Ewing, and was an inspiration for one of his contemporaries there, in the 1830's. That other boy was Sam Clemens. Sam was not allowed to play with Tom but he observed Tom's ways and, as he readily admitted later, used Tom Blankenship as the basis for Huck Finn.

In Huck's story his father is everything, furnishes the central theme of the book and of Huck's life, and Huck's adventures are often viewed as the search for a father to replace Pap.

"Drifting down the river toward a goal he can neither define nor scarcely imagine, Huck is in fact looking for another father to replace the one he has lost," writes one critic. And, writes another, "in Jim he finds his true father." Moreover, Huck wasn't simply running from his father to save his life physically; Huck had to put Pap out of his mind to have any life of his own. That is what gave the intensity to his search for a replacement for Pap. That is why he could choose a black man.

James Earl Ray was to go off from Ewing down the river, live almost all the rest of his life in the towns (Alton, Quincy, St. Louis) on the banks of the river — and if The Boy and The River are the two symbols of Huck Finn, if the river gives a structure to the novel, it gives a geographical shape to the adventures of James Earl Ray. He was to end his adventures on the river, with one that shook the world, the adventure he planned and executed in Memphis. That final adventure was also at least in part the search for a father.

# Chapter 9

The old Adams place was just about *wore out*. The frontier log cabin, built with hands inspired by God knows what dreams and hopes, was now about to come to an ignoble end at the hands of a family who were contemptuous of the virtues of the land, whose dreams had nothing to do with an open sky and ripening fields.

This scruffy clan, the Raynes family, were now pulling the old place apart, plank by plank, for firewood, forcing the old house to consume itself in its own gizzard.

The old place had hung on beyond its time. The frontier spirit was gone. Well, dust to dust. If the Camels don't get you the Fatimas (or the Rayneses) must.

---

It's not easy to figure out what the quality of Raynes family life was in those last years in Ewing, before they broke up their home there, in the years from 1940 until 1943.

The difficulty is that the members of the family who were living there then are not altogether reliable reporters. Their recollection is not trustworthy. It has become mellowed by time, and by something else: They all look back on it as the happiest time of their lives. Wretched and squalid though their lives were in Ewing, everything was to turn out worse for them after they left Ewing.

An example of this view of Ewing is at hand in a letter from Jack Ray, written in 1973 from the federal penitentiary at Marion, Illinois, where Ray is serving time (eighteen years) for driving the getaway car in a bank robbery. It was one of a long series of letters exchanged between me and Jack in which he turned out to be the most detached and objective member of his family.

I once asked him why, during her travail in Ewing, Ceal did not get up and leave there, take the children with her. He replied:

"I expect that you know that Ceal and her best girlfriend [Emma] used to attend Square dances up in Godfrey, [Illinois,] and when the ole man came by in his Dodge Roadster strumming ole Suszanna [sic] on his banjo, Ceal fell in love. Emma died in her twenties.

"The Rays usual got married late in life and very few divorces. The Old Man, his dad, brother and sister, all was only married once. Jimmy, Melba, Frank and me was never married. Jerry is the Black Sheep of the family [he did get married].

"This brings me back to your question. Where would Ceal go if she did want to leave Ewing? Those days persons did not run to Judges to get there problems solved. Especial our family. The Law always hound, persecute the Ray's for over a century, and they still haven't let up.

"Why would Ceal leave Ewing anyway, she had her children, the old man didn't drink, I have never saw the old man lay a hand on her. All this stuff about nothing to eat! Do you know anybody with land who can't eat? In fact, Ceal use to can berry's, beans, tomatoes, etc., for winter.

"I believe the only place Ceal was happy was in Ewing. Ceal, or the rest of us do not have many friends. But we don't want none, having friends is the quickest way winding up on the end of a rope."

Ceal did try to leave once. She packed a tow sack with clothes, and set off with the children down the road toward Ewing — and for what destination beyond that she never told anybody. Speedy ran after her and begged her to return. She listened to him patiently, looked down the road where she had been heading and then, as if she had not seen anything on the horizon more attractive than what she had left, she returned to him.

What had been true all these years was still true for her and for Speedy. They loved each other with their capacity for love. They did not hate each other; whatever the atmosphere was at the old Adams place, it wasn't one of warfare between a husband and his wife.

"You only love *once*," said Speedy in his later years, referring to Ceal.

Because the old Adams place was falling apart, Speedy took it on himself to find some new shelter for his family. He had had his eye on a small C.B.&Q. building that once sat on the railroad right-of-way. He started, as they say in that part of Missouri, "talking around a little bit" with the owner about the price — half-threatening, half "poor mouth." Finally $50 passed hands. Speedy had no sooner moved the house to the Adams place than another man turned up claiming *he* owned the building, demanding $100 for it. Speedy paid over the hundred bucks, but complained bitterly:

"If that had happened to Earl," he told Ceal and the kids, "he would have gone down there and *killed* all those people and wound up in the electric chair." Speedy's way was different. "About three months later," one of the Ray boys now remembers, "those people found themselves missing three cows worth about six hundred dollars, and we had three new cows on our place."

There was one good day a year. It was Christmas. To children like the Raynes children, it must have been a little bewildering to find that on one day a year, people turned out to be generous and kind. Mom Maher always came from Alton, bringing with her money for Ceal and gifts for the children. Mabel Fuller did not come (it was too depressing) but she sent gifts, something especially nice for Jimmy. He was her favorite. Those two maiden Fitzsimmons sisters were the most generous of all. Sadie sent presents and usually something in cash. Aunt Rose Maher, a typist at the Navy Department in Washington, lived frugally and sometimes, the children believe, sent as much as $300 or $400 to help Ceal out.

Those hard years in Ewing riveted them together. You can see how much so by looking ahead to the present. They are in touch with each other. They know each other's whereabouts at any given moment. Nor is it that they have maintained a series of one-to-one relationships, say Jack with Jerry, or Melba with Jimmy. They are in touch as peers. No one of them is in closer touch with another than he is with the group. What's more, they seem to be attuned to each other's feelings, and to know how to interpret these feelings correctly even though none of them has a vocabulary of sentiment. They accept each other no matter how unacceptable they may seem to others. When one of them has, say, done some pimping, they all seem to understand that perfectly, not only give moral support but immoral support if that is the form that moral support must take. If one of them is on the run and needs a gun, the other will get it for him as a matter of course. They are welded together by those searching years at the old Adams place, loyal to each other as only people can be who are loyal to an all-consuming shared experience, like men who served at Valley Forge or Guadalcanal.

Ewing left them emotionally maimed. They did not form attachments to other people because they could not. They were emotionally incapable of doing so.

The children were all showing scars before they left Ewing. One day Jerry became so outraged at Speedy's teasing him that, in the night, he stuffed the privy full to the ceiling with old newspapers and set fire to it. It burned to the ground. Jack was less violent on the surface, but he had speech trouble, seemed to be swallowing his words when he tried to talk, almost as if his talk was being played back on a tape over a rumble of his anger. "Melba never was right from the day [1939] she was born," one of the children has recalled. One day in the school lunchroom Jimmy suddenly stuck a knife in Jack's ear during school lunch recess.

In the first week of school in the fall of 1942 some boys were playing scrub football at recess and Jimmy got a chance to carry the ball. When he was tackled, there was a crack. Jimmy had broken his leg. He did not cry. He lay there silently and uncomplainingly on the ground. He would have to be taken to Quincy, to the hospital. There wasn't a doctor, or even a nurse, in Ewing. Mr. Graves, the eighth grade teacher, offered to take Jimmy to the Quincy hospital. Graves had a car even on his $52 a month (for nine months a year) — a salary he supplemented in the summer by keeping time for a WPA gang.

It fell on Mrs. Graves to do the driving. Someone by this time had taken Jimmy home, and she went out to the old Adams place to the back of the house where she found Ceal in "this huge kitchen with a wood stove." Mrs. Graves offered to help Ceal carry Jimmy out to the car, but Ceal lifted him up by herself. "She was *so* gentle with him," remembers Mrs. Graves, who thought "Mrs. Raynes was about as well dressed as any of us were back in those hard times. She was neatly groomed.

"I drove as near to the doctor's office as I could, and Jimmy's mother carried him in her arms to the elevator, and from there to the doctor's office, and back the same way. All this time Jimmy was very quiet. It seemed that every movement brought much pain but he lay very still and hardly spoke a word.

"I made several trips after that. I can't remember of getting any help in paying the expenses and didn't expect any. The bridge fare cost fifty cents for a round trip and it did take gasoline. But I was thankful that we had a car and could help."

Ceal was grateful. One day in Ewing she saw Mrs. Graves: "I've got some baby chicks, and when they get big enough I'm going to bring you some," Ceal said. Several weeks later Ceal turned up at the Graveses' door with two frying chickens.

At this point an odd thing happened. Jimmy, who was known for keeping his distance from everyone, even members of his own family, began to turn tentatively to Graves for friendship. "After he broke his leg," Graves has said, "he was always coming to me for something."

Graves was very far from being the kind of man one might have thought Jimmy would turn to. He was at another pole from Speedy. In fact, Speedy did not like him, had once, because of something that happened between Jimmy and Graves, threatened to "go down there to that schoolhouse and thrash Jack Graves." Graves, whose real name was Virgil, was soft-spoken, gentle, anything but violent, moral if not pious. In fact he was a part-time reverend who ministered to a small evangelical sect in Ewing. In rural areas in those days the preacher and the church functioned somewhat as the church did in medieval times, when the church was as much the source of the artistic life of the community as it was the religious life. Children who were interested in the arts, in music, turned to Graves. He had protégés, none of whom were at all like Jimmy Raynes.

Some of the rough-and-tough boys disdained Graves. A school basketball star remembers Graves as a "likable man who could sometimes be quite cocky and pompous.

"One day he came into the room and asked what caused there to be a hole in the wallboard partition. I told him it was where the half-pints came through. He was sensitive about his shortness and proceeded to slap my face. I was pretty cocky myself so I placed my hands on each of his shoulders and gave him a 'gentle' shove that propelled him backwards and he fell under a kerosene stove. He was burned, required to doctor for some time, and I was suspended."

Jimmy once asked Graves: "Are you ashamed of me?" "He was very self-conscious about his appearance," says Graves.

There were children who couldn't afford even the few cents the hot lunches cost and Jimmy was one of those. It was taken for granted that they would never be able to pay, that their circumstances wouldn't change from week to week. Nevertheless, at the beginning of every week, Jimmy would go up to Graves and explain that he didn't have any money that week but that he hoped he could eat anyway.

Once when Jimmy had broken a school rule he appealed to Graves: "Aren't you mad at me?" Graves said that he was not.

Not long after that Jimmy brought to Graves's desk at the end of the school day a hickory whistle which he had whittled himself.

"I can't remember a single incident," says Graves, "where Jimmy showed a malicious or a wanton heart."

---

Nobody ever accused James Earl Ray of being a student. It would have been surprising if he had been one. Where would he have studied? What would have been his incentive? Where in his world was there a model for him to take academic work seriously?

He wasn't stupid. His IQ was 108. Graves believed that Jimmy could have finished high school, that if he had done so he would "never have got into any trouble." Well, he didn't finish. And he did get into trouble. And speculation like that simply fuzzes the chance of understanding what did happen and why.

What happened was that Jimmy did have a certain interest, and a latter-day version of Graves might have seen it and exploited it as a way of making Jimmy a better student.

Graves noticed that Jimmy did pay attention when the class took up history. "That's the time his hand would go up," remembers Graves. It was an interest broader than that, that extended not only backward to the past but to the present, in what in school in those days was called "current affairs."

As a practical experiment in science, Graves's class (which included the sixth, seventh and eighth grades) built a crude one-tube radio receiver. Jimmy Raynes was fascinated with it, not in building it, not in how it operated, but in one of its products, the news. When other students had fled to the playground for lunch recess, Jimmy often stayed behind, crouched over the radio, listening to news broadcasts.

Graves denies any knowledge of Jimmy's politics, says that the boy never discussed politics with him. Perhaps not, perhaps Graves now believes that it would be unfair of him to talk about Jimmy's boyhood political interests.

But the Raynes family readily acknowledges Jimmy's early political bent, and took it as simply another piece of evidence of how different he was. These were the days when baseball was still the national pastime, its heroes national heroes, the days when the Gashouse Gang of the St. Louis Cardinal team — Pepper Martin, Dizzy Dean — were the reigning heroes. Everybody in Ewing was for the Cardinals. All of the Raynes family were.

"But Jimmy was for Detroit and his hero was Schoolboy Rowe," remembers Jack Ray.

Also, as it turned out, "Jimmy was about the only Republican in Ewing. The Old Man and Ceal was strong for FDR, just like everybody else was in Ewing. Jimmy used to argue them up and down. He was very strong for Willkie. But mostly he was *against* Roosevelt. Jimmy said Roosevelt wasn't doing anything but throwing off propaganda on Hitler. He kept saying all that stuff Roosevelt was saying about Hitler wasn't true at all."

What on earth did Jimmy Raynes know about Hitler? How on earth did ideas like that get into the boy's head there in that little town at the end of nowhere? Wasn't he too young to be interested in politics? Wasn't baseball a more appropriate interest?

The answer is no. He was at the very point in his life when boys (and girls) first show an interest in politics. Boys at this age, at twelve and thirteen, are at the threshold of ideology. Until a child is twelve or thirteen, his whole world is a world of the concrete, the specific, the immediate, the here and now. He lives in a world of vivid, present images. But somewhere between twelve and fourteen, a child becomes capable of dealing with time in a much wider perspective. He becomes aware of the past, and of a future. He becomes capable of thinking abstractly, of having *political* ideas.

It is not surprising that Jimmy had the *kind* of ideas he

had, for it is an illusion that adolescents are dreamy idealists, looking for loose, unregimented utopias. Just the opposite is true. "The young adolescent has only a dim appreciation of democratic forms, little sensitivity to individual or minority rights," says a study. "His morality is absolutist. He has a pervasive authoritarian bias."

---

Might Graves have changed Jimmy, and the course of history, at this stage of the boy's development? Yes, he might have, or at least he might have done something toward that end. He might have leavened Jimmy's views, given him some sense of historical objectivity, other books to read, introduced Jimmy to other views and approaches to politics. Jimmy was educable, as tests of his intellectual capacity were to show. Jimmy was interested, eager to hear more about politics. There is no doubt that Jimmy had accepted Graves to some degree, as another father, a father with more warmth and gentleness than Speedy.

But Graves was overworked and underpaid. Graves is not to blame for the missed chance. It is more plausible to blame the school for not giving James Earl Ray a clearer understanding of the nature of American society, American ideals, American democracy. The failure is an institutional one more than it is a personal one.

It is very important to understand that Jimmy was *not* some foredoomed kook who was going to turn out the way he did turn out no matter what help he got or didn't get.

# Chapter 10

The time had come for Jimmy to leave Ewing. By the standards of the world he lived in, he was a man, big enough to go out into the world and get a man's job. In 1944, when he was sixteen, he left the old Adams place for good.

For a young man like him, with no money and no special job prospects, he had to go someplace where he would have a place to stay, and this came down to either Quincy or Alton. All of Speedy's family were in Quincy, and Mom Maher and her son Willie were in Alton where Mom was now running a rooming house on the second floor over some stores on Broadway, the main street of Alton.

Jimmy knew Quincy better than he knew Alton. He had, in fact, been going over to Quincy off and on all through his early adolescent years, while he was still living in Ewing. Sometimes he stayed with his uncle Earl, that is, when Earl wasn't in the state penitentiary down at Menard, Illinois. As Jimmy had grown older, out of boyhood, he had lost most of his awe for Speedy, only to transfer his affection and respect to Earl. "Jimmy worshiped Earl," according to Walter Rife, a friend of his own age Jimmy made in Quincy. With Earl as his vocational inspiration, Jimmy began to do small jobs with Rife in Quincy — "boy stuff," Rife has since described these activities. "We would just be walking around the streets," recalls Rife, "and one of us would say, 'Let's go in there.' We never planned it or anything. I remember I couldn't take my money home for fear my mother would catch me with it. I used to hide what I stole in an old tin can and bury it in the alley."

Jimmy sometimes stole enough so that he could take a room in a hotel, just like a man. Sometimes he would spend the night at the Victor Hotel, sometimes in a whorehouse, at "Gene and Rusty's," at Second and Oak streets. Jimmy did not have much to do with straight girls.

"We'd meet girls. He just couldn't talk to them. He was shy. I'd get him a date and we'd go on an excursion boat and his girl would be gone off with another guy before the boat got halfway on the trip. And when we got back to Quincy, he'd go to a whorehouse. He'd just take any prostitute, didn't care whether he ever saw that same girl again."

Stealing seems already to have come quite naturally to Jimmy by those teenage years in Ewing. He tried it elsewhere, not only in Ewing, not only in Quincy, but in Alton when he went down there to visit Mom Maher. The first time Jimmy was arrested Jack was with him. Jack was eleven and Jimmy was fourteen. "We was going down the street and we pick up a stack of newspapers that a truck had toss off,"

Jack recounts in a letter. "The Alton cops arrest us, him on one corner me on the other Selling these paper. I was scared of the police, and Jimmy was getting tough with them, I'm trying to shut him up. They took us over and Lock up in Jail. I got scared and Started hollering for Mom. Mom Jump on the police For having us Lock in a cell," and the boys were released with a warning.

The Alton episode wasn't the first time Jimmy had been caught in a theft. When he was in the sixth grade at Ewing, in Miss Inez Kitson's class, he stole the school lunch money out of Miss Kitson's desk, ran to town with it and hid the money under a porch where it was soon discovered and Jimmy's complicity established.

Thus he had not only acquired some experience as a thief, but there was also Quincy itself, a ready-made environment for a man who wished to spend his life outside the law.

------

Cities can have personalities, foibles, eccentricities, ups and downs of morale, and can give off atmospheres, gain and lose identities, just as people do.

Quincy was all hope at its beginning, full of the bounce, bustle and optimism of the 1840's, an uproarious river port, the most important settlement on the upper Mississippi, the second largest city in Illinois. In 1846, twenty thousand hogs, "long-legged, long-snouted, fleet as a deer," were shipped out of Quincy. Five steamboats a day stopped there. The town exported $15 million in goods a year during the 1850's.

But in that same decade, Quincy was riven by racial strife. It was only across the river from Missouri, a slave state. One of the Lincoln-Douglas debates was staged in Quincy in what is now Washington Park, a place that became one of James Earl Ray's hangouts. A Quincy Abolitionist society met in a church called "The Lord's Barn." An ugly, hateful mob gathered outside one night and began to throw stones at The Lord's Barn. But the Abolitionists had been forewarned: "They seized clubs, hatchets and muskets hidden under the pulpit, and, led by deacons, rushed forth brandishing their weapons. The mob fled."

When the railroads came and took the river business away from Quincy it had nothing left to grow on, to hope on. The town lay stagnant for many decades. It had its eccentrics, like Major Thomas B. Baldwin, a pioneer balloonist who made a four-thousand-foot parachute jump in Quincy in 1887. Fortunately for Quincy, it was the only city within a hundred-mile radius and it became a trading center for western Illinois, southeastern Iowa, and northeastern Missouri. This was the state of things in Quincy from the last quarter of the nineteenth century through the first half of the twentieth.

But it had lost its unity as a political, social and cultural organism. It had no particular civic pride, no sense of itself. It was only its disparate parts. It added up only to "the Quincy syndrome, that is, to keep everything here on dead center," says a college teacher in Quincy. Those in power in the town wanted to keep it like it was. A prominent lawyer was quoted as saying that if he had his way he would freeze the population of Quincy at fifty thousand. It was then forty-seven thousand.

This has made for bitterness. "If somebody had done away

with twelve pairs of grandparents two generations ago, Quincy would have been all the better for it," believes one resident.

The suicide rate in the 1960's was twice the national average, attributed partly to the presence of so many old people in Quincy. Fourteen percent of the population was over sixty-five.

The fact that the town was on dead center deepened the lines that divided the social, economic, and ethnic class structures in Quincy. "There is less mobility than in a rapidly growing urban area," is the finding of a careful study of Quincy.

The ruts are deep. A large German Catholic population has always given a deep conservative hue to Quincy. They live and work uneventfully in a section called Calftown, in narrow red brick houses with unusually long deep lots where they could keep a cow at home.

There were never many Negroes in Quincy, the proportion has run about 3 percent of the population, but they represented a problem out of all proportion to their numbers. Quincy had its race problem, and in Quincy it was *unresolved*, bore that air of diseased unreality that comes when one group of people has a distorted and unknowing picture of another group of people. Blacks couldn't go to a downtown movie until 1964.

There were and are a few rich families who without too much trouble dominated everything, kept Quincy on dead center, successfully held on to their accumulations of economic and social power.

At the other end of the scale were those country people

who came in with cow shit on their shoes and worked, off and on, in the "chicken-factory," plucking and packing poultry, the lowest status and lowest paying work in Quincy. "My brother, him and his wife, worked down there years and years ago," said a former river ward resident. When his sixteen-year-old daughter wanted to work down there part-time in the summer, he told her: "I don't care where in the hell you get a job, but you're not working at that place!"

These chicken pluckers were among the "river people," Quincy's lowest class. A University of Chicago team of sociologists studied Quincy in the 1960's. They located people by status, numbering them from 1 (highest) to 7 (lowest). All of the Number 7's were along the river, and so were all of the Number 6's. The grading system worked upward in status the farther you got away from the river, out toward the city limits where all the Number 2's and Number 1's lived.

There's a local saying that, in the light of the map, is not at all surprising: "In Quincy, two blocks is a lifetime."

Living along the river, in the "river wards," was fateful; if you were an adult, it proved you had failed in life, and, if you were a child, it foretold your almost certain failure. The graduates of the four elementary schools in the river wards did poorly in high school. Less than half finished; only 9 percent went to college, and almost all of these were athletes. By contrast, 76 percent of the upper middle class children went to college, and only 5 percent of them dropped out before finishing high school. "The area of town a child comes from, the house he lives in, and his parent's occupation are all rather well known and profoundly affect the community's educational expectations for him. Almost any child growing up in the neighborhood was to a degree disadvantaged."

Vice can't exist in a community without the consent and cooperation of The Good People. They are not guiltless. It simply won't do for the "respectable" people to say they don't know what is going on. They do know and often, as was the case in Quincy, give their silent support. The police, the members of the bar, judges, businessmen, hotel keepers, drugstore owners, pharmacists, doctors, and many more people in a community like Quincy know that there is vice in their midst. And of course this applies to every politician, office holder, from the mayor to the garbage man, and includes the whole apparatus of social work, family welfare workers, probation officers, schoolteachers, principals and school administrators. The newspapers know it, down to the names of every whore and bartender in town.

The entrepreneurs of vice are catholic in their choice of cities in which to conduct their business. They don't care where they go; for them the critical thing is to have the cooperation of the police and the indifference of the general public. Once they find a vacuum of law enforcement, they fill it.

In the 1930's, and until after the Kefauver investigation of the 1950's, there was vice in Quincy out of all proportion to the size of the place. An investigation in the 1950's showed that there were 572 slot machines in Adams County, with 165 bars, three times as many as in a typical Illinois town of that time, and the gambling take was put at $5 million a year.

Gambling was going on at a rate which, if the dollar cost had been shared equally, would have cost each family in

Quincy about $450. But that isn't the way it worked. The burden fell on lower and working class families, on the ones who could least afford it, taking from them the margin of financial security, keeping them in a sort of bondage to their low-paying jobs. In this sense, the sinful world of Quincy functioned for the most "respectable." Hence, though the two worlds seemed worlds apart, they were in fact and sinful practice interdependent.

But as far as social mobility was concerned, the criminal world of Quincy — and the Ray family — was self-enclosed in those river wards, as much a "district" as the old open prostitution district of New Orleans, in Quincy a district of shameless whores, rough and tough bars and hotels with hotbeds of pimps, robbers, fences, and knowing, infinitely tolerant tavern keepers.

---

But, surprisingly, Jimmy decided against Quincy. For some months, Mom Maher had been talking to him about coming to Alton. There were jobs in the huge, booming International Shoe Company tannery just south of Alton, at East Hartford, Illinois. He moved into Mom Maher's Broadway rooming house and went to work in the dye room of the tannery.

There was a time when he would go to Quincy. But now, in 1944 at sixteen years of age, he had other things in his head. He was imbued with all the things the family had told him about himself, full of the sense of mission they had given him, determined to live up to their expectations of him. It was true that he had slipped off the straight and narrow now and then himself, but he dinned it into the younger boys, into Jerry and Jack, that stealing was bad medicine.

Speedy had always told him that he could amount to something, that he was smart, and Ceal and the other children had always treated him as if he were the smartest member of the family, and he had come to believe them.

He had come to a time of decision in his life, the kind young men have always faced, of seeing what part of himself, of his younger self, was worth carrying forward into adulthood. In the 1970's, this is called "the identity crisis," but it isn't really a crisis so much as it is a mutation, and the person he was to become would still be made up of, in large part, the hopes, fears, ideals and unspoken dreams of the people who had been closest to him.

Their hopes and passions were passed on to Jimmy, the oldest child, with special intensity. The oldest child always bears the special hopes — and the responsibility for revenging the parents' disappointments. The oldest son must make up for the lacks in the Father. He has the perilous task of linking his family and the world all over again for his generation. He sees, sometimes merely senses, what is missing in his parents' relationship with the outside world, and the responsibility for making up for what is missing falls heaviest on him.

Jimmy was going to be powerful where they (and especially Speedy) had been powerless. He was going to act where Speedy had merely talked. He was going to do something about the political situation Speedy had merely griped about. The family's hopes were pinned on Jimmy. He was the one who was going to make it outside.

———

Jimmy knew the vocational rewards and hazards of being

a thief, and he, at least at this point in life, wanted no part of that trade. He knew the cardinal fact about being a thief, and much else: that the thief is willing to pay a higher price than the rest of us to get the material things he wants: the loss of his freedom.

The thief knows better than anyone else the odds against his success. He knows that he is going to get caught. He knows that if he steals and gets away with it, he is going to steal again, and again, until he *is* caught. To the thief, the attainment of the object is the important thing, more important than keeping it, for what he seeks is to dispel his deep feeling of deprivation, and once he has the object he has dispelled that need. The thief has no confidence whatsoever in the established social order or that he can get anything from it by honest effort. He is sure it is rigged against him. He is not a radical or a revolutionary, not a Robin Hood or a Raffles. There is no such thing as a "criminal mind" unless it is a collection of more or less paranoid estimates of what the straight world is like.

He is likely to make some half-hearted passes at a regular job, but each defeat he suffers in the straight world only deepens his suspicion of it. A thief's life is a descending scale of failed possibilities as he moves back and forth between prison and the "outside" which he inhabits, as he grows older, for ever-briefer periods. In the end, he is more comfortable "inside" than "outside." The outside world becomes chaotic, frightening to him, and he is happier, safer, more comfortable, more secure, behind prison walls. The criminal life is so different that the people who live it find it necessary to create a separate and quite distinct environment, a self-enclosed world. Once a man or woman has moved within it, made an adaptation to it, accepted its underlying despair and defeatism, it is very difficult for him or for her ever to leave it. People tend to be jelled within it, even intermarry, produce children who grow up within it. The problem is in fact to get out of it. That was one of James Earl Ray's problems as he grew into adolescence: to fight his way out of an environment that would define his future just as certainly as if he had been born blind. He was determined to turn his back on that as he moved down the river to Alton.

Not long before Jimmy left Ewing, something happened at a carnival that opened his eyes. It was one of those times that Earl was visiting Ewing. A barker invited anyone in the crowd to come forward. Earl knew the ropes of the carnival world, and having a few drinks under his belt anyway, went forward. He lasted three rounds, came out of the ring, battered but undaunted. The barker turned to Speedy, taunted him to come forward and fight, "like your friend there fought." Speedy hesitated. He took off his shirt as if he were going to fight, but then drew back.

This was disillusioning for Jimmy and Jack. "We wanted to see for ourselves," says Jack, "see this man who always told us he could hit harder than Gene Tunney, who told us he could drive his fist through a concrete wall, who told us he had so much power in his arm he scared he break his wrist if he hit at his maximum."

And they saw their father chicken out.

In fact, Jimmy was very much disillusioned about Speedy as a man and as a father by the time he left Ewing.

From that time on, for the rest of his life, Jimmy was forever afterwards to insist, whenever he was asked:

"Father?"

"Dead," Jimmy would answer, and his police and prison records show it. Of course, Speedy was very much alive, and Jimmy knew it.

# Chapter 11

When Jimmy arrived in Alton in 1944, he was determined *to amount to something.* But to what?

What particular *mix* would Jimmy — and circumstance — make of the elements of his identity, of the fact that he was to bear the responsibility of being smart, of being ambitious, of being powerful where his family had been powerless, of righting the wrongs of his family politically, for of course Jimmy was political.

At the beginning in Alton it seemed unlikely that these elements would come together, particularly his ambition and his politics, that he might give meaning to his life through politics.

There seemed little if any promise for him in the job he was able to get at the International Shoe Company tannery at East Hartford, Illinois. East Hartford was a tough mill town, one of those places, as Ewing had been, that bragged: "No nigger ever spent the night in East Hartford."

In those days, Jimmy was able to get back and forth by streetcar from the plant to Mom's boardinghouse in Alton. Jimmy was paid seventy-seven cents an hour, but, as the factory struggled to meet World War II orders, Jimmy made plenty of overtime, often worked so late that he slept there.

He did not drink. Mom kept beer in her icebox for her roomers, but Jimmy never took a beer for himself. She would have known it if he had done so. She was generous, but she was also a woman used to living close to the line. He did not smoke. He did not have a girl friend. He told Mom once that he thought dancing was "silly," and that only sissies wore ties.

"Never went out, never runned around," is the testimony Mom later gave in an affidavit. "As far as girls, he was backward. He was bashful with girls. No pals of men, either. Just stayed home. Always comes in with a smile on his face. He's quiet and easy."

He was very straitlaced about stealing, too, got quite self-righteous with Jack and Jerry, warned them every time he returned to the family for a visit: "Stay out of trouble. It's easier working."

He was saving his money and telling people that he was going to open a filling station.

He knocked around some with his uncle Willie Maher, Mom's son, who worked in a steel mill below Alton. Willie was older than Jimmy, unmarried, and a man who liked a good time. The two of them went to ball games in St. Louis, mainly to see the Browns. They shot pool at the Elks Club where Jimmy soon established himself as a young pool shark.

Between Mom's boardinghouse and the river there was an improvised ball field, and Jimmy occasionally went down there and joined the game. His position, when he played, was shortstop.

This was all to the good, and normal enough. But what about Jimmy's political side, his political ambitions?

---

Jimmy's closest friend at the tannery, the man who taught him how to mix colors, was a much older man. The son of German immigrants who brought him to the United States, he had spent much of his adult life at the tannery. His was a narrow, insular, ethnic life, almost all of it lived within a local German community. In fact, it was even more constricted than that. He seldom moved outside the world of his own family. He spent a large part of his life taking care of his mother. He never married.

He was a meticulous person, on the job and off. At home, he did the cooking. He kept the kitchen spotless and the rest of the house just as orderly, to the point of placing clean newspapers on the floor under each of the easy chairs in his carefully organized living room. He cultivated a kitchen garden in the backyard. His roses were his pride.

He loved Germany, and German culture, as he knew it, German religion (he was a member of and attended the Lutheran church), and as time passed he came to love German politics. He carried a picture of Hitler, his idol. He would show it to people. This was not popular in 1944. And his heavy German accent did not help, for most people knew that he had grown up in the United States.

He and Jimmy became close friends. They were together

a great deal. It got so that he would ride the streetcar home with Jimmy and they would go to "Boob's" restaurant — Boob for Boob Roberts who is (1969) a civil servant in Alton and remembers the two coming in after work, late in the afternoon, taking the two back stools, waiting for those stools to be empty if they were not, and then talking lengthily, heads close together, as other customers came and went. Jimmy's choice of food was chili, and of subject politics, "Hitler politics," as Boob remembers. Mom Maher noticed the friendship, and did not understand it. "Jimmy came down and wanted to work during the war," she said, "and he was sixteen in 1944 and he worked in a tannery and was laid off after nearly two years. He worked with a man in the tannery from Germany and learned the trade of dyeing leather. Jimmy got a job mixing dyes. Got promoted. He and this man, I don't know his last name, showed him his picture and said he was a friend of Hitler's." Mom meant that he showed Jimmy Hitler's picture.

Eric Duncan, of Hartford, was shop steward when Jimmy worked at the tannery, remembers Jimmy's friend, remembers that he and Jimmy were "together all the time. They were bosom buddies. It looked like Ray looked up to him. He went around the shop calling Germany the Fatherland. Finally, one day a fellow got sick of it and bumped the man's head against the wall." He came to Duncan about the incident, but Duncan didn't do anything.

As for Jimmy, Duncan remembers one incident: "One day Ray pushed a table into a woman there and it looked like he did it just for the hell of it. If there was a way to break the rules, Ray did it. I'd call Ray a little on the prick side."

There is no doubt but that the relationship between Jimmy

and his friend was a deep one, a resonant one, and one that at that moment was at the center of both their lives.

This friend has refused to talk about Jimmy, but I wandered into his backyard one day in 1969. He was hanging up laundry on the line. He was dressed in loose-fitting khaki, and wore heavy black overshoes (although the skies were clear) over white athletic socks.

When I identified myself he grew nervous, and when I presented my credentials he said that he could not read them. When I asked him if he had known James Earl Ray, he became almost hysterical. His whole body shook. For a few seconds he did not say anything, and then he cried out, loudly, there in the open: "Sharmans, Sharmans, why don't they like Sharmans?" He of course meant Germans.

He did invite me into his home, talked briefly to me, and I asked him if I might come back the next day to talk with him again. I tried to explain to him the importance of understanding James Earl Ray's life story. I did not try to deceive him. I did not pretend that my interest was anything but what it was. He grew thoughtful, and then told me to let him think about Ray overnight, and that he would see me the next day. But when I rang the bell next day at the time we had agreed upon, there was no answer.

Knowing so little about him, it is neither wise nor fair to speculate on exactly what the relationship meant to him. But we know more about Jimmy, and it is obvious from what happened to him before he knew the man and from what he did afterwards that he was a catalyst. Jimmy had thought Hitler was right and President Roosevelt wrong about World War II even before he had left Ewing. But after he had chewed over politics with his friend at Boob's for a while,

Jimmy had become an impassioned proponent of the Nazi philosophy.

In him, Jimmy had found yet another kind of father, different of course from Speedy, and different from Jack Graves certainly, a father who could articulate the son's feelings, give them direction. Adolescence is a time of idealism, and there isn't any doubt but that this time with his friend was the apogee of James Earl Ray's political idealism. It was one of the most hopeful and emotionally satisfying interludes in his life. Jimmy *did* feel smart, he did feel he could do something important, he did feel he could do it through politics.

His pledge to nazism was itself peculiarly satisfying. To a young man like Jimmy, for whom so many things were unsettled, troubling, unresolved — not the least problem of which was his own personal sexual definition — Hitler was powerfully alluring. Nazism can attract those who are emotionally fragmented, who want to believe it will make them whole.

And for a young man like Jimmy, nazism was alluring in detail. It was absolutely, self-consciously free of the feminine image. The Nazis had a strong, decisive way of dealing with threats. They knew how to put an end to Jews, Negroes. The regimentation of nazism was comforting; that everyone knew exactly who he was, where he belonged in the scheme of things, was reassuring to a young man whose family was always slipping and sliding around the borders of social class, a family more often than not collapsing into deviance and criminality. Besides, the Nazis were clean, not dirty, not lazy, and not sex-ridden. Speedy had once said that "niggers just lay around and fuck all the time." That is one thing that Nazis did not do, or did not seem to do. For it cannot be overemphasized that Jimmy's ideas, his ideals, existed in no perspective but the present clouded vagueness of his own immediate personal needs and intensities.

---

Jimmy was laid off at the tannery in December, 1945. But before that happened, he had a plan for what he was going to do. At that time, as an incentive to enlistment, the army offered the volunteer his choice of duty and choice of place of assignment. Jimmy was determined to go to Germany. He felt he had a mission there. If things worked out as he hoped they would, he was going to stay in Germany, give up his U.S. citizenship.

A few weeks after he was laid off, on February 19, 1946, he went to the nearest recruiting office, down at East St. Louis, Illinois, and signed up for the regular army. He was seventeen. He was given the service number 16-163-129.

By then he was giving the Heil Hitler salute in public, did it when he visited home. It frightened Ceal. She begged him to stop. And she wept bitterly when Jimmy told her he was going into the army.

---

# Chapter 12

On his first visit home on leave from Camp Crowder, where he did his basic infantry training, Jimmy was full of high spirits and hope. He felt that the army was something he could handle. He told the family that he was going to be a captain soon. If they did not exactly believe the "soon," they believed in the eventual probability of his success. They knew Jimmy was smart, and they had no doubt but that what they thought of as his exceptional sharpness and mother-wit would lead him to rapid promotion.

That was the first impression they had of Jimmy's career in the service. The second one was of a different kind. No sooner did Jimmy get to Germany than he started sending home for cigarettes. There wasn't any doubt about what Jimmy meant to do with those cigarettes. He wanted them for the black market.

If Alton represented the positive side of Jimmy's life and Quincy the negative, then Germany was turning out to be a kind of Quincy-in-hell. It was not a place for a young political idealist, not in 1946, though it would have been for Jimmy's ideals in 1936. Jimmy was ten years too late for Hitler's ascendant Nuremberg festival and just in time for the Nuremberg war crimes trials of Nazi leaders. His first army assignment was at Nuremberg, where he served as a jeep driver in an MP unit from August until December, 1946.

"I think he went over there," his brother Jerry has said, "with the idea in his head that he would work to support the Nazi party, even though the war was over. But he got discouraged after the Nuremberg trials. That was the turning point. He saw what happened to the Nazis and gave up hope.

"What appealed to Jimmy in the first place about Hitler was that he would make the U.S. an all-white country, no Jews or Negroes. He would be a strong leader who would just do what was right and that was it. Not try to please everybody like Roosevelt. If Hitler could win it would be a different world. Jimmy didn't think Hitler would kill Jews and Blacks, just put them in their own country someplace. Jimmy thought Hitler was going to succeed and still thinks he would have succeeded if the Japs hadn't attacked Pearl Harbor."

In December, 1946, Jimmy was transferred to the 382nd Military Police Battalion doing guard duty in Bremerhaven. Bremerhaven was then an inferno of vice and wickedness, of moral corruption, where prostitution was not a peripheral parasite but an industry, where the whole economy was based on contempt for the law. It was a challenge to all that was worst in Jimmy's life and training.

The physical scene in Bremerhaven in 1946 was a gray, bleak nightmare of rubble. Ninety-seven percent of the buildings in the center of Bremerhaven had been destroyed by bombing raids, especially one on the night of September 18, 1944. There were no street lights; the city was dark, shuttered and terrifying at night. Roving through these somber, shadowy ruins were bands of defiantly violent toughs who called themselves Werewolves. They enticed Americans into the ruined buildings by offering to trade something. But once inside, they jumped the Americans, robbed, killed them if necessary, stripped their clothes, their shoes, everything. The ruins were in fact dangerous.

The result of all this was that American soldiers began to travel in pairs, never alone. They began to carry arms, not army weapons which would have got them in serious trouble, but handguns, usually of German make, of which the Luger was the favorite. Shoot-outs between Germans and Americans became frequent evening events in the streets.

The focus of almost all the life in the ruined city was the black market. The area around the Dom, the Bauhaus, the cathedral, and a Red Cross center was the trading hub. Every transaction was illegal, but if an MP did interfere, it would as likely as not be to carry off the loot himself.

The currency was cigarettes. "It worked like this. A soldier received two cartons of cigarettes a week, and if he wanted to get into the trade, he'd buy up cigarettes from his buddies, or steal them, and when he got enough, he'd buy, say, a case of Leitz lenses, then he would sell the lenses for occupational currency to his fellow soldiers. Let's say that he got a thousand dollars in occupational currency, he could buy a money order (in American currency) and send that home."

It was not one-way. The Germans did their share of hustling. They carried leather attaché cases filled with stuff they wanted to sell on the black market. "You'd be walking down the street and Germans would stop you and ask if you wanted to buy potatoes, eggs, cameras, clocks, which they were carrying," remembers an ex-GI.

The black market encouraged the GI's to steal; it was an atmosphere so amoral that stealing was not even called that. It was only "big-dealing" when a GI in the quartermaster corps "appropriated" something from a warehouse, or a cook took steaks out of the larder.

The breakdown of the usual marketing and trading mechanisms inevitably produced not just thieves but a new breed of illicit entrepreneur. James Earl Ray became one of these. If there was no place in Germany for Jimmy's Nazi idealism, there was a place for his other qualities and experience. He had learned at Uncle Earl's feet how to be a "fence," how never to betray the thief who delivered up the stolen merchandise. Jimmy was a quiet fellow, anyway, one who kept his own counsel. Nor did it surprise the family at home that Jimmy asked them to send him more and more cigarettes and that, in return, he sent more and more money home. "We never lived so well as we did when Jimmy was in the army," a family member recalls. "He sent money home nearly every month." He sent some home to Ceal, and some went to Mom Maher in Alton to make a stash for himself. She deposited it for him in the Alton bank. All this to the family was a well-understood role. They knew it from prison, for there "the merchant" is a useful and respected figure, a man who has to be ultimately trustworthy, one who will not betray the guards who take part in or tolerate his illegal activities, nor the prisoners who buy (and stand to suffer for it) his contraband merchandise. It was in the Bremerhaven black market that Jimmy perfected his skill as a merchant, training that was to be invaluable to him later.

While the people of Bremerhaven picked through the ruins for food, dressed in rags, the Americans turned flamboyant. The GI's began to go for flashy clothing, to turn their uniforms into zoot suits. They used the Germans to clean and press, to keep a knifelike crease in shirts and pants. They had the German women embroider and crochet insignias. They had the Germans tailor, cut down their army overcoats into car coats, peg their uniform pants, make them wide at the knee, narrow at the ankle. The GI's used the Germans as servants, not only as cooks, but as handservants, to carry their bags, to pack the things they were sending home. And inevitably, as prostitutes.

The official quarterly reports of the 382nd Military Police Battalion, Jimmy's unit, during 1946 and 1947 show that about 1,600 women a month were arrested as "venereal disease suspects" in Bremerhaven, while yet other unspecified numbers of women were arrested for "illegal possession of U.S. government property," and for "harboring AWOL's," soldiers without leave.

The Jimmy who was a habitué of Gene and Rusty's in Quincy was not a stranger to prostitution or to prostitutes. It was a world in which he moved with assurance but with, in Bremerhaven, certain consequences, as his official army medical record shows:

| | |
|---|---|
| July 5, 1947 | gonorrhea, acute, urethral |
| September 29, 1947 | syphilis, early |
| March 25, 1948 | headache, lumbar puncture |
| March–June, 1948 | gonorrhea, acute |
| June 14, 1948 | coryza |
| June 17, 1948 | pharyngitis |
| July 6, 1948 | pediculosis pubis (lice) |
| August 16, 1948 | tonsillitis |
| October, 1948 | boils |
| October 25, 1948 | furuncles, neck |
| October 28, 1948 | spinal puncture |
| December 14, 1948 | sore throat |

---

The longer he stayed in Germany, the more contemptuous Jimmy became of the Germans. He was forced to conclude that they were *weak*. His friend in the tannery had told him that Hitler and the Germans knew how to handle black people. But Jimmy found just the opposite was true; he saw it in his work as an MP, doing patrol of nightclubs. He saw German girls freely associating with American black GI's, easier than they could have done back home in the States. It made him furious, and he was in a position to do something about his rage. He was an MP with a billy in his hand — and he used it. He and the buddy patrolman he worked with (who shared his views) found occasion to take some of the black guys out in the alley and work them over. This didn't go on very long. Somebody complained, Jimmy was called on the mat, given a verbal going-over, and taken off that duty. No charges were filed.

He got in one bad fight, a barracks-room brawl, a result

of his airing some of his political views, but this did not result in any charges against him, either.

Jimmy seems to have had some contact with a man in a neo-Fascist group in Bremerhaven. He met this German in a bar, refused invitations to go to his house. Jimmy was disillusioned, and told the German so. This German tried to reassure Jimmy: "They can't keep us down, we'll rise again," he said. Jimmy told him: "If you all ever get straightened out, I'll come back."

"Jimmy had really believed he could be in on reviving the Nazi party," a family member says.

---

Jimmy began to drink heavily in Germany, and, with his growing disillusionment with Germany, he had less and less patience with army rules and regulations. On November 18, 1948, at the headquarters of the 16th Infantry Regiment at Fürth, Germany, he was charged with violation of the 96th Article of War, specifically of being drunk in quarters on October 31, 1948, and with violation of the 69th Article of War, "in that recruit James E. Ray, having been duly placed under arrest, did, on or about November 3, 1948, break said arrest before he was set at liberty by proper authority." He was found guilty on both counts and sentenced to hard labor for three months and to forfeit $45 of his pay per month for four months. Jimmy was locked up in the stockade at Nuremberg. His career as a Nazi ended at the same spot where so many other Nazi careers ended.

The army at this point gave up on Jimmy. On December 10, 1948, that part of his sentence having to do with hard labor was commuted and he was returned to the States directly from the Nuremberg stockade and discharged on December 23, 1948, for ineptness. Army Regulation No. 615–369, covering discharge of enlisted men for "Ineptness," gives three major reasons for granting such a discharge: one is enuresis (bed-wetting); a second is: "does not possess the required degree of adaptability for military service..." A third lists many other more serious emotional disturbances (schizoid, paranoid, etc.) as reasons for such a discharge. His record is confidential, but the evidence suggests that he was discharged for the second reason. It seems probable that the army concluded that James Earl Ray was more trouble than he was worth. Ray was authorized to wear the World War II Victory Medal and the Army of Occupation Medal with Germany clasp. He had served thirty-four months and four days in uniform, and he had not made captain. His highest rank was PFC, and he held that only briefly. He never did tell his family why he was discharged.

Jimmy seems to have been in a racial brawl on the transport back home. Jack Ray writes:

"What really burn Jimmy and the rest of soldiers coming back from Germany was the orders that all married couple ride first class and singles ride second. They almost had a riot on ship when white soldiers who did the fighting had to ride second. The Black soldiers who were the kitchen workers had all married German girls and rode first class. The Blacks would parade around on the deck with a white gal on his arm, getting the best service."

One thing is certain — by the time he got out of the army, Jimmy was a deeply confirmed bigot; his anger and frustrations were turned on black people.

# Chapter 13

We are all ready to admit, when we don't loudly proclaim, that we are our brothers' keepers. But we don't really mean it, or at least we mean it only up to a point. Sometimes when our brothers — and sisters — need us the most desperately, need our understanding, our compassion, when they have lost all hope and pride and are in the gutter, at that moment, we turn our backs on them. Our excuse is that there is a point at which people no longer *deserve* our help and sympathy. The way we get them off our consciences is by stigmatizing them, by abstracting their humanity from them. We dismiss them as "good-for-nothing," or as "trash."

That point has come with the Rayneses when it is easier to turn our backs on them for, as we saw their raw-boned poverty in Ewing, we are now about to have to face their often sordid degradation and spiritual destitution.

Jimmy had no sooner left for Alton and the tannery job than the rest of the family pulled up stakes, left Ewing, left the old Adams place, left, more exactly, the *site* of the old Adams place, for by the time *they* left there was nothing but the site: a bare rectangle of Missouri earth was all that marked the spot of James Earl Ray's childhood home.

The family left Ewing with, for them, unusually good prospects. That is to say, Speedy had a job, a regular job, working on the railroad as a switchman in the yards of the C.B.&Q. at its division headquarters at Galesburg, Illinois.

World War II was a happy time for many Americans. To those who had been through the Depression, it marked the end of a period in which many had come to think that there never would be Good Times again. There seemed to be good jobs everyplace and at good wages, too. Even the Rayneses were drawn into the job market.

The nine months that Speedy worked for the railroad were the only Good Times the Raynes family ever had. Jimmy was sending money home from Germany to supplement Speedy's regular pay envelope. Speedy still slept every minute he wasn't working, but for once Ceal had some sense of status. She was a railroad wife among railroad wives. Ceal had no airs or pretensions, and she made friends. Those Ray children who remember Galesburg remember it in a golden glow of recollection. It was in Galesburg, however, that Ceal began to drink a little, if only beer, if only companionably with the railroad people.

But the boom didn't last, and as soon as it was over men like Speedy dropped out of the job market just as abruptly as they had fallen into it. After nine months on the C.B.&Q., Speedy was laid off.

This time Mom Maher suggested that Ceal go to work. Mom found Ceal a job in Alton, at the Western Cartridge Co., and the family a place to live in the countryside outside Alton in the village of Hamel, Illinois, where Speedy was supposed to farm — or at least take care of the children while Ceal was at work. By then there were more children, for if there was one thing Speedy and Ceal seemed able to cooperate successfully on it was bringing children into the world. By the time they left Ewing in 1944, the children were: Jack, thirteen; Jerry, nine; Melba, five; Carol, two; and Franklin Dennis (Buzzy), a few months old, having been born in Ewing just before they left, in June, 1944.

Speedy didn't farm, and the children went dirty, undisciplined and hungry while he snoozed. In 1947, after a year in Hamel, they moved to Quincy, down into the river wards, and into a descending spiral of misery, unhappiness and deepening discouragement.

Speedy had always hated cities; now Ceal found that she couldn't deal with them. City life was too much for her, with children and a husband like Speedy. On the farm in Ewing, she had a simpler life and, in a way, more resources and few if any temptations. Her life was encompassed by her family and she had found support from her children and, even, from her husband. The family was a stable, cohesive unit there. If they stuck together, it was largely because circumstances stuck them together. If the rest of Ewing thought of the Rayneses as outside their world, they at least did not threaten the inside of the Raynes world. If in Ewing Ceal had no close friends or any circle of acquaintances, then neither was she challenged nor threatened by keeping up with the Joneses. She was able to avoid places and people who would make her feel ashamed of herself, as a woman, as a wife, as a mother.

She had been able to provide for her family in Ewing. There she had had a garden, chickens, sometimes a cow. She could always stir up something for the children.

But once they moved smack into the middle of a city, into the heart, the disreputable heart, of Quincy, she felt helpless, vulnerable. She did not seem to be able to get a grasp on the simplest elements of her life. When she went out to make a living, she realized how poorly she was dressed, how badly she looked, how *well* other people looked — this she learned when she went to work as a waitress at the big downtown hotel in Quincy, the Lincoln-Douglas, which faced on Washington Square. She was ashamed.

Ceal and Speedy began to drink together, but Ceal could not handle the stuff. It was cheap wine, and the more she drank, the more they drank together, the worse the children behaved, the crummier their living quarters looked. She found herself in a struggle where she had no help and which she was not strong enough to fight alone. She lost her self-respect.

"Lucille didn't make much, the old man wouldn't work," remembers Jerry. "The old man slept all day so we slept, too. We had a wood stove upstairs and down to keep warm.

"Very often they would both be drunk, Ceal and the Old Man, on wine four or five nights a week. They would have awful fights, hit each other. That's why we older children stayed out all the time. I wouldn't come home until one o'clock, go straight upstairs to sleep, sneak in without their hearing me, the stairs I used were on the outside of the house. And John would be gone two or three days at a time, robbing. The younger kids had to stay home and suffer.

"When Jimmy used to come to Quincy, he wouldn't stay overnight with us. He was ashamed of the way we lived. He had got away from that stuff of sleeping on the floor. Jimmy didn't like what was going on, but he always took up for the Old Man. Actually, the Old Man and Ceal didn't fight in front of Jimmy. They didn't dare. They were afraid to. He was too violent."

It did not help that Ceal was often pregnant. It was one thing to be pregnant out in the country without proper clothes, another to be so visibly pregnant out of shape in the city. In May, 1947, soon after they moved to Quincy, Ceal was delivered of another daughter, Susan Jane, and in 1951, she gave birth to another son, Max Raynes.

Mom Maher moved up to Quincy into the Tremont Hotel. Although she didn't live with Ceal she came around every day. She was still fiercely determined to hold this family's head up, although by now it must have been obvious that she was losing in her struggle. She insisted on giving Ceal advice which Ceal either could not or did not take. She stayed with the children some, baby-sat, and often took the children to the Catholic church where, one by one, she had had them baptized.

The older children were not really any help to Ceal. Jimmy of course was away. There were too many strikes against Jerry and Jack; they knew too many people in Quincy, too many of the wrong people. Jerry set up pins in a bowling alley for a while, carried papers, remembers hiding in a back room to get away from Speedy and Ceal when they were in their cups. "I fell in with some fellas my own age there in Quincy, began to roll drunks, snatch purses, and the next thing I knew I was on the way to jail." He was committed to the Illinois State Training School for Boys at St. Charles in 1950, was returned there in 1951. Jerry has some fond thoughts of St. Charles. A kind psychologist there helped Jerry with his speech — "taught me with a recorder to say 'lamp' where I used to say 'yamp.'" But while he was in St. Charles he took part in a prison riot which got him another one year to eighteen months' sentence at the Illinois State Industrial School at Sheridan. .

Jack stayed on after the family left Galesburg and worked there. But he was soon down in Quincy with the rest of the family — and in trouble; was convicted on two counts of second-degree burglary in Adams County in 1950. He went, he says looking for work, to Gary, Indiana, but ended up on January 23, 1950, with a two- to five-year sentence for burglary and in the Indiana State Reformatory at Pendleton.

The two people from the world outside the family who saw the most of Ceal were Mrs. Eda Jansen, the Quincy police matron, and a juvenile court probation officer. The probation officer remembers going to the Ryan house on a bitter cold day in 1946 when they lived at 214 Spring Street. The children weren't home. Speedy was down on his hands and knees under the sink, trying to thaw out a frozen pipe with a candle. "I only got into the kitchen that time," says the probation officer. "After that, things kept getting worse, worse, worse. One time I went down there and somebody opened a closet and nothing fell out but empty wine bottles, dozens upon dozens of wine bottles. Mrs. Ryan had just become a drunkard. She was picked up in the south end of town drunk. She wasn't a bad looking woman. She had black hair, but she wasn't clean. Mostly she'd be wearing dirty blouses. You could see that she had been a pretty girl. I went down there once and Lucille was as big as a house. I asked her if she was pregnant and she said no it was a liver condition."

Mrs. Jansen says: "By the time I knew Mrs. Lucille Ryan she was a beaten woman. The family did not have enough to eat, and she had turned to drink. She was arrested a time or two for drunkenness. But Mrs. Ryan was not a woman you could really dislike."

In Ewing there had not been any such thing as a social worker, and now Ceal could not seem to get rid of them. She became obsessed with the idea that "they" were going to take her children away from her.

---

In 1952, Speedy gave up. He went off, as people in his world say, with another woman, went off to St. Louis with a Quincy woman named Ruby Carpenter. "The only thing that made me and Ceal separate," declares Speedy, "was I figured that if I left her she'd straighten up. I don't understand drinking. Drinking never bothered me. I'd stay drunk for a week and then just cut it out right now and never drink no more for a long time. But I see now I should have stayed with Ceal. Women are just like babies."

Mom Maher took up the cudgels for Ceal, would go to the courthouse and argue with the probation officer who remembers Mom as "a neat little thing" who "didn't want those children taken away. I think she really loved those children."

One county juvenile judge who became involved with

them during this period remembers the Ray (Raynes, Ryan) family well. "They were a lousy outfit," he says. "No doubt about it, Mama [Ceal] was a lush. She was a wild gal. She would come to my office and curse me. I have never seen a worse parent as far as understanding what was best for her kids. She was an extremely immature person. I think she loved her children and wanted to keep them but simply was not able to manage even her own affairs let alone those of a family.

"She had the look of a schizophrenic. She had that *look* in her eye. Her hair was wild, stood straight out."

His philosophy was that children should be taken from their parents only as a last resort. "A poor home is better than a good institution," he says. The children were later placed under custody of the court, and remanded to Mrs. Ryan's care, to give her a final chance to get a grip on herself and her family.

---

It got so after a while that Quincy saw the Ryans through Melba. Melba was very visible. She was enough to keep two or three social workers busy.

Melba seemed to have made it her mission to act out the anger for the whole Ray family. By the time she was twelve (1951) the probation officer had more or less taken over, or tried to take over, Melba's life. The first place she put Melba was in a Catholic school in Maumee, Ohio, a small town near Toledo. This was one of the benefits the Rays got from the change of name they gave themselves in Quincy, where they called themselves Ryan, and claimed to be Catholics. Melba wrecked the school. She tore up her mattress. She set fire to her room. She didn't last two weeks. They called the probation officer to come and get Melba, and when she got there she found that they had placed Melba in a cell. They claimed that Melba had done $1,000 in damage.

The probation officer next put Melba in a detention home where Melba flooded her cell and set fire to her mattress.

Once Melba hit Mom Maher with a chunk of coal. Once she hit Jerry a punishing blow in the jaw. Once the police picked her up, and she "tore the jail apart," pulled out her hair by the roots, broke the lights, tried to set fire to a mattress. When she was picked up it wasn't for drinking, or for having anything to do with men. "She didn't like men," believes someone who knew her at the time. "She wouldn't allow them in her room. She never did date."

For a while Melba was a familiar character in Quincy. She walked with a stoop, shuffled along, looking sideways at people from under her eyelids. Sometimes she would hang around the courthouse, sometimes ride a bicycle around it, screaming obscenities, sometimes she would go into a courtroom and sit quietly. She made friends with a young secretary in the courthouse, who used to keep candy for Melba. One of the judges began to speak in a kindly, friendly way to Melba and he noticed that she began to touch his sleeve, his arm, "as if," he remembers, "she had some desperate need for affection."

It came to the point where the probation officer took her to the Jacksonville, Illinois, state mental hospital, but *they* called the probation officer to come and get Melba. Melba ended up spending the years between sixteen and twenty-one in Jacksonville. Her IQ was discovered to be 90. A friend she made at Jacksonville said that "Melba talked all the time about her brothers who were in the penitentiary. She sure was fond of them."

Now, as for Earl. Earl had got married in 1942. He married the woman with whom he had been traveling on the carnival, Patricia Garrison. But he got caught up in the fever of World War II, caught up to the point that he decided to follow the gold rush of skyrocketing wartime wages in Alaska, left Patricia, got a job as second cook up there, and stayed until 1944 — these dates appear on the records of the Alaska Travel Control agency which gave him a permit on June 5, 1943. By January 29, 1944, he was in Wilmington, Delaware, where he registered with the police department on that date. By then his ardor and affection for Patricia had run out, absence had made the heart grow colder, and he divorced her that year.

In 1945, Earl (then forty-one) made the mistake that many men in their forties make: he married a much younger woman, eighteen-year-old Audrey Ferguson, in Kansas City. He did a little better with Audrey than he had with Patricia. They stayed together until the summer of 1947 when, then living in Quincy, they separated. They had begun to fight. Earl wanted her to come back to him. He wanted custody of his children, Larry Lee, born in 1945, and Mabel Myona, born in 1947.

There was one ugly, *horribly* ugly incident. Because of it, Earl was arrested, tried on September 23, 1948, in the circuit court of Adams County. The official trial record reads:

THE COURT: What are the facts in this case?
MR. DELBERT LOOS: (representing Earl Ray): If the Court please, as I understand the facts, on August 23, 1947, the De-

fendant, Earl Ray, went to the Owl Drug Store in the city of Quincy, Illinois, and purchased a bottle of phenol, which is pure carbolic acid, and said it was to be used for disinfecting purposes. He then went to the home of his wife, Mrs. Audrey Ray, and I believe that was about 12:30 — it was in the morning, anyway, about ten o'clock, I believe — and there was a party in the house who witnessed the act of what went on. It was briefly this.

His wife was on the kitchen floor, scrubbing the floor. He tapped her on the shoulder and mentioned her name, and, as she looked up, he threw the contents of the bottle into her face, burning her face and arms and shoulders, severely burning her face and mouth. He then left the house.

MR. SCHOLZ (a court-appointed defense lawyer): I made as thorough an investigation of this case as I could. I did learn that Mr. Ray and his wife had been having some trouble. They had been separated off and on. I do feel this. Mr. Ray has been in some trouble before, but in that ten or twelve years I believe he has been a law-abiding citizen. His wife told me ... he always provided for her. She does not want to cause her husband any trouble. I think this act was caused by a mental condition, and while it is not excusable, I hope the Court will take that into consideration.

THE COURT: You can't take much into consideration a justification in a thing like that. It is just a miracle the woman wasn't blinded. He went down to the drugstore, buying that, he said, with the deliberate intent to do that. There are no mitigating circumstances that I can see. Whether they were having trouble or not, that would certainly be a brutal way to settle an argument, having her down on her hands and knees, looking up at him. The sentence of the court will be a sentence of one to fourteen years, with a minimum of three years and a maximum of ten years.

A later report showed that Audrey had to have extensive surgery on her face. Even then a few permanent scars remained. Her child, too, was severely burned.

Earl fled from this tough rap but was eventually caught in Kansas City and returned to Menard where he did six years.

Well, at least Earl wasn't lonely down there at Menard. He was soon joined by Jerry and Jack. In fact, it was Earl who broke them into prison life, gave them the mental preparation, the support, the counsel, for learning how to "do your own time."

A kinder world, a world whose institutions reflected an interest in helping, not blindly punishing miscreants, would have been more temperate with these two Ray boys.

It is true that they stole, but their stealing was plainly only the larceny of despair. Jerry was eventually to spend nearly a decade in prison for stealing less than $60. That's punishing the powerless, the unlettered and the inept.

Here is an excerpt from the official court record of February 11, 1954, again in Adams County, this time involving Jerry. The state's attorney told the court:

"This case was on South 8th Street approximately in front of the State Theater. Jerry Ryan [Ray] and three other boys had been riding around and parked the car on 7th Street between Kentucky and State. Jerry and Mickey Walker got out of the car and walked up to 8th and State, and saw Mr. and Mrs. Edgar Schaefer going northward. Jerry ran past and grabbed her purse and Mickey Walker bumped into Mr. Schaefer, and then they ran on back to the car. They got between $75 and $80 out of her purse which they divided among the four boys and then they took that purse down the river bottom road where they divided the money and burned the purse and its contents."

Jerry got $20 and paid for it — "not less than one year

and not more than ten years, and the minimum will be fixed at two years and the maximum will be five years."

As for Jack, he too is in the Adams County court records: "On the afternoon of May 5, 1953, Ryan [Jack Ray] and one other person stole a 1941 Hudson two-door sedan parked in front of 217 4th street. During the next approximately thirty-six hours the Defendant was in and about that Hudson sedan, having traveled out as far as Burton or Adams and back to Quincy. On the morning of May 7, 1953, at or about 3:30 A.M. Ryan was discovered in this car parked in Riverview Park. The officers cruising in the vicinity noticed the front seat was on fire. They aroused Ryan who assisted the officers in putting out the fire." For this — but not entirely for this alone — Jack, then twenty-three, got "a minimum of five years and a maximum of ten years." Jack Ray was in Menard from June, 1953, until February, 1960, nearly seven years in prison for stealing a *twelve-year-old* automobile.

And what kind of stealing was *that*, to take a heap of junk, cruise around in it, joy-ride for a couple of days, out to the unpromising suburbs of Quincy, and then go to sleep in it, undoubtedly drunk, in a city park where you are certain to be found by the cops? If Speedy had been asked what the car was worth, he would have replied: "Put it on the scale," meaning it was worth its weight in scrap metal, worthless as a vehicle.

This was not stealing for profit, for the thief's permanent gain. Jack didn't try to sell the car. It wasn't money he wanted and he didn't really want a car or obviously expect to keep that car very long. If he had wanted a car to sell or to keep, he might as well have stolen a good car, a late model.

Jack stole that old Hudson for a momentary pleasure, not giving a shit about any of the car's qualities except its mobility, that it put wings on a man, that it lifted him, if even for a moment, out of dull and listless routine. And Jack was the one in the family who clearly didn't give a damn. Jack was the most clear-headed of all the boys. Not the smartest: Jimmy was that. Jack was the one who had his feet on the ground. He was more direct, more open, would tell you straight-out what was on his mind. He had his own tics but, among the Ray boys, he was the one who, admitting everything to be relative, was in the closest touch with reality. The reality of his life being what it was, it is not surprising he didn't measure the odds in his acts of loony larceny. The odds were all against him anyway.

The Ryans became regular clients of the court's probation officer. The neighbors complained about the Ryans more and more often. The probation officer warned Ceal that the court was going to take the children away from her if something wasn't done to improve things down there on Spring Street.

"When we went down there the children were throwing garbage out the windows and yelling filthy names at passersby. They were filthy and covered with lice," is the probation officer's recollection of what it was like on one of her visits.

But nothing changed, except that Ceal began to come up to the courthouse, sometimes pleading, sometimes arguing, often weeping. The day came finally when the probation officer went down to get the children, with a Mrs. Roberta, a Catholic Charities worker, because the court gave custody of the children to that agency. But when the two women got there, armed with a court order, the house was empty. Mom

Maher had scooped up the children and carried them away.

"We went in the front door and Mrs. Maher went out the back with the children," says the probation officer who had by this time changed her mind about Mom. "I don't know how she got out of the house. Oh, she was a devil! She was the limit! She sided in with Mrs. Raynes about everything."

Mom took the children across the bridge to the Missouri side of the river where they hid under the bank, where police found them the next day, found them and returned them to Quincy. Mrs. Roberta took the youngest children, Buzz, Susan and Max, down to Alton to a Catholic home for children. The probation officer put Carol, Jean and Melba into foster homes. Of course the three older boys had even more secure accommodations: Jimmy, Jack and Jerry were all in prison.

———

Ceal was alone. Everyone in the world that she loved most dearly had either left her or been taken away from her. Ceal began to weep terribly, and to drink more than ever. She became a habitué of certain bars in Quincy.

This kind of sousing eventually put Ceal in the hospital and on the operating table. She developed a "knot in her side," hesitated to go to the doctor for fear it was cancer, finally did go. He operated on her in St. Mary's Hospital in 1953, took *something* out of her but nobody in the family was sure what it was. One of the prices of being poor and disreputable, when you fall afoul of the medical system, or was in those days, is that doctors and nurses don't bother to tell you what they are doing to you and why.

Willie Maher is bitter and angry over the way things

turned out in Quincy for Ceal. "My sister's degradation," he has written, "followed Jim's [Speedy's] running away with a housekeeper simply because she had a nice bank account. You have to remember that Quincy was his home town. He picked the house at 214 Spring Street. The neighborhood was a cesspool of crime. It was bad enough when the boys all went bad, but when the man she bore nine children to ran off with a bank account, Lucille, haggard and middle-aged, just plain gave up."

It will put us slightly ahead of ourselves to do so, but we might as well finish Ceal's story while we are about it. After the children were all gone in their different ways, Ceal and Mom found a place where they lived together for a while. What with Ceal drinking and Mom nagging her about it, that didn't work. Then Ceal tried living alone in Quincy for a while. That of course didn't work, for who was going to take care of her even if, as one of her children says, "Ceal could always get home, no matter how much she had under her belt."

At this point Mom decided that they had better get out of Quincy. Mom's mind turned toward St. Louis and toward running a boardinghouse as she had done in Alton. When Ceal's Aunt Rose Maher died in Washington about this time and left her $3,000, the move from Quincy was sealed. Mom and Ceal together bought (in 1958) a three-story, nine-room house at 1913 Hickory Street in the Soulard section of St. Louis and opened it to boarders. The place did not attract the quietest clientele. "It was the kind of rooming house where people drank and cursed all night," said a woman who lived next door to it. But this did not last indefinitely and the outcome was that Ceal moved out, around the corner to Mississippi Street to live alone — well, not quite, for she had acquired a friend, an older man. The other members of the Ray family accepted him as if, in him, Ceal had acquired something like an old chiffonier, a worn but comforting piece of furniture. They accepted him as, simply, "Ceal's Old Gent."

Ceal's acquisition of a living companion did not offend Speedy or create in Ceal's mind a situation where she could not maintain relations with Speedy. In fact, whatever awkwardness might have been created by Speedy's living with Ruby Carpenter had also worn off. Poor, down-and-out people cannot afford the luxury of pride, of hurt feelings, of "face." If they are to have any relationships with each other, share any affection and warmth, they must accept the fact that every emotional link may have a short tether, and that the middle-class conventions of respectability cannot be observed in their world.

It was not long before Speedy and Ruby weren't, as they would have said, "staying together," anymore. When Ruby left him, Speedy and Carol made what by then came to seem a natural and congenial alliance, for Carol had grown increasingly fond of her father. Speedy and Carol moved in together, not far from where Ceal and Mom lived, all in that down-at-heel Soulard section. Carol was more like her father than, well, he was. She was determinedly self-sufficient, somewhat dogmatic and categorical in utterance. Carol was determined to move out of the social netherworld in which the Rays had lived, and she worked out the details which put her and Speedy into a dry cleaning business.

While Speedy and Carol were living together, it was quite usual for Ceal to visit them. Carol thought that Ceal would like to go back to Speedy. It was as if, in fact, their relationship had never been severed, only temporarily interrupted by circumstances over which neither of them had any control.

But by this time in Ceal's life, visits to Speedy were of small comfort. She was down to the threads of her emotional kit bag. What seemed to have robbed her of her last hope was the news from Jack that Jimmy had been arrested. She had placed so many of her hopes in Jimmy, her first child, her favorite child, her brightest child. Jack was at this time a parole violator working in an Oaklawn (suburban Chicago) riding stable, when he read the item about Jimmy:

"I pick up a paper and saw where Jimmy was shot in a robbery. I sent a clipping to Ceal. A few days later I couldn't believe it. Ceal was walking down the gravel road, she had walk all the way from La Grange. It must of been six or seven miles. I told her I could of borrow my employer's car and pick her up, she said she didn't want to bother me. They was a few cabins behind a tavern for rent, no lights. I got her a room there.

"Ceal look very sad that time sitting on side of the bed white and wore out, with her head down trying to keep from crying. The next day she went into Chicago and saw Jimmy. I found out later she was broke, had to work as a dishwasher to pay her way home."

"After that," says Jerry, "Ceal didn't have nothing else to live for."

Toward the end of 1960, she got sicker and sicker. Her liver was giving her serious signals of its distress. Finally, the day before Christmas, 1960, she went into the city hospital in

St. Louis. They operated on her that day. Word passed along the family grapevine that Ceal was sick, and the family began to assemble in St. Louis, at her bedside.

Jack, who had by now clearly established himself as the man of the family, took over, and handled such things as there were to be handled. Ceal needed blood, and Jack went out to get it. He had a kitty of about $1,200 at this time, and he went out and rounded up "a scummy looking crew of winos," paid them to give blood.

Together, Jack and Jerry told Ceal that they were going to find her a nice place to live, buy her a TV, and help her out from that point on in her life. She had tubes in her nose, and they were not sure at first whether she heard them. She made a kind of affirmative motion with her hands.

At one moment, when they had the tubes out of her mouth, she asked Carol, who was at that moment in the hospital room, "Is Pop coming?" She was asking for Speedy.

But blood was not enough. Her desire to go on with the life she had lived ebbed away in four days into nothingness.

Almost everybody was at the bedside. Jerry and Jack, Carol and her husband, Albert Pepper, Buzz, Mom Maher, and Speedy, and Ceal's Old Gent . . .

Practically everybody was there except Jimmy.

# Chapter 14

Jimmy got out of the army in January, 1949, and the first thing he did was what most veterans do when they return to the civilian world they left behind: look on in bewilderment for a while, and do nothing else much.

It wasn't that easy for him to put his political dreams behind him. He hated to admit his defeat to himself. He was still giving the Heil Hitler salute. He was angry and disillusioned about what had happened to him in Germany. It may look to us, as outsiders, that he never had any real chance of doing anything anyway in postwar Germany, of reviving nazism. But you don't have to know history to dream of having a place in it. It didn't matter that his dreams were politically illiterate. Their content didn't arise out of what he *knew* or didn't know about politics. His political ambitions grew out of his emotions, not out of scholarship. His visions of political history, of political causes and results, were like a series of brilliant flash cards, illustrations etched with the acid of his passions, vivid symbols not actualities.

He moved in with Mom at her boardinghouse in Alton. He could not think of moving in with Speedy and Ceal and the other kids in Quincy, in that mess. When he went to Quincy, he stayed in a cheap hotel. He began to withdraw his savings, the savings he had accumulated from his black-market operations in Germany. He did what every young man wants to do, bought a car, a "late model" Mercury.

In a kind of vague, almost hallucinatory way, he talked around Quincy about starting a nightclub, even went to the VA people to see if he could get a veteran's loan to carry out the idea. It turned out he couldn't make a proposal that would satisfy the government people — a good thing: what he really had in mind, he told his friends, was starting a high-class whorehouse, "turning out," as they say in the world of prostitution to mean the professional training of girls, the finest whores in Quincy. He played with the grandiose idea (considering the talent) of starting a filling station with Speedy on a busy downtown Quincy street corner, even talked with the property owner about a lease. But this was only a vapor.

He was balanced between the straight world and the world of deviance and crime. At first he took a straight job in Chicago, at the Dryden Rubber Company, went to work in June, 1949, was laid off in September, grew restless, took off for Los Angeles because, he said, he hoped to find a job through Willie Maher who was working on defense construction on Guam.

But on the night of October 7, 1949, a man named Strayhorn, the manager of a seedy cafe in downtown Los Angeles called The Forum, switched on the light of his second floor office to find a man hiding behind the safe. Strayhorn grabbed the intruder. The intruder struck at Strayhorn, picked up a chair, flung it at the manager, climbed through a window and fled down a fire escape. An attendant in a parking lot below saw the fleeing man and grappled with him, but lost his grip. Some papers dropped out of the man's pocket as he took off. One was an army discharge bearing the name James Earl Ray. Four days later, Strayhorn saw the same man coming out of a bank in the neighborhood. He called the police and they arrested Jimmy.

The criminal in his first crime, like the poet in his first ode, is likely to show the major themes of his later work, and James Earl Ray revealed, in his first "serious" robbery in Los Angeles, the characteristics that were to mark his subsequent crimes, including his most ambitious one.

In all Ray's crimes, there is a certain ineptness. In all of them there is a certain sordidness of setting. All are marked by some physical violence, of which as often as not he is the victim. In many of them Ray behaved in such a way after he committed the crime as to lead to the suspicion that he wanted to be caught. Or, if he does not actually appear to seek capture, there is almost always something self-degrading about the way he acts during his pursuit. Yet, in every crime, Ray is no sooner safely locked up than he seems to have an infusion of self-confidence, self-confidence that becomes contempt for the whole structure of justice, not only the cops, but the courts. He then defiantly concocts his own alibis and defense, mocking the police and making disparaging comments on their methods.

What seems to distinguish Ray from the ordinary thief is the intensity of emotion he puts into his dreams. With Ray, the process of stealing may start out in an ordinary way, but he no sooner enters into the commission of the crime than it becomes an important emotional event for him. What sets Ray apart is the way he infuses his crimes with his own anger. It is as if the execution of the crime is only a facade for the unconscious purpose of giving outlet to his brooding anger. The original purpose of the crime is lost in its commission. That is why Ray has seemed to be a bungler. He loses his concentration.

His anger explains why he returns to the scene of the crime, or sometimes seems reluctant to leave it. It is as if he has not yet gone through the emotional process of his act even though he has gone through the vocational process. He has not lived through the rage that has been sparked off by it.

It is another aspect of his anger that makes him appear to want to be caught. What he really wants is for the event and its high emotions to end. When his rage begins to subside, he wants quiet, relief from the tension, stress and hazards of the event. Only then is the crime finished for *him.*

And when the crime is finished, he is once more the *smart* Jimmy that he has been told he was since he was a child, with, added to it, all of Speedy's and the family's contempt for all the forces of law and order. In Los Angeles, Ray did a con job on the probation officer. The picture of himself he drew for that official was of a foursquare, all-round American boy, one who "spent much time on dates with girls," one who "went to movies a lot," who liked "to read common ordinary books," and one who played baseball, "quite a bit," according to the probation officer's report on the case.

Having thus described himself, Jimmy then gave the probation officer an alibi in his own handwriting: "I had left a theater approximately 30 minutes before I entered the restaurant. I did not enter the building to commit a theft. I was stopped a few seconds after I entered the building by an employee. He grabbed a hold of me and told me to leave the building which I did. After I got down the street about half a block he started hollering for the police."

Then Jimmy made his typical sarcastic comment about the police and their stupidity. "He said," the probation officer reported, "that if there had been as much fighting as had been alleged, it would have been easy [for the police] to get fingerprints to substantiate it."

Anyway, it worked for Jimmy: he was given only ninety days, a light sentence.

---

Something, maybe it was that stretch in jail, caused Jimmy to try the straight life again.

He hitchhiked back to Quincy, found a job at the Quincy Compressor Company, worked there for a few months in the late spring and early summer of 1950, until he moved to Chicago and began a series of jobs on assembly lines at which he worked steadily *for two years.* His work record:

| | |
|---|---|
| July, 1950–August 14, 1950 | Neo Products Company |
| August 14, 1950–June, 1951 | Arvey Corporation |
| September, 1951–May, 1952 | Borg-Erickson Company |

For a while, he went to school during the day, and worked at night. He told the family he was going to Northwestern University but he was actually enrolled in the Academy for Young Adults at 30 Washington Street which could have given him, had he stuck to classes, the high school diploma he was trying to get.

In the two years, he lived only at two addresses, 853 West Fullerton Street and 352 West Armitage Street.

What's more, he had a girl friend. She had a job something like his, on the assembly line at Neames-REM. Jimmy took her out for a long time, up through the end of this phase of his life — to movies, and frequently to stock car races in a Chicago suburb.

Through this Chicago period, Jimmy's strongest rooter was his Aunt Mabel Fuller, who seems to have been one of the people in his life who cared most about his making something of himself. She called him once in a while from Quincy; he would go see her when he went to Quincy occasionally on weekends. She met and liked his girl friend.

She told people that "Jimmy's girl friend looks just like Ceal when Ceal was a young girl."

It was a crucial moment in Jimmy's life, and the odds were overwhelming that he would fail. Everything in his life from the moment he was conceived was pulling against him as he made this stab at the straight life. Even Aunt Mabel was not wholly a plus; after all, she was one of the Quincy world and Quincy was a pull in the wrong direction. One of the worst liabilities was the fact that he had no one to look to who was living the straight life. No one close to him was carrying on a normal life in the ordinary world. He had trouble conceiving of himself in that world. It was a struggle to keep believing that he might succeed; no matter how hard he tried to stick out those routine, unrewarding jobs, he had trouble doing so because he could not create in his mind's eye an image of himself in that world of regular hours and regular paychecks. In fact, it was the last attempt he was ever to make to hold a regular job.

---

On the night of May 6, 1952, Jimmy hailed a cab at the corner of Clark and Maple streets in Chicago and asked driver Louis Knox to take him to 67 East Cedar. When the cab reached that address, Ray put a pistol to Knox's head and robbed him of $11.90. A man named Robert Everhard saw the robber, and ran for and found a police cruiser.

Jimmy took off down an alley, but it was a blind alley. The cops drove into it and blocked it, then jumped out and drew their guns. For an instant, Jimmy appeared at the end of the alley. The cops ordered him to stop, fired a warning shot, but Jimmy vaulted over a fence. The cops fired at him, and the bullet creased his arm. He took off again, but tripped and crashed through a basement window. The cops found Jimmy crumpled in a washtub, like a trapped wild animal, bleeding from glass and bullet wounds. They dragged him up the stairs of the house, out into the street, propped him up until the paddy wagon came.

Here for the first time was something that was to become another trademark of Jimmy's crimes, a kind of absurdity, a bathos, like his ending up in that washtub. Here was another meaning: an element of self-hatred, of self-contempt, of self-debasement.

In a subsequent trial in Chicago Jimmy was found guilty of robbery and sentenced to one to two years in the state penitentiary.

---

Prison and crime go together like fish and water, and prison was the logical next step in Jimmy's life. He was going to have to learn to live in prison, to be a prisoner, to adjust himself to prison society, a society that is as different from the world outside as, say, the world of some New Guinea mountain tribe which paints its faces with mud and eats its enemies.

The irony of prison life is that the more successful you are at meeting its requirements the less chance you have of ever returning to the straight life. If you're good as a prisoner, you'll almost certainly never again be any good in the "free world."

Our prisons mock and pour contempt on every pretense we make that ours is a humane and civilized society. Don't be misled: there is no such thing as a "good" prison. Prisons are shockingly different from what most people think they are. Prisons don't build character. They don't rehabilitate. They don't do *anything* to help a man go straight when he gets out. They destroy character. The process of criminal justice is a series of "status degradation ceremonies" whose goal is "the ritual destruction of the individual's identity," says a criminologist. It is not just that he must make some kind of temporary adjustment while he is in prison. In fact, he is *reconstituted* by prison. He must give up his former self, his identity, and take on a new one. He must change his sense of what is real to him, and what is real in prison is *worse*. His new identity is lower on the social scale than whatever identity he had outside.

County prisons like the one Ray served time in in Los Angeles are one thing. They are transient holding pens, chaotic, anarchic, poorly controlled, the kind of place, not surprisingly, where homosexuality is commonplace, where many young male prisoners find themselves brutally raped. Anything goes.

But to go into one of the Big Houses is another thing. A certain kind of *order* is their trademark. The Big Houses are run by a hierarchy of the prisoners themselves. "Having been denounced, degraded, segregated and confined, many prisoners renounce the legitimacy of the invidious definitions to which they are subjected," and themselves create a system designed to give them a substitute selfhood. It is their answer to degradation.

Would Jimmy adjust himself to the system? Would he take on a new identity? Would he be able to reconstitute himself?

He was taken by bus to old Joliet prison, the place that had grown famous for housing the Chicago gangsters of the twenties. Among other things, it is a reception center for the Illinois prison system, and Ray was given a medical exam, prison uniforms, a haircut and some tests. He scored 110 on an Army Alpha test. On an Otis test, whose purpose was to establish his level of academic achievement, he came out above second-year high school. The test showed that his best subjects were Geography, Reading and History, and that his worst were Spelling and Language Use. His Otis grade was 102.

The psychologist who interviewed him at Joliet found Ray

to be "quite an able personality." He said that Ray had made a "pretty good" adjustment to the authoritarian situation in the army, but noted that Ray was "pretty much a loner," and that he was "somewhat evasive to questions." One of the things these comments prove is that everything is relative, that the psychologist was a prison psychologist, that he was "inside," in that "inside" value system, and that Ray probably did look pretty good to him by the standards of behavior he had become used to in the prison world. He gave Ray the best assignment he could give him in the Illinois prison system — to Pontiac prison, the place for "younger men with a possibility of improvement."

Ray's criminal background, his close attachment to Earl and Quincy, now turned out to be an advantage rather than a disadvantage to Ray. Although technically, in prison jargon, he was a "fish," a newcomer to prison life, in fact he knew everything about it and above all how to "do his own time," the mark of the veteran time-server.

There is not even an inkstain, not to say a blot, on his record at Pontiac. In the time he served there he did not have a single punishment "sheet," a rare accomplishment for a first-timer. From the first, Ray seemed "quite reasonable and cooperative," his file at Pontiac says. He asked to be assigned to the farm, he was assigned to the farm, and he did well there. "He knew how to conform, there's no doubt about that," said the sociologist at Pontiac who handled Ray's case. "Of course we tend to know only what happens to a man outwardly, not inwardly."

Prisoners are scheduled for routine interviews at six-month intervals at Pontiac, but Ray's record was so uneventful that he was never called in, or interviewed a second time. But he made no friends in prison — prisons keep up with such things — and had no visitors, and he wrote only to Ceal and Jerry. He failed to get parole, but that was only because he had two previous offenses on his record. He was fully discharged from Pontiac on March 12, 1954.

---

That spring and summer of 1954 Jimmy hung around Quincy and Alton, now and then doing a little house-painting for Willie Maher, by then a painting contractor. He did a lot of TV-viewing in taverns, some of it with great absorption, for it was the time of U.S. Senator Joseph McCarthy's hearings into the alleged influence of Communists in the federal government. Ray became a passionate supporter of McCarthy's, told people he *hated* Eisenhower for trying to interfere with McCarthy. At the climax of the hearings, when Joseph Welch, the Boston lawyer, wept before TV cameras, "Jimmy just laughed and laughed," says Maher. "It broke him up."

In Quincy Jimmy picked up again with Walter Rife, who had been having troubles, too. Rife deserted from the army in 1947, was captured, sentenced to Fort Leavenworth, from which he escaped. In 1951, he was convicted of forgery, and was sent to Menard. Earl Ray and Jack and Jerry were then all imprisoned at Menard. Walter and the Rays, and for that matter, Walter's brother Lonnie, had all known each other in Quincy. When Walter got out of Menard, he went back to Quincy and he again ran into Jimmy.

They shared more than the Quincy setting. Both Ray and Rife had grown up in small towns near Quincy, both were members of large poverty-stricken Depression families. The small town Rife came from was Kellerville, Illinois, a place

---

so small that its post office was a shed beside the general store that sold only $900 worth of stamps in a year. Rife had not forgotten how small — and vulnerable — that post office was. And he was not interested in stamps. He discussed the possibilities with Jimmy. What they would be interested in was postal money orders which, because they are insured by the government, are easy to cash with very little identification.

On the night of March 7, 1955, Rife and Ray robbed the Kellerville post office and took sixty-six postal money orders and the rubber stamp that would validate them. The two of them, Rife, big, heavy, dark, somewhat lethargic, and Ray, moderately small, intense, together took off on a sixteen-day orgy of forgery during which they drove south to Miami in an old car, cashing (and forging) the stolen money orders as they went. At Miami, they bought another car, turned back home, but went by way of New Orleans and Hot Springs, Arkansas, a gamblers' and gangsters' hangout. They touched base with some old friends in Kansas City, and then returned to Quincy.

I looked up Rife on one of my research trips to Quincy, for after all he had been about as close to James Earl Ray as had anybody outside Ray's immediate family. I knew how to reach his brother, Lonnie, in Quincy and I called him.

"Why should my brother talk to you?" Lonnie said in a gruff voice. "I wish you cock-suckers would leave him *alone*."

I gave him my number and asked him, without much hope that he would do so, to give it to his brother.

In a few minutes the phone rang: "This is Walter Rife," said a friendly voice. "Do you want to talk with me?"

I did.

"Well, answer me this: Are you colored?"

I went out to his place beyond the city limits at about 10:15 that night, stopping on the way to buy a bottle of Cutty Sark which I put down on Rife's kitchen table. Rife remembers his spree with "Jimmy Ray" vividly and with unqualified pleasure.

"The first thing we did was get I.D. We went in this tavern on South Broadway in St. Louis. We bought a driving license from this fellow for seventy-five cents. We was ready then.

"The trip was Jimmy's idea. I can't remember whether it was an old Chevy or a Ford we started out with. He drove. It was a stick shift. He couldn't drive worth a shit, but at least he didn't go fast. After we got to St. Louis, going south (we started from Quincy), he did very little drinking. He didn't have more than two drinks in any day between St. Louis and Miami. He'd drive along, and he wouldn't talk too much.

"The way we worked it, one of us would sit in the car. Either one of us could go inside because the I.D. fit both of us. When we drove up to a store, I was usually the one who went in. I could get out and in faster than he could. Jimmy was bashful. We probably went in a hundred places. I would buy something, a watch, cigarettes, a radio, clothes, and when they laid the merchandise down on the counter I would throw our check down beside it. I never had any trouble. Nobody ever questioned me with our I.D.

"Sometimes I'd get Jimmy a date, and he wouldn't know what to say. That was true even back when we were just young fellas.

"We'd be in a bar and I'd pick up these girls, and get one for Jim. He might talk with her for a little while, but he wouldn't dance with her. Sometimes he would just go out on the street and ask a cop where there was a whorehouse.

"He would only stay with these whores ten or fifteen minutes. He didn't have any favorite girl. He would go into a whorehouse and he would take a girl and the next time he would go to that whorehouse that girl might not be there and he wouldn't care. He'd take another girl. When he talked about women it was in the most contemptuous way. 'All those fucking whores,' he would say.

"Now I don't know what he *did* with those girls, but I know he wasn't no freak. We slept in the car together many nights and he never went for me.

"Ray had a good heart, in some ways. He gave up his old car to me. It was worth about two-fifty. That was when we started to buy another car in Miami, a maroon Oldsmobile. He just gave me his old car and we traded it in right there.

"But we never stayed in no decent place. It always looked to me like he would be a fella that would be easy to find because I don't think they would ever find him in any other place than on Skid Row. That's the only place he ever lived. Like right here in Quincy he'd have hundreds of dollars in his pocket and he'd go down to that old Baker Hotel and pay a dollar and a half a night.

"That's the kind of people he feels comfortable with. He isn't the kind of guy to get in a job where there's a big payoff. He wouldn't be likely to be associated with people of that type. Where would he be acquainted with people like that?

"As I say, he didn't talk too much, he was in a way a little backward, his personality. You have to know him real well to understand him.

"He never talked about his father, but if he talked, it was most likely to be about his uncle Earl, what his uncle was doing, something like that. He'd call Earl most every day. There was a little hero worship in there somewhere or other. Sometimes he'd only stay in that booth talking to Earl for five minutes. When he'd talk he'd say his uncle did this, or did that, something like stealing or gambling or conning somebody. Even when Earl threw acid on his wife, Jimmy seemed to approve. 'That's what my uncle did to *his* wife,' Jim told me.

"When Jim was stealing he would carry stuff to Earl. He'd carry it to Earl and Earl knew a fence that would take it.

"I don't know about Ray's politics. Well, I know he didn't like colored people, I know that. But politics, he wasn't more radical about that than anyone else would be, even myself. I hated Kennedy, absolutely. If I ever hated anybody, which I hardly ever had, it was Kennedy. And not because of . . . he, Kennedy, just hurt me personally, down through the wire, me and a lot of other people, people like us. Kennedy is more responsible for Quincy closing down than anybody, stopped the gambling, stopped the prostitution. There used to be a lot of money in Quincy till Kennedy got in there. I wouldn't shoot him, but I hated him for that reason.

"Yeah, Jimmy was a little outraged about Negroes. He didn't care for them at all. There was nothing particular he had against them, nothing they had done to him. He said once they ought to be put out of the country.

"Once he said, 'Well, we ought to kill them, kill them all.'

"I'll tell you what, I myself have probably made a statement like that. I don't understand how King lived as long as he did. He was a rabble-rouser. Well, a lot of people will tell you that. They don't understand how he lived as long as he did. The man caused too much trouble. He went all over the country rabble-rousing. Everyplace he'd go they had riots, sitdowns and all. Hell, he *had* to go.

"Well, about Jim, it's just like I told you. He was unreasonable in his hatred for niggers. He hated to see them breathe. If you pressed it, he'd get violent in a conversation about it. He hated them! I never did know why.

"With most people, it's just something they grew up with. That's what it was with Jim. I tell you, most of the people who talk about Negroes, it's just something that's come down through their families.

"He was quiet, Jim was, but he had a *temper*. We were sitting once in this tavern in Kansas City. Somebody at the bar said something to him, nothing serious, like move your glass down. And Ray said, 'Oh, forget about it,' and he didn't look mad, and he just walked out the front door as if he was forgetting about it. But he went around the place and came in the back door, walked up behind this fella and stuck a knife in him. The fella fell off the stool, and we just walked right out of there.

"Well, like I say, Jim never mentioned his mother and father. I always figured they was dead. I don't talk about my mother because my mother is dead. A lot of people don't like to mention things like that. And unless they give you some indication in conversation, well, you don't want to mention it, either. Like I say, it was hard to get into a conversation with him at all."

When they had come to the end of their spree, emotionally, they began to get careless, to act suspiciously. Finally, a filling station man reported their plate number to the police.

They didn't know that this had happened, but with the high wearing off, Jimmy wanted to get back to Quincy. It was as if he thought that if he was going to be caught, he wanted to be caught at home.

This led to a fight when they were in Kansas City, with Walter not too eager to leave their friends and connections there. "The snow was three feet deep, nothing could run, there was no reason for us to leave there *that minute*," Walter has said. "But Jimmy *had* to leave. The car skidded all over the road, went off the curb. I wanted to wait. But he called a wrecker. We got in a fight, the first fight we ever had."

So they drove on silently together eastward across Missouri, toward Quincy until, on March 23, 1955, a Missouri highway patrolman, who had spotted their license plate as being on his list of hot cars, followed them a while, called for help, and, when he got it, ordered them to pull off Route 36 just south of Hannibal. There he arrested the two of them. When the cops booked him, asked his occupation, Jimmy sarcastically replied:

"Lover."

When the two men were tried in federal court in Kansas City, Ray got forty-five months at the federal penitentiary at Leavenworth, Kansas; Rife, thirty-six months there. The two of them arrived at Leavenworth on July 7, 1955.

It was only a few weeks before Jimmy was writing from prison to the judge who had sentenced him: "Your honor, I would like to take a few minutes of your time to ask for a

9 month reduction in sentence if you see fit. AL-though I realize you gave me a lenient sentence, July 1-st, 1955, of me and my codefendant I equality guilty you would base the sentence reasonable close. I recd 45 months, my codefendant recd 36. We both plea guilty to the charge of forgery. Thank you. James Earl Ray, Prisoner No. 72498."

Once again Ray was giving the legal system an arm-twist, to see how much give there was in it, but in this case there was none. The sentence stood.

---

Jimmy now found himself in old Leavenworth, the prison for big-timers, for long-term habitual criminals, for those who had "succeeded" in their craft. "There were no piss-ant people at Leavenworth," says a man who served there. I asked a friend of mine who was a longtime civil servant in the Federal Bureau of Prisons, working "inside" them as a sociologist, to characterize Leavenworth as an institution for me. He is John Boone, former commissioner of corrections in Massachusetts.

"If prisons can be considered 'progressive' and/or 'humane' at all, the United States Penitentiary in Leavenworth, Kansas, would be considered a good prison," said Boone. "The staff of Leavenworth, despite strong policies concerning humane treatment, can do very little that would be useful in helping an individual adjust in the community. It would mainly underscore the misunderstandings that are already too much of the inmate's makeup.

"For every kind of disorder that occurs in the free community, there is a similar kind of disorder in prison in actuality or in the minds of the men imprisoned. This includes polarization of the races in prisons, and at that time Leavenworth was not really integrated at all."

Jimmy was offered a chance to go to the honor farm. "On September 12, 1957," reads his Leavenworth record, "he was approved for our Honor Farm but was never actually transferred due to the fact that he did not feel he could live in an Honor Farm dormitory because they are integrated."

Rife became a nurse, went into group therapy, ended up in charge of a group. He claims to have won a meritorious award of $50 for nursing. "Leavenworth was segregated," Rife says, "but there wasn't any racial tension there, no problems. They [Negroes] were fed and housed in separate dormitories. But that doesn't mean feeling wasn't strong. One white guy was heard to say that Negroes are as good as we are, and he was killed for saying that.

"At Leavenworth, the guards were educated, treated you like a man," says Rife, "I never had a feeling I was really in prison when I was at Leavenworth. It was more like a hospital. They were stern if had to be, brutal if you asked for it. They taught you respect for the law, for the public, for your fellow man.

"Leavenworth is where you grow up," he says. "It did me *good* there. I'd say Leavenworth did Jimmy Ray more good than anything that ever happened to him. Leavenworth is where he grew up. Jim didn't have no trouble there at all, never got a ticket. Neither did I."

What Rife meant by Jimmy's growing up at Leavenworth may not be the kind of maturation the rest of us mean. Jimmy's record shows that Leavenworth represented only another stage in his adjustment to prison society, a willingness on his part to cooperate with the prison system and prison society — as he had done at Pontiac — in the reconstitution of his personality. There was less hope than ever that he would lead a straight life again.

"This man has no trade nor skills, is not interested in Vocation Training or Self-Improvement programs," says a Leavenworth report on Ray. "His only interests are to work in the Culinary Department." And as those in the prison *know*, working in the culinary department meant working in the key spot in the prison from which to operate in the prison black market, or, in prison parlance, as a "merchant."

Another report, written after Ray had been in Leavenworth a year, was even less promising: "He apparently lacks foresight, or is afraid of the future, as he absolutely refuses to look forward. He claims that he can do his time better if he doesn't have any trouble at this time, and apparently is enjoying his present situation."

He did take some courses — in Spanish, Composition, Typing, Culinary Sanitation, Applied English and Elementary Vocabulary — but to those who knew Ray, these only indicated preparation for a long crooked career. The typing and English classes suggest that he meant to prepare himself as a jailhouse lawyer, to be able to write and even type up his own briefs and petitions. The Spanish shows that he meant to go to Mexico, perhaps as an escape route if someday he should need it.

Nor was it a good sign that Jimmy began to be worried about his physical condition. "You're getting pear-shaped," Rife used to tease him, and Jimmy began to go to the gym, work out on the pulleys with weights. But in prison this is often a signal to other inmates that a man has begun to worry about his sexual situation. It's a sign in prison that a man may be "building himself up" against homosexual threat.

There were other clues that Jimmy was not prospering emotionally. He complained to the prison doctors of "chronic difficulty in breathing through his nose, thinks he may be allergic to the climate in this region."

Jimmy did not have a visitor the whole time he was in Leavenworth. Certainly Speedy didn't come to visit his son. He had warned his boys time and again: "You boys bust your way *into* prison, bust your way *out*." But, as at Pontiac, Jimmy corresponded with Jerry, creating a deepening loyalty and interdependence between the two brothers.

# Chapter 15

St. Louis was once an orderly little community made up of about two hundred grass-covered Osage Indian lodges spaced fifteen feet apart along the banks of the Mississippi River. These rude frameworks began to disappear when, in 1762, the village became a trading post. Since then the fate of that river-bank site has risen and fallen almost as often as the crest of the muddy old river.

Its heyday was the decade 1840–1850 when steamboating was at its brief romantic height; in 1860 there were 3,454 steamboat arrivals in St. Louis. The railroads of course did in the steamboats, and the Civil War nearly did in St. Louis, throwing a lot of the old city's business to new thriving Chicago, the railroad center. But eventually, it got its footing again, began to grow outward, in widening concentric arcs from the now quiet but still muddy river. In this way its history was like that of Alton, Quincy and Hannibal. And in another way, too. For St. Louis left behind, there along the river bank, at the center of its arcs of growth, a decayed area, like a rotten core at what had once been its very heart. This river-bank area was, and is, called Soulard, and Soulard was like those river wards in Quincy.

By the late 1950's Soulard had become "an expanding area of physical and social deterioration — aging houses, mobile population, high rates of delinquency, death, morbidity, mental disorder."

It was to the Soulard section of St. Louis that James Earl Ray came from Leavenworth. By 1958, most of the family had lived, or were living, in Soulard. Speedy had lived there as early as the 1920's, when it was already run down.

But by the 1950's, an unusual, yet typical, situation had come about there, a typical situation, that is, for many cities in post–World War II America. Those German and other earlier migrant families who had built homes and lived respectably for several earlier decades in Soulard were swamped with folks coming from the country, particularly dirt-poor white families from the Ozarks. They were of two markedly distinct kinds, the "good country people," and the "hoosiers."

Hoosier is a lower class and underworld expression that has come to mean something quite different from merely describing a resident of Indiana. As early as 1899, it was being used to describe a rube, a rustic, a simpleton, often by hoboes who called anyone a hoosier who did not know the world as the hobo knew it. It evolved into a yegg's word, meaning an easy mark, a victim. To some it came to mean a *rat*. In other circles, a "hoosier stiff" came to denote a worthless check, and a "hoosier fiend," an inexperienced drug addict.

The definition of hoosiers in Soulard was that of people who are "dirty, disrespectful and ignorant," people who "fill the air with drunken arguments and the landscape with garbage, trash, broken down cars. A hoosier is the man who sits with his bare feet in an open, unscreened window overlooking the street, propped back in a chair watching TV, beer bottle on the window sill, from late afternoon until ten or eleven o'clock. The hoosier's children are the ones who throw bricks through the windows of temporarily vacated buildings, and who, when the building is then vacated, rip out the plumbing and other fixtures and sometimes even set the building on fire," says a study of the section.

Hoosiers quit jobs, then don't have any job seniority and are the first to be laid off; they don't pay their rent, raise hell with the landlord for "not fixin' nothin' 'round here," and then move and never pay rent at all.

As the hoosiers gradually obliterated the decent housing in Soulard, the industrial city grew up around the plagued section until it had become "an interstitial area bounded on three sides by heavy industry with foul air, noise and heavy traffic." In an environment like this, mental decay quickly follows upon physical decay. The spiritual atmosphere in Soulard was one of hostility, alienation, suspiciousness, resentment, lack of self-respect, low self-esteem.

This was the moral slum James Earl Ray now moved into. In these surroundings he was not likely to find any counterweight to his now almost irresistible pull toward crime. He was no longer balanced between the straight world and the crooked world. He was inside the criminal world, a criminal, his chances of doing anything else slim.

Jimmy was back in that world of oilcloth tablecloths, unshaded dim light bulbs, cracked linoleum floors, greasy wallpaper, and stained bathroom sinks and tubs. Sometimes he stayed in the rooming house that Mom Maher and Ceal ran, sometimes he took a room of his own, sometimes he holed up in "missions" and "halfway houses," of which the St. Louis Mission, a seedy flophouse, was one of his more or less regular haunts.

This grim establishment was housed in a run-down former movie house and was operated by a Reverend who it was rumored had been a Tennessee moonshiner. It was here that Jimmy ran into Blackie Austin — Joseph Elmer Austin, a sixty-year-old ex-convict who had spent most of his life in Menard, in fact had been inside there thirty-three years when he was paroled in May, 1959. Austin was one of those men who had been behind bars so long that his skin is translucent.

But there was one thing Blackie felt comfortable with and that was a pistol. Blackie was a man who could be *trusted*. Jimmy knew that. He knew it from Walter Rife who had once been Blackie's cellmate. The result of this mutual trust was that Jimmy and Blackie got their heads together on a job. And, on the morning of July 11, 1959, a little less than three months after Jimmy had gotten out of Leavenworth, Jimmy and Blackie entered the Kroger Supermarket at 131 North Euclid Street in St. Louis, and Blackie told the manager: "Open the safe and give me the money and you won't get hurt." The manager turned over about $1,200 and Blackie and Jimmy fled, but not before they had both been photographed by a camera set up to identify check cashers.

Blackie and Jimmy ran from the store, got into their getaway car, scratched off only to hit another car a couple of blocks away. They were able to go on, change to another car, and make their getaway. But they were later identified from the photographs, and the store employees said that Ray was "the number one man." It turned out that one of the aliases Jimmy was giving then was William Marr, not too far different from his uncle William Maher. It also turned out that the getaway car had been stolen from the Jack Randolph used car lot where Speedy had worked.

---

Jimmy had not become a big-time criminal in Leavenworth; that was clear. But he had graduated from those two-bit holdups like the taxi job in Chicago. In these supermarket jobs, there had to be at least a perfunctory casing of the joint. He had to plan for a getaway car, steal it, and get guns. He also had to recruit and select an assistant. "The supermarket job was just about right for Ray," says a man who knew him at this time. "He didn't want anything bigger than that. He was too much of a loner to work with a group, too suspicious to work with anybody who hadn't been tested and who wouldn't work *for* him." But if Jimmy had taken one step upward in his criminal career, he apparently, during those years in Pontiac and Leavenworth, had taken two — maybe many more — steps backward in his emotional development. He was more angry, angry at *something*, than he had ever been.

The next job Blackie and Jimmy did together was proof of it. They turned up together on the morning of August 21, 1959, at the IGA grocery run by Mr. and Mrs. Henry Wegener at 901 Alby Street in Alton, just after the store had opened. Pistols in hand, they demanded the money in the cash registers, and insisted that the manager open the store safe. Wegener told them that he had only one key, and that it took a second different key to open it. This set Jimmy off. He could not bear this frustration. He suddenly began "acting wild, like he was crazy," Mrs. Wegener later told the Alton police.

Even without what was in the safe, they got about $2,200 and took off on what ended as a wild police chase, with both of them having to abandon the car they were in, and ending up by fleeing through the woods. Austin was captured, returned to Menard as a parole violator, told the police that he was relieved, glad to go back. But Jimmy escaped, although he was later identified and indicted on October 27, 1959, by a grand jury in Edwardsville, at the same courthouse where Speedy and Ceal got their marriage license.

Before that indictment was handed down, however, Jimmy found another friend at the St. Louis Mission, and, with him, entered another grocery store with a gun in his hand. On the morning of October 10, 1959, Jimmy and James Owens, an ex-convict, held up a Kroger store at 3417 Ohio Street in St. Louis.

The St. Louis police made a detailed report on this crime. It is Complaint Number 222,015 of the Metropolitan Police Department of St. Louis and is on file in the Police Bureau of Records. It is a case history of a prototypical James Earl Ray crime.

It tells how Owens met Ray at the St. Louis Rescue Mission and "due to the fact that they both had something in common that they were both ex-convicts," they struck up a friendship. It tells how Owens and Ray next met in a restaurant on Olive Street, "and both spoke of financial difficulties, during which time they made mutual agreement to accompany each other at a later date for the purpose of a holdup."

The report tells how the two men cased the Kroger store, how Ray gave Owens a snub-nosed revolver, how the two of them stole a getaway car, using a "jumper" Ray owned, how they parked their second car some distance away from the Kroger store, and how Ray led the holdup with Owens standing at the front door of the store acting as lookout, how they drove the stolen car around for a while, and then dumped it for their second car, how they then went to Ray's furnished room, where Owens gave Ray back the revolver (Ray had used another revolver in the holdup), and how Ray then gave Owens six $10 bills which Ray told Owens was half of the money he got in the robbery.

The report tells how a bystander saw the two men change cars, reported it to the police, how the police waited at the second car until Owens returned to it, captured him, how he betrayed Ray, and how the police then went to Ray's rooming house to capture Ray.

Two St. Louis detectives went up the stairs to Ray's room. When they got to the top "they observed a white man coming from the north end of the common hallway, from the bathroom, and upon identifying themselves as police officers and commanding the subject to halt and to raise his hands, the subject instead turned and began to curse and ran back towards the bathroom, and in a matter of a few seconds, the officers overtook him and placed him under physical arrest.

"At this time, the prisoner began to scuffle with the officers and grabbed a hold of Detective Connors about the waist.

Detective Connors then struck prisoner Ray over the head with his service revolver. This action caused the prisoner to release his hold on the officer's waist. The two officers started to escort the prisoner to his room and the prisoner broke away and managed to elude the two officers and began to run towards the bathroom. Detective Connors fired one shot in the direction of the fleeing suspect at which time the prisoner halted and submitted to arrest without further restrictions."

Ray showed the detectives where the two pistols were, acknowledged he was the owner of the weapons, and said, in what was an about-face of attitude, from violent resistance to passive compliance with authority:

"I guess you want me for that Kroger store stickup," and went quietly. The cops took him to the hospital to have his head checked. It was, except for lacerations, OK. They then took him to jail and booked him for Suspected Robbery with a Deadly Weapon.

---

For two months Jimmy sat in the St. Louis city jail waiting to be tried. He was a three-time loser, and there was every reason for him to think that his criminal career, like his aborted political career in Germany, was a failure. It did not help him that he had an outbreak of his venereal disease as he waited. His mood was black. It was one of the blackest moments of his life. A date was set for his trial. It was December 15, and on that morning a deputy sheriff came to take him to the courtroom. The two men started off through an underground tunnel that led from the jail to the courthouse, went up a special elevator for prisoners, entered a courtroom cell where the deputy unlocked one of the handcuff bracelets on

Ray. Suddenly Ray broke loose, pushed the deputy violently away, kicked him hard, and ran back to the elevator. Jimmy had one elevator door closed and was pushing at the second one when the deputy thrust his hand through. Jimmy gave him a hard angry push, flung himself out of the elevator and ran down the hall of the building. He was met there by another policeman who pulled his pistol and challenged Jimmy to stop. At that, Jimmy became strangely passive, compliant, backed against the corridor wall, and covered his face with his hands.

---

The sum of a human being's emotions is called his personality, and the pluses and the minuses in Jimmy's personality were now showing themselves in sharper and sharper outline. There were weaknesses in that emotional structure of his — as of course there are in all of our emotional structures — and he had done what all of us do, more or less, about them. He had built *defenses* against his weaknesses, defenses against his vulnerable spots. One of the things he feared was that he might be (emotionally) overwhelmed; he was afraid of his own passivity. There is proof of that. It is not a fanciful or a theoretical guess.

He proved it in that hall of the courthouse, he proved it in the hall of his boardinghouse where he was trapped by the cops: he proved that when he felt crucially threatened he would cast his lot with the most powerful symbol of authority around him. His emotional defenses broke down at the same time that his physical defenses failed him.

In fact, he did not need the threat of physical danger to seek to make himself identical with those potential aggressors around him, those symbols of authority. That was one of Jimmy's most needed defenses. Jimmy's relationship with his tannery friend, Jimmy's attraction to Hitler and nazism proved that. Jimmy had followed the Swastika to Germany like the Holy Grail. With Jimmy, the gain was that when he became one with Hitler, with the cop who threatened him with a pistol, he gained some of that other person's power, authority, some of his *rightness*.

Like many people with some inner weakness (which they themselves may not understand), Jimmy hated weakness.

When Jimmy finally got in the St. Louis courtroom that morning, he had regained his composure, and was once again Jailhouse Lawyer Ray, and a far more ambitious "member of the bar" than he had ever dared or pretended to be before. Indeed he told the judge that he wished to represent himself, although every criminal knows that is foolish. He also asked to take the stand, an unwise step because it meant that his past criminal record could be introduced into the proceedings. What's more, he demanded and got a jury trial which meant, if he was found guilty, that he would probably get a tougher sentence than he would have had he pled guilty.

Jimmy's defense was not good. He said he hadn't been able to locate a witness. Then he said: "It seemed to me that the police officers shooting at a man ought to at least get his name. I think my constitutional rights were violated."

There was some point in that but not much, not for a man who was standing trial on a charge and a record that could get him a long sentence as a habitual criminal. His behavior suggests something that had now happened to Jimmy. His image of himself was out of focus. He was out of touch with reality. He had reached the point where he thought he was a lot smarter than he was.

During the trial, he repudiated his confession and later appealed his conviction to the Missouri Supreme Court — insisting that his confession had not been freely given. "The only thing I admitted was what they more or less beat out of me," he claimed.

His try at being a lawyer was a grave disaster for him. He got twenty years while James Owens got only seven. On March 17, 1960, he got aboard the prisoner railroad car that runs once a week from St. Louis to Jefferson City, the site of the Missouri state penitentiary.

# Chapter 16

For more than a hundred years a motley, forbidding collection of gray stone buildings has been spreading like some insidious fungus along a ragged bluff above the Missouri River at Jefferson City. These godforsaken structures, which age has not been able to mellow, together make up the Missouri state penitentiary. It is an institution well known to — and hatefully regarded by — most criminals as "Jeff City." When it opened in 1836, during the second term of Andrew Jackson, it was the first prison west of the Mississippi River, and ever since then it has been considered the *worst* one. Its crawling walls and turrets enclose forty-seven acres of land — "and square foot for square foot it is the bloodiest 47 acres in America." In their publication, the *Jefftown Journal*, the prisoners themselves label Jeff City, with masochistic pride, as "The Big — The Bad — The Ugly."

It says something about *something*, perhaps about the state of Missouri, perhaps about all of us, that this warren of violence sits only two blocks from the governor's mansion and seven blocks from the capitol building of Missouri. "It is deplored by politicians, neglected by entrenched officials, damned by a persevering press, and run by its hapless inmates," was the conclusion of Patrick J. Buchanan in 1964, later to be a speech writer for President Richard Nixon, but who was then writing in the liberal *Nation*.

Waves of "reform" have swept over the prison with no more effect than to leave behind more discontent. As early as 1854 it was thought of as "a school for rogues." An early warden bragged to investigators: "I guess I have whipped more men than any man alive." He flogged inmates with cat-o'nine-tails "until blood filled their shoes." In the 1930's, President Franklin Roosevelt sent a team of prison experts to Jeff City who were shocked most by A-Hall, a wretched old structure where Negroes were segregated, and crammed seven and eight to cells designed for three. They said A-Hall should be torn down. A-Hall was still standing and still segregated for many years after that.

Times changed, but Jeff City did not. In 1954 (the 1950's were years marked by many outbreaks in the old state penitentiaries of the country), there was a fifteen-hour riot at Jeff City, leaving five inmates dead, a number of guards and other inmates injured, and seven of those old buildings in ashes. A marine colonel, who had proved himself running tough marine brigs, was brought on to restore order. But this old leatherneck was himself soon telling the legislature that Jeff City was "the roughest damned prison in the country."

He urged the state to abandon the whole works, *all* the buildings and the acres.

Conditions inside the old prison when James Earl Ray went behind its walls in March, 1960, were probably as bad as they had ever been, if not worse. A joint Missouri legislative committee made a careful study of the prison not long after Ray went inside.

The state of things in those forty-seven acres in the 1960's was like "a medieval twilight zone," this committee found.

In the two-year period from 1961 through 1963, the committee, by carefully studying hospital records, found that there had been 489 violent acts. This is an astonishing, shocking statistic. In a relatively well-run federal prison, there is only one stabbing a year on the average.

The committee's summary of violent acts reads like the casualty report of some bloody battle:

*Acts of Violence — All Types*
1961–1963

| Stab wounds: | 145 |
|---|---|
| | 6 died |
| | 14 required surgery |
| | 37 required hospitalization |
| | 88 sutured, bandaged and treated as out patients |
| Struck with some object: | 134 |
| | 1 died |
| | 12 required surgery (8 jaws wired, 2 eye removals) |
| | 36 required hospitalization |
| | 85 sutured, bandaged and treated as out patients |

| Fist fights: | 199 | |
| | 12 | required surgery (wired jaws) |
| | 12 | required hospitalization |
| | 175 | sutured, bandaged and treated as out patients |
| Burns (lye, acid, coffee, etc.): | 11 | |
| | 11 | required hospitalization |
| Total acts of violence: | 489 | |
| Custodial officers injured: | 1 | |
| | 1 | struck in head; required 2 sutures |

"In there, I could have you killed for a carton of cigarettes," an inmate claimed.

One of the worst outrages was the prison hospital. "It would need a Jonathan Swift to do it justice," the legislative report said. The psychiatric ward was run by a man who had been discharged from the armed forces for emotional instability, and who had often been under the influence of either drugs or alcohol while on duty. There were tin cans under the hospital bed and table legs to prevent vermin in the food, "but thousands of bugs scampered before the committee's eyes during our visit." One emaciated prisoner patient with rubber tubes in his nostrils and through his stomach wall had the diagnosis: "upset stomach." Prison authorities had allowed a private doctor the right to conduct experiments on prisoners (during which a needle was stuck from the front of their necks through to the cervical disk) who were given sixty days' "good time" (off their sentences) for submitting to this cruelty. One ward-size room had been converted into a luxury suite by two inmates with no apparent illness. "The sight of ten electric fans blowing on the two beds had a smack of indulgence not commensurate with the other surroundings," was the committee's sour comment.

But the violence and corruption only proved something else about the prison that was far more significant, far more important, something that directly affected what James Earl Ray was to do in that prison for seven years. *The prisoners had taken control of the prison.* This happens everyplace, and it is an axiom among criminologists that "Prisoners inevitably and always control prison life."

But not to the point that it happened in Jeff City while Ray was there. Things had reached the stage where guards had to *buy their safety* with favors and gifts. The inmates were forced to pay other inmates (and the worse elements among them were running the place) to get medical and dental treatment. Ray paid $40 for a set of teeth. Inmates were allowed to become "switchmen" and "lever men" with the right to open cells, to allow inmates to transfer from one cell to another, most often for sexual purposes. For a price, prisoners could even "marry." The guards, for their part, were so poorly paid that they were moonlighting to make a decent living, working in Jefferson City as bellhops, taxi drivers and clerks.

The consequences of this lack of control spread throughout the prison. The time had come, for example, to integrate the penitentiary, to get those black men out of A-Hall. The old building was simmering and seething with hatred and resentment, casting a pall over the whole prison. The legislative committee found that A-Hall was "a terrible example to the inmates." But where was the warden, where the guards that would dare try to integrate Jeff City when they couldn't be safe in their own shoes? It was a time when one warden was afraid to come into the prison at all.

But, a prison where the prisoners were running the place, a prison out of control, was just exactly the kind of place James Earl Ray was looking for. If he was going to have to do time, there couldn't be a better place to do it than Jeff City in the 1960's. It offered a special vocational opportunity.

---

It seems obvious that to the prisoner the single most important fact about prison life is that *you can't get out.* What this means is that whatever you're going to get in the way of *pleasure* you're going to have to get *inside.* You can't go out to a movie, to get a girl, to drink a beer, buy a steak, a candy bar or even pop pills or shoot dope. When you're inside and have to try to learn to do without these things, you begin to realize how far you will go, what a price you will pay, to get some of these pleasures. "A candy bar in prison is like a diamond outside," is the saying.

In a prison that is out of control, or that is in the prisoners' control, there is quite naturally going to be a lot of pressure to produce some of these pleasures *inside.* In fact, there is more than that at work inside a prison which the prisoners run. They try to create a system that will restore, to some degree, to a degree that may seem only pathetic to us outside the prison, their dignity, their humanity. They create a system of status, a system that will work *inside.*

As the guards lose control, an elite of prisoners emerges to take over, and to take care of themselves first, as did those men who were living under the cooling breezes of ten fans in the Jeff City hospital. In the time Ray was there, the prison was actually run by an inmate named Bradley who lived in a cell with upholstered furniture, draperies, a TV set and other amenities. It was a legend in the prison that the warden had allowed his picture to be taken with Bradley's arm across his shoulder.

Bradley was the prototype Politician or Big Shot, the fellow who is at the top of the prison status system. He actually runs the prisoner organization. Below the Politician comes the Right Guy, the charismatic hero of the prison. There were men like that in Jeff City, fellows whose names still bring tears of pride along the cellblocks. The Right Guy is the man who will be loyal to the inmate code whatever the sacrifice, against *any* show of official force. They say of one of these guys in Jeff City: "They could have *welded* Jack in The Hole and he wouldn't squeal."

On the next step down comes the Merchant. It is the Merchant's job to get into the prison, or to divert from official sources within the prison, as many of those Goodies of outside life as he can provide. Everything he does is illegal, against the rules; thus, the one attribute above all others the Merchant must possess is, in the eyes of the inmate elite, absolute trustworthiness. If he talks loosely, he will upset a network of intricate relationships throughout the prison that has taken a long time to develop. Naturally, no guard would do business with a prisoner who wasn't also, from the guard's point of view, trustworthy, and who could be coerced or bribed into betraying the guard to the warden.

If his system of contraband merchandising is to work, the Merchant must be tough on the people under him, or people who owe him. He must not let a debt go uncollected. He must, if necessary, coerce the inmates who trade with him, at the same time that he is, on the other side, intimidating the guards, usually lower echelon guards, with whom he does business by buying them off. The Merchant is a man who is capable of "sharp dealings in the exchange of goods stolen from the supplies of the mess hall, workshops, and maintenance details." He is never "giving" but always "selling!" The Merchant's motto is "con them, chastise them, coerce them, but don't give credit."

If there was ever a man who combined the emotional attributes with the right kind of background and experience for being a Merchant it was James Earl Ray when he entered Jeff City, and he quickly made the right contacts to become one.

It is a misconception to assume that the status a man has in prison depends upon his status or rank as a criminal. It doesn't. The fact that James Earl Ray was a small-time criminal didn't keep him from becoming a Merchant in Jeff City. What matters is a man's proven capacities to understand the ways of the prison community. James Earl Ray understood prison life and he knew how to operate with Big Shots, with guards, and with other prisoners.

At Pontiac James Earl Ray was a fish. But he obviously knew how to behave. The fact that he did not have one mark against him during his whole stay proved that he already had the savvy about prison life and values. He knew how to do time before he ever had to do any. Earl and Speedy had taught him — they and everyone in that world in Quincy which he inhabited. What's more, he learned a skill that he knew would put him in a strategic place in prison. In the commissary, where there were goodies.

But, as Rife said, "Jimmy grew up at Leavenworth." He met big shots there. He made the final adjustment. He learned how to behave around big-time criminals. It meant that he had given up on ever making it in the real straight world. He was permanently committed to a life of crime.

It was almost automatic that he would get back in prison after he left Leavenworth. And when he got back in prison — in Jeff City — he was prepared, he was educated and trained by previous prison experiences to be a Merchant.

Whether James Earl Ray was or was not a Merchant at Jeff City is not just something that would make an item for the *Jefftown Journal*. It is a matter of crucial historical importance. On it hinges the central mystery and uncertainty about the Martin Luther King assassination. If Ray was paid, as he has alleged, by a man named "Raoul," who was an agent of a foreign government, then that is where the money came from and there was a conspiracy in the assassination. If Ray was a Merchant at Jeff City who made several thousand dollars in the seven years he was in there, then the question of where Ray got the money for his travels, and to buy his white Mustang, then that question of "Where did that little punk criminal get the money?" is answered.

The history of Ray's illegal dealings as a Merchant in Jeff City has been very difficult to document. The prison authorities are not helpful. Just the opposite. They can no more admit that they have lost control of the prison, that the prisoners are running it, than they can fly to the moon. See no evil; hear no evil; and certainly speak no evil of the prison is their determined policy. Those legislators up there in the state capitol at Jeff City don't want any bad news from the prison, the prison which they have been so reluctant to improve.

There are two reasons the official denial that Ray was a Merchant carries weight. One reason is that the only way to challenge the official version is with the testimony of convicts, or ex-convicts, whose credibility seems questionable on the face of it. The other reason that the official denial carries weight is that the truth, the facts about what Ray did, seem so outlandish, bizarre and improbable to the person who has not been in prison.

"Ray was just a *nothing* here," I was told by Fred Wilkinson, Missouri corrections commissioner, when I visited Jefferson City and the prison. The warden was just as flat about Ray and his role in prison. "If James Earl Ray had amounted to a hill of beans here, I would have a card on him in this pack of Big Shots and Bad Actors," said Harold Swenson, pulling out a bundle of three-by-five index cards, and riffling through them as he talked. "And Ray isn't in here," he said.

I asked Swenson if it wasn't true that Ray had on his record a violation for carrying contraband goods into the prison hospital. It was true, Swenson admitted. The contraband was, in fact, five packages of cigarettes, one jar of Maxwell House instant coffee, one pack of razor blades, and one can of Campbell's soup. These all are highly negotiable items inside Jeff City.

Swenson volunteered to let me talk to a prisoner named Bill Miles, who had known Ray, and I went down into the prison to a room set aside for the interview. I was suspicious of Miles. I knew he had been brought out before by the prison officials as an authority on Ray.

It turned out that Miles had usually been questioned about Ray's racial views. He did not like it, he grew uncomfortable and began to squirm, when I asked him about Ray as a merchant and hustler. He looked questioningly at the prison official who had come down with me. He got an official nod in return, and began hesitatingly to talk with me. It turned out that Miles had in fact worked for Ray. He had run a "library" in the yard. Miles's job was to carry books into the yard and trade and rent them on Saturday and Sunday mornings. "At one time Ray had two or three of these libraries going," Miles said. "He had about three hundred books in his cell. One pack of cigarettes would get two books for one week. There was about five cartons a month in it for me."

But he ran into trouble with Ray once. He borrowed $12 from Ray and agreed to pay up on "Draw Day." "When I didn't have it that *day*, Jim was waiting in the yard for me. He wanted the money, and he wasn't kidding. I could see *that*. So, I scratched around and *paid* him."

I asked Miles if he had helped Ray in dealing drugs. He looked up quickly at me, and then turned to the official: "Do I have to answer that?"

"No, you *don't*," the official told him.

With that, Miles got up and moved to the door where a guard was waiting to take him back to his cell.

But the question of whether Ray made money in Jeff City and how much was too important to drop right there, with that rebuff.

# Chapter 17

One bright afternoon in May, 1968, I left Atlanta to drive
north to the little Piedmont town of Dalton, Georgia. I was
on my way to see Raymond Curtis, a man who had claimed
publicly that he had been a friend of James Earl Ray at Jeff
City. To get to Dalton, I had to reverse the route General
Sherman took; he drove his men southward from Chattanooga, through Dalton, to Atlanta. Since Sherman's time,
Dalton's history has ebbed and flowed until it has ended as
a rug manufacturing center. At Adairsville, the road nar-
rowed and I began to see signs of the life of the hilly-
mountain South. All along the highway there were chenille
stores, small rabbit box–like structures, with wooden wings
stretched out from them, crude frameworks on which were
hung cotton bedspreads in lurid patterns. The most popular
item was a huge towel imprinted with the Confederate flag.

When I turned off an interstate to go to Dalton, I saw parked in a saucer cut out of a red clay hill a truck billboarding an evangelist's office: SOUL SAVING AND FAITH HEALING, and as I drove into Dalton, I passed the national headquarters of the Church of God, a strict evangelistic sect. When I parked to get gas, I saw a small factory down the street bearing a sign, GOSPEL TENTS. These mountain people have for two hundred years been hugging the hills and clasping their fundamentalism. They are hard-fisted people, used to the poor living, who vote unfailingly to keep their mountain counties legally "dry," and fight violently over the right to make and drink moonshine.

Curtis was in jail in Dalton. Sheriff Jerry Malden had told me I could talk with Curtis, and Curtis's attorney had said, with a note of bitter despair in his voice: "Sure Raymond can talk with you. There's nothing more he could do to hurt himself with the juries of this county." Curtis was charged with the murder of one man and the gunning down of three others in a dispute over a poker game. His father was a preacher in the nearby hamlet of Tunnel Hill, Georgia. The jail was out of a western movie, a two-story mellowed red brick house with bars on its windows. Sitting in the outer hall of the sheriff's office, there was a copper liquor still which no doubt would someday, somehow, find its way back to a creek bank, and more distillations.

To reach Curtis's cell, I turned right at the top of the stairs and into a narrow aisle that separated his cell from the outside wall of the old jail. I said hello and made myself a seat by pulling up a dented galvanized water bucket. Curtis handed me a stained brown GI blanket which I folded up into a cushion.

I opened my notebook, looked him in the eye, and said:

"Listen, maybe I'm getting my courage out of these steel bars, but I'm gonna tell you flat out that I don't believe your story that Ray was paid to kill King by a group of Mississippi businessmen." Curtis had got national attention by telling press associations and TV newsmen this story, and it had become one of the permanent "truths" about the Memphis assassination.

He looked at me a moment and then turned away, moved his hands along the top bunk, as if to gain a moment to think. Stacked there in neat rows was a mini-market, four large cartons of Premium soda crackers, jars of instant Maxwell House coffee, cans of Prince Albert tobacco, cigarette papers, and at the end of the bunk was a new Bible, its gold lettering gleaming. It was clear that I was talking to the Merchant of the Dalton jail.

He turned around and pushed through the bars a copy of *Jet*. The magazine had used and added something to Curtis's story, that the Ku Klux Klan had also offered a bounty for King.

"This *Jet*," Curtis said, "they got me all fucked up." His tone was whining, complaining, not so much angry as entreating, as if asking me to accept the fact that this injustice from the media he had suffered canceled out any guilt he should feel for having lied to the newspapers. "I ain't never said one word about the Klan. We did use to kid around Jeff City, using 'KK,' to mean kill Kennedy or kill King. But if this *Jet* gets down to Reidsville, the state 'pen' where I'm going, I won't live thirty days."

As we talked, and I got used to the light (a bare bulb shaded by cardboard), I began to perceive that the "store" on the empty top bunk was only the beginning of the vast amount of *things* that Curtis had packed into his tiny cubicle. From the bars of the cell, he had suspended good luck charms, a transistor radio which hung by a leather strap, and two plastic bags of his dress clothes, being saved there perhaps for his next court appearance, for, although he was convicted, people like Curtis are always "on appeal." He had even used up most of the *space* that was in the skinny walkway between his bunk and the bars. Sitting on the floor at one end was an electric fan, whirring and turning in monotonous cycles. At the other end was a TV set resting on a wooden crate.

I thought how frantic I would be if I were in that cell and I no sooner had that thought than it came over me that Curtis did not seem crowded in there at all. He moved around easily, deftly, as if he were in a ballroom at Versailles. I realized that to a man who had spent, as Curtis had, a great part of his adult life in just that amount of space, he would of course have habituated himself to that crimped dimension, as *his living space.* I thought to myself: if this fellow had any *more* space, he would be at sea, lost, adrift, probably quite confused and unhappy.

"I first knew Ray in 1955 in Jackson County jail at Kansas City," Curtis told me. "Me and him used to work a card game there. With two men working together you could pretty well clean everybody out. He'd run it up, and I'd false cut. Sometimes we'd loan money, me and Ray, two bucks for three back. He used to talk to me about little jobs he did in Chicago, before he was caught on the taxi job. He robbed a lot of beer and liquor stores, the Little Brown Jug, too, at Indiana Avenue and a Hundred and Twenty-seventh Street.

"We used to walk the yard together at Leavenworth. They called it the 'plotting circle' because when you saw two men walking the track, like two donkeys abreast, you knew they were thinking out some big scheme, something they were gonna do when they got out. But he didn't run no store there at Leavenworth, or get in any business that I know of."

Curtis had the color of a man who had spent his life in a cave, that is, no color at all. But what was even more notice-able, and unpleasant, was that he seemed to have no *sub-stance*. All that distinguished him as a person were append-ages, huge ears and a long knobby nose, arms that were covered with tattoos in a sickly blue that looked as if the dye had been drawn from his pale veins. His dingy hair was glued down and parted sharply as if he had not changed his hair since the days of the "Sheiks" in the twenties. He was in what were obviously his casual, workaday, at-home clothes, frayed leather house slippers, a pair of faded magenta cotton knit pajama pants, and a worn, spotted T-shirt through which his fish-colored flesh showed.

"But he was a peddler at Jeff City, all right," Curtis went on. "I've seen him work on a plan as long as thirty days to get a dozen eggs halfway across the prison yard. He stole many a case of eggs in his time, sold them for a dollar a dozen, thirty dollars a case. The way you handle eggs is to take a case of toilet paper, lift out the middle section, put in the eggs — or canned fruit if you're selling that — in the middle, then put toilet paper back in on top to fool the guards.

"Sometimes we made raisin jack, sometimes homemade

beer. Ray supplied the yeast because he could get it in the bakery where he worked, and I made the stuff. The way you did it was to take the stuffing out of a mattress, and then take a plastic mattress cover and stick it inside the mattress. It will ferment right in there. Thirty gallons.

"You seal that plastic bag with an iron, use the kind of hose you give blood with. Take a quart jar and put it at the end of your bunk and fill it with water, and just let the booze drain down into it. That kills the smell. It takes seventy-two hours to make. If there's a shakedown, the guard usually just picks up one end of the mattress. He doesn't figure what's in it.

"Ray was tough, but he came to see me every day when I was in the hospital at Jeff City. [Curtis had hepatitis.] He brought me things that if he'd been caught they would have put him *under* solitary. But if he got mad he would *hurt you*. To get him really mad, take something of his, push him, you'll get him *killing* mad. He'd steal a nickel off a dead man's eye.

"The way he worked it so that he never got caught, was that *he wouldn't even talk to you* unless he could get the stuff to you. If he knew he couldn't deliver to where you were, what was the use of gabbing with you. He wasn't much of a talker anyway."

Curtis began to reminisce about his own "jobs," about going up and down the Mississippi River, doing holdups, and I began to suspect that he had a glow on, that he was getting "high." I let the interview taper off, and I left to let him come down. Outside the jail, I called someone who visited Curtis regularly, to ask about Curtis and drugs. "Oh, sure,"

I was told, "he has his pills in there with him. Sometimes when he thinks there's gonna be a shakedown, he'll ask me to carry out his stash."

I knew Curtis wasn't going anyplace, he was appealing a life sentence, so I waited a few weeks, and then drove back north from Atlanta to Dalton, found that copper still resting in the same spot in the jail corridor, and went upstairs to find Curtis, still operating his store, still wearing what seemed to be the same pair of house slippers, frayed T-shirt, and pajama pants.

This time I asked him about drugs at Jeff City. This was a more sensitive subject. Curtis told me that to his knowledge Ray had used pills and amphetamines since he had first known him fifteen years before. "At Jeff City he was in that business," Curtis said. "Him and another boy had the connection. Ain't but one way to get it in — the guard! Keep in mind that in penitentiary your mind is alway depressed. Ray was a user, but I never saw him take hard stuff — and there was opium out there at Jeff City — nor an overdose. He drank a lot of mineral oil and a lot of juices, to put oil back in his body.

"Ray would take Splash, lay down on his bunk, he would think. With that amphetamine your mind will clear up. You will go all the way back till you are six or seven years old. Ray would go over a job and see the mistakes he had made.

"I can't use no names," said Curtis, "but Ray's connection was in the culinary, doing a life sentence. There was a lot of stuff in that prison. There was Y-mine inhalers that went for ten dollars, there was yellow bennies, and white bennies, Spaniels — take three of them and you'd jump off the moon.

"Mostly Ray had it fixed so that certain people could get to him, like the hall runner. There's ten or twenty of these fellas in prison, the Major's runners, fellas allowed to move around the prison, go most anywhere. Ray worked with them, got a couple of them, also the hall tenders and the night man, anybody who could move around. The runners would buy the stuff from him, they would pay him, and deliver for him.

"One thing you could do is give a guard a hundred dollars to buy a plane ticket to St. Louis and pick it up for you, or even five hundred dollars to go to Kansas City. A fella like Ray would end up paying about seven hundred fifty dollars a pound. With pills you make more. You buy a thousand for fifty cents apiece, and sell them for a dollar apiece.

"Of course one way to make more money out of Speed is to cut it with powdered sugar, dump it all together and stir. You may sell a whole pound to somebody for thirty-five hundred dollars. Or, you can sell it out by spoons, but there was only two or three men in the whole penitentiary who were selling it by the spoon. You take one of these small plastic spoons and measure it out. That's fifty to seventy-five dollars. The fellow that buys a spoon's worth may sell it by the paper. The way you do that is take a fingernail clip, and measure out your Speed on the tiny corrugated point. You cover the third mark and that's five dollars. That much you put in a cigarette paper. You use a cigarette machine to make up the cigarettes, and you put these papers folded up very small in the middle of the cigarette, hidden by tobacco at both ends of the cigarette. You might have four or five of these Speed papers inside one pack of cigarettes.

"That's the way they packaged pills, too. Roll them up ten

to a package in wax paper, put them in cigarettes, or in the hollow end of a shaving brush.

"For a while I was making it good myself. I was a tower runner, I'd go out early in the morning to carry food to the tower guards. They'd let a bucket down, there might be a pound of Speed in it. I'd carry it all the way across the yard, and I might get three hundred for that, and take three or four spoonsful of it for myself besides. I've made as high as six hundred dollars in one day.

"Sometimes we worked it that Ray would supply me, I could supply other suppliers, and they'd supply others down the line.

"I've seen two murders over a pound. One guy had the money and he ordered a pound. The guy that brought it switched it, gave him a pound of sugar, and he got killed for doing *that*. Then his buddies killed the killer.

"The way you shoot it is with an eyedropper. You put a needle on the end of it. You can also use a golf ball. That way you'll get a faster reading than a regular syringe.

"There were four big-time merchants in Jeff City who ran everything, or everything they wanted to run. One was in the commissary, that was Ray's buddy. One was the industrial officer in the tag factory; one was in the dry cleaning plant, and he was a big one; and another was in the soap factory.

"I could give you the names of nine guards who worked with them, and with fellas like Ray. I myself once loaned a guard the money for his wife's hospital bills."

We talked on into the late afternoon, about many other things. I asked him about Ray's family, about other things in Ray's life history, to check Curtis out, to see if he had known

Ray as well as he claimed to have known him. He did. He was undoubtedly close to Ray at Jeff City. He knew almost as much about Jimmy's brothers and sisters as had Rife.

As I showed signs of getting ready to leave, Curtis's eyes began to water. He seemed sad. He began to talk faster, show me letters, one an appeal for money to Howard Hughes. But about that he said: "Oh, even if I won this appeal, they've got five other charges they can throw on me."

"Listen," he said entreatingly as I left, "I'm in here on a bum rap. I know you don't believe me but I *am*. I used to laugh at guys when they said that. But this time it's true. This *one* time."

As I drove back to Atlanta, the songs that had been playing softly in the background on Curtis's transistor radio from a Dalton station began to flood my mind. Their lyrics had been engraved in my mind from childhood, the plaintive, wistful, revival hymns I had sung myself, when my father used to take me 'round to big revivals in tobacco warehouses in East Tennessee where I was born and grew up.

> *I come to the garden alone*
> *While the dew is still on the roses*
> *And the voice I hear*
> *Falling on my ear*
> *The Son of God discloses*
>
> *And He walks with me*
> *And He talks with me*
> *And He tells me I am His own . . .*

Curtis did go on to Reidsville, he was not murdered there, and got transferred to a county road gang in the swamps of south Georgia near Waycross where, in 1973, he escaped. The last word I had was from the F.B.I. who came to ask me if I knew where Curtis might be. I didn't and don't. But I send him a greeting out there wherever he is.

One day in 1972, I was talking about this book to a famous sociologist in William James building, a modern tower that is the palace of the social sciences at Harvard University. "Listen," he said suddenly, "there's a fellow out here in prison in Massachusetts who must have been in prison with Ray in Missouri. Why don't you go interview him? Of course, he's a black man."

I checked, and it was true that this man who had taken the Muslim name Malik Hakim was an escapee from Jeff City. His case had become a cause in Boston because he had come there and worked in Roxbury, the Boston ghetto, doing community work so successfully that his acclaim led to his discovery. He was being represented by a well-known Boston civil rights lawyer, who cheerfully gave me permission to see Hakim while a fight against his extradition to Missouri was going on in the Massachusetts courts.

I met Hakim in the visitors' room at Norfolk prison, a maximum security institution a few miles south of Boston. The room was filled with that inevitable handmade, poorly designed furniture that is made in prison, and which is always covered with several coats of varnish. The room was packed with visitors, and several couples were locked in immodest, passionate embrace, while their children played innocently around them. The guard led Hakim to a cubbyhole off the room where there was a table on which I could rest my note pad. Hakim was a quiet man who seemed perfectly at ease. I had taken for granted that Hakim, a Black Muslim, would passionately hate James Earl Ray. But I was to be surprised.

"To be honest," he said, when I had identified myself, "if I knew something bad about James Earl Ray, I wouldn't tell it. He's still serving time. He's got a big charge over him. No matter what Ray has done since he got out of Jeff City, I wouldn't have much to say about him there. Hearsay can cost you your life in Jeff City. You can get killed in Jeff City in a flash. I may have to go back there. I never had to watch my back before out there, and I don't want to be watching my back if I go out there again.

"I'll tell you about Ray," said Hakim. He paused and then said with great emphasis: "He was a *concrete* con." He said it in such a way that he embodied in the word, concrete, a virtue that rose above all others he could ever imagine. The extremes of his differences with Ray about race seemed to be as nothing compared with their agreement on the importance of acting in conformity with another code, and a far more relevant (to Hakim) and crucial one, the code of prison life and the prison system. "He was trustworthy," Hakim continued.

"Ray wasn't a snitch. If you wasn't a snitch you got a chance to hustle. He was in with the 'in' crowd. The 'in' circle controls what goes on in joints like Jeff City. They're the cats who have guards on their payroll. Hospital people on their payroll, too, so that they can turn into the hospital, lay up, shoot dope, fuck kids and eat steaks.

"Everybody had a little ol' jive business in Jeff City. The way it worked was this. Say that one of that crowd was able to get a large quantity of drugs into prison. They would split it up with the others and sell it throughout the joint. When they got ready to sell, that's where a guy like Ray would come in. What they needed was a guy with free movement, who went to work someplace, like Ray did in the bakery, and they'd pass the stuff while waiting to go on the 'out count.' For those guys Ray was a delivery man.

"Ray sold food, too. In a place like Jeff City, where food is so poor, selling food is a good business. Ray sold stuff right out of the commissary, like butter, raisins, even steaks. They make wine out of the raisins, they even drink 'potato water.'

"The way you get Splash [amphetamine] if you're a user is for three or four of you to go together on an ounce at fifty dollars. It was common. Anybody with money could get it. If you wanted to sell your part, you could measure out a little in a cigarette paper, fold it twice, and get five dollars for it.

"But that Splash makes you *paranoid*. I've seen guys go off their rocker on it. You begin to suspect your best buddy. You begin to imagine that this or that guy has it in for you, and you strike out at him. More guys are hurt at Jeff City because of Splash than anything else. You begin to imagine things. You begin to say to yourself, 'Why is that motherfucker looking at me like *that?*' And then you stick a knife in him.

"Well, you learn something in that joint. Either you settle your own differences or you don't. If they're too big for you, they're too big for the guard to handle."

I asked Hakim about sex at Jeff City, and how Ray fit into the patterns of whatever sex life there was there.

"There's no question," he replied, "but that homosexuality

flourished at Jeff City. Any kid from seventeen to twenty who was reasonably good looking was preyed upon. Only the strong survived. A kid would be confronted, approached. You can count on your fingers and toes all the young white kids in Jeff City that didn't end up that way. They would come off the farm not knowing anything . . .

"Some young kids survived by fighting, but then they ended up in disciplinary court. Some old guys just sit and talk to the young kids, actually convince them to become their punks. If this young kid is gonna be in four or five years, this first protector may be the first of fifteen or twenty guys who will come into his life.

"The old guys played con games on the kids. They loan the kids money. They'll get two or three kids to threaten another kid. The old guy will sic two or three of his young kids on the innocent young guy — and then when they are really on him, the old guy will intercede, protect the young innocent, and then get the kid himself, be his protector.

"These older fellows sit around and get drunk on raisin wine, get their young innocents drunk, and then screw them while they are drunk. Then they tell the kids: 'Well, now everybody knows you've been had, you might as well go ahead with me.'

"Then what happened was the whole cycle — fuck in the ass, fuck in the mouth, the hand thing, or the old guy might force the kid to screw him, or force the kid to beat the old man up.

"Having a kid was a status thing in Jeff City, like having a Cadillac on the street. Most of the guys in Ray's clique had a kid. They'd fight over a kid, kill somebody over one. Fooling around with somebody's kid was a good way to get your throat cut in Jeff City.

"But I never remember Ray having a kid. I don't remember him ever having a fight. People in prison tend to leave quiet people like Ray alone."

I started to leave with the other visitors when a bell rang, but Hakim pulled me back for a moment. "I just want you to understand," he said earnestly, "I'll never put no jacket on that man Ray, no matter what he done."

A few months later, Hakim was put on parole to his lawyer, and disappeared. Wherever he is, I send him a greeting, too.

# Chapter 18

I got the clearest picture of how James Earl Ray operated as a merchant at Jeff City from his brother Jerry. It was Jerry who told me the details of how Jimmy made the stash he put away against the day that he would escape from the old walled city of felons on the banks of the Missouri.

I first met Jerry on Wednesday afternoon, February 12, 1969, when I searched him out in a sleazy furnished room at the rear of a decrepit building at 710 Ann Street in the Soulard section of St. Louis. The room was heavy with the sweet smell of kerosene burning in a rusted space heater. His only companion was a German shepherd puppy who played at my shoestrings as I talked with Jerry. We sat on tubular metal chairs with split plastic seats pulled up to a shaky folding card table on which rested only two items: a glass ashtray and a round Morton salt carton on the top of which was scrawled in pencil, "property of Jerry Ray."

From the look of the room, that carton of salt seemed to be just about the only property Jerry Ray possessed, and through the years that I have known him since then I can say pretty surely that it is just about as much property as Jerry has ever possessed in his life. He told me once that he had served a total of ten years in prison for stealing the sum of $60. He has never had a job with any future. He has made a career of working as a busboy, grounds keeper, or night watchman in country clubs in suburban Chicago.

Jerry is almost always cheerful, jolly, playing out the clown that his father always told him that he was: long after Jerry was an adult, Speedy was still calling him "Igg" for ignorant. But there hangs over him, as over many clowns, a sad, pathetic air. He dresses like an undertaker, as if to let his clothes speak louder than his words or feeble jokes. I have never seen him wear any color, but only a pair of sharply creased black slacks, highly polished pointed black shoes, a white shirt open at the neck, and slicked-back black hair. He is short, but heavily muscled. Sometimes his humor wears thin, and he becomes sullen, angry, resentful, bitter, and tense. Then his left leg begins to shake up and down in fast rhythmic pumping motions, and he jerks his head in a nervous tic, as if he were trying to pull it off his shoulders. He can be very serious. Jerry has shot a man through the lungs since I have known him.

I have talked with him *hundreds* of times. For long periods we talked at least once a week on the telephone. At one time he was living in Savannah Beach, Georgia, then headquarters of the National States Rights Party, and working as a body-guard for J. B. Stoner, the irrepressible Ku Klux Klan organizer and anti-Semite. At that time, we met frequently in a go-go bar in Savannah, but we have met in restaurants and in Chicago, Quincy, St. Louis, and in Atlanta.

There was no reason for Jerry to see me. I was writing a book whose assumption was that his brother was an assassin. He did not like that, but I would not have it any other way.

He prided himself that he was smart, and that he knew what to say and what not to say to help his brother. More often than not he told himself that he was conning me. What's more, he almost always demanded some money from me, and I did pay him from time to time. I saw that this was with him as much a matter of saving face as it was the money itself. It was as if the passage of money between us made what we said serious. Of course he lied to me anyway and we laughed about it and remained friends — for I think that is what we were becoming and did become.

But I would not let him think I believed a lie. I would not place any value at all on any of the stories he told me about his brother's innocence.

I eventually got to know other members of the Ray family, Speedy, Carol and Jack, and my relations with all of them were somewhat like those I had with Jerry.

I told them all without pussyfooting that I was writing a biography of their son and brother and that the book assumed he was the assassin. They would sometimes be furious about this, be enraged at me. But over the years, it got so that they *liked* to talk with me in the only vein in which I would talk with them. Sometimes they would lapse, and *want* to talk with me about why Jimmy did it. I never grew angry at anything they said to me, and I never pretended to believe something I didn't believe.

The first time I went to see Speedy in his little shack in the Missouri countryside, he brought a pistol to the door with him. For a while after that, he used to carry the pistol around the room, and place it carefully on the bed beside him, for he usually sat on the side of the bed to talk with me. He never threatened me with it. It was just there. And then finally, when I went to see him, it wasn't there any longer.

One day Speedy said to me: "Well, why do *you* think Jimmy did it?" but then, without waiting for my answer, he went on: "Do you realize that if Jimmy hadn't done it, King would be President today?"

Sometimes one of them would ask me what I thought of a situation Jimmy was in, for my "honest opinion." It was as if they had no other source for an honest opinion, and that they could not allow themselves to admit that their brother was guilty, even among themselves.

At one point they began to give me reports on the family health. I would be told when Speedy was sick, or when he had an operation. I began a correspondence with Jack, who had gone into federal prison convicted of driving the get-away car in a Missouri bank robbery.

I sent some of the manuscript of the book to him, and his comments were simple, candid, detached and quite moving.

Sometimes, when the family would gather at Carol's house in St. Louis, they would call me up, and laugh at me and tease me, but then give me their best regards in the end. I had been in a kind of perpetual pursuit of more information about Ceal, and it was Jack who began to tell me a little bit about her. I asked for permission to see him, was refused by the Federal Bureau of Prisons, and filed suit, with the help of the American Civil Liberties Union, to see Jack, then at Marion, Illinois. My suit became a thing in itself, was won in the lower court, went to the First Circuit Court of Appeals, and was thrown out there when the U.S. Supreme Court ruled against the Washington *Post* in a similar case.

Well, I could write a book about myself and the Ray family, but I am quite sure I never will. I have either written it with this book, or I haven't.

I once told a psychiatrist about my relations with the Ray family. "Why, don't you see what you are doing with them?" he asked me. "You're giving them through you a chance to piece together the truth about their lives."

I hope that I have done so, even if it is only to a small degree, and if only for a transient moment.

What Jerry and I talked about mainly was the Ray family life in Ewing and Quincy. Poor people have no written history. The Rays wrote few letters, kept no diaries. It seemed important to me to keep the living material of my book in front of me as I went along. When I discovered some new fact that seemed to show that Jimmy had no links to anyone except himself, I told Jerry of my discovery. He became interested in what I was doing, especially in my attempt to understand *why* his brother had done what he had done. I read the early chapters of my book aloud to Jerry.

It gradually became an assumption of our talks that Jimmy had done it. Finally, Jerry began to tell me, not on the phone, but when we met in person:

"Listen, Georgie-boy, some day I'm gonna tell you the *whole* story, all of it. Not yet. The time hasn't come. But I *will.* You be thinking about how much you're willing to shell out for it."

But there were many reversals. Sometimes when I reminded him of his promise, he said: "*What?* I never told you I was going to tell you anything like *that*. If I knew anything you would be the last person I'd tell it to. You're trying to lock Jimmy in prison forever."

And sometimes he would meet me, tell me a few facts I wanted to know, and then regret it, and call me collect or write me:

"I have enjoyed our meetings and its a shame it have to come to a end as i like to live good and why we were together we went first class.

"Mr. McMillan people like you try to act like you are for the poor people and also for the Black Beast but if you had to live around a Beast then you would be against them more than I am.

"Believe it or not Mr. McMillan i dont hate you as there isnt enough room in my heart for hate, i hate what you stand for but i dont hate human beings.

"I only hope that we could have been Friends and you could have wrote a truthful book, as personally you have good qualities. You was right when you told me on the phone that one part of me liked you and the other part hated you.

"What susprised me even tho you are a liberal how i with a limited education could get a fee from you without telling you anything and making up all that Bull.

"In closing i hope there is no hard feelings.

"Ill keep in touch. Sincerely, Jerry."

And he did keep in touch. A time came when he called me

and, in a voice heavy with mystery, asked me to come out to Chicago. "Bring your money," he said. I went, and we holed up in a hotel room and talked for three days. I agreed to pay him so much down, hear his story, go home and check it carefully, then come back to Chicago for another stay, and go over the whole story with him again. This is what we did. I paid him $1,000 in all for what he told me, and he signed a release freeing me from liability for printing what he said. We had it notarized in the hotel office (the Regency Hyatt Hotel at O'Hare airport). The year was 1972.*

During our talks in Chicago, Jerry said to me quite unexpectedly, "I used to run a business in Jeff City myself." I had forgotten that Jerry did time there, too. What he had sold, he said, was "green." Sometime during the 1950's at Jeff City, United States currency — "green" to the prisoners — was outlawed, as it is in most prisons today. It was too powerful, too dangerous. It will buy the help a man needs from his fellow prisoners when he wants to escape, wants to go into the drug business. Real money breeds real trouble in prison, and the only legal exchange inside Jeff City from the 1950's on was the commissary ticket.

---

* The help of the Ray family was essential to me in writing this biography. All of them demanded money before they would talk with me, and I ended up paying the following sums to them over the six years I worked on the book.

| | |
|---|---|
| George Ray (Jerry Rayns), James Earl Ray's father | $1,000 |
| Carol Ray Pepper, James Earl Ray's sister | 1,000 |
| Jerry Ray, James Earl Ray's brother | 2,100 |
| Jack Ray, James Earl Ray's brother | 250 |
| | $4,350 |

In addition, I have paid for Jerry Ray's hotel room several times, bought him many meals and many drinks.

"I was selling ten dollars green for fifteen dollars in tickets," said Jerry, "and never mind where I got the green. There was lots of it in Jeff City, though. Anyway, I ran into trouble with one of the Menard [not the prison] boys. There was three of them. They was good friends of Jimmy's later. I had a place in the yard where I stood, that was my stand. But one of the Menards came up and challenged me, told me I was in *his* territory and to move the hell out of there. He was doing business there. We had to fight to settle it. I won that time, went on doing business, and we became friends again. That's the way things are at Jeff City. You have to establish yourself.

"Personally," Jerry said, "I think a man is born to be a hustler, like he's born to be a baseball player. Not everybody's got it in them to be a hustler. I haven't. Rife was a good hustler, a real bullshit artist. A lazy person can't be a hustler.

"There would be ten or twelve of them in Jeff City, but most of them got too well known, had to go out of business at one time or another. Like, many of those hustlers begin to live good and show off, keep their clothes pressed, have extra candy, orange drinks and ice cream. Then the heat gets on you, and the guards don't want to fool with you.

"But Jimmy was *so* quiet. Mostly there'd be a shakedown only if somebody was under suspicion and Jimmy didn't do anything to make them suspicious of him. He just wanted to make money, didn't put on no show.

"He was a natural hustler. As you know, Jimmy's the kind of fella that's got to have something to do. If he didn't, he'd go crazy in there. And he was the kind of fella that did have that something extra.

"You have to be close-mouthed. Jimmy talked to a lot of people but he didn't have no friends. They could shake him down and nobody could break him. Nobody could make Jimmy talk. That's the key to being a merchant, the guard's trust. It was known that Jimmy hustled, but nobody wanted to mess with *him*. He wasn't gonna give nobody no trouble, and nobody was gonna trouble him."

At first, according to Jerry, Jimmy dealt mostly in commissary wares. You could buy a steak from him, a can of soup, things like that.

But in 1963, James Earl Ray began to deal in drugs, Jerry said. It was in that year that he began to make substantial sums of money at Jeff City, and to get it out to members of his family.

It was then that Jimmy had established himself with a guard. "Jimmy got all kinds of stuff, hard stuff, stuff you sniff, mainly amphetamine. That hard stuff was expensive. When the guard brings you the stuff he wants money for it. He wanted cash. He'd bring the stuff in his socks sometimes, sometimes taped under his balls."

Two comments by James Earl Ray, in his own handwriting, in the notes he wrote for William Bradford Huie, show he was not unaware of these systems of value. "Getting money in prison is very easy and I could spend the rest of the day explaining all of them," wrote Ray. And further: "It's a simple matter to give a prison employee $20.00 to bring you a hundred dollars in."

The guard with whom James Earl Ray had his connection worked in the cell block. It was, in the end, a two-man operation, and no one else was in it. The money was brought out by the guard, who took his share off the top and mailed the rest to one of the Ray family members in plain envelopes that bore no return address. He sent it in $100 bills, wrapped in a piece of plain paper. He sent some to Jerry. It was addressed Box 22, Wheeling, Illinois. When Jerry got the money, he would write "OK" on a piece of paper and mail it back.

# Chapter 19

Something had to be done about A-Hall. A revolution in civil rights was taking place across the country, in the 1960's, but at Jeff City black men were still being crunched together in the old building. Jeff City was still a segregated institution. Warden E. V. Nash, the ex-schoolteacher and highway patrol officer who had led his patrolmen into the prison in 1963 to end that riot, knew well enough the state of things inside the prison. Things were in fact so bad that he wouldn't go in there anymore. He stayed in his office, and people, his assistants, the guards, came to *him*. He decided in 1964 that the time had come to integrate Jeff City, and to take some of the steam out of A-Hall.

There are people who say that Nash planned the change with the *worst* intentions, so that it wouldn't work. "He took six of the most militant Negroes and tried to put them in the toughest white cellblocks in Jeff City," says one man who knows the prison's history.

At first the experiment in tokenism seemed to be working. "They took eleven blacks out of A-Hall and split them between F- and G-Halls," says the Jeff City *Journal*'s history. "Ominous quiet existed for days. The unaware blacks in A-Hall began to send in requests for transfers to F- and G-Halls. Then on the afternoon of June 9, 1964, the explosion came. The F- and G-Hall inmates were coming in from the yard (the whites and the handful of blacks), chattering as they went, when at the corner where the corridor turns, it happened: a dozen inmates, pillowcases over their faces, came from nowhere, cursing, stabbing and cutting..."

When it was all over, the walls along that corridor "looked like a slaughterhouse." One black man died, and three others were badly cut up.

Nash was in more trouble than he knew how to handle. The blacks in A-Hall refused to eat. The men in F- and G-Halls had their privileges taken away from them. The situation was getting worse. There were beatings and stabbings (one with a mattress needle) on through the fall of 1964, until a few days before Christmas, while the employees were holding a Christmas party, "there was a shot in the night and Warden Nash had fallen heir to a self-inflicted wound," goes the *Journal* account. Nash had killed himself in his office. Nothing ever happened in the prison that was not almost immediately reported — and interpreted — along the grapevine. This time the rumor was that Nash did himself in because his daughter was pregnant by a black man.

All the black men were moved from A-Hall to other quarters, but the prison remained segregated, and racial hatred became a common denominator of Jeff City life, and a highly articulated one in certain circles. There was a coterie of forthright Nazis, led by three brothers: one, a former engineer, taught the German language, another taught Nazi philosophy, and the three of them led discussions in the yard about Hitler. They pushed the circulation of *Mein Kampf* and Goebbels's *Diary*.

Another clique was made up of the white men who had been in the 1964 riot; they stuck together with all the camaraderie of men who had shared a battlefield. There was a right-wing group, self-conscious conservatives, who claimed to be American Legionnaires. There was yet another racist group whose shared quality seemed to be that they all came from small towns.

There was talk in the prison about the Ku Klux Klan, and many inmates boasted that they belonged to it.

Jerry Ray claims that Jimmy told him he was one of those who wore a pillowcase that afternoon. Prison authorities say that James Earl Ray wasn't even in the area, that a thorough investigation of the 1964 knifing was made by the state highway patrol, that those who took part in it were identified and punished, and that Ray was not in the group.

It would not have been like Ray to have been there, to have acted with a group, to have risked his chance for escape, always one of the foremost things in his mind when he was in Jeff City. But he showed his temper in two known episodes: once, when the black inmates struck because one of them had been called "boy," and once when he got into a fistfight with a black man who called him "Gray," instead of Ray. When he saw a Negro guard, Ray was heard to say, "That's one nigger that should be dead."

Everything he had felt about race and politics was underscored by the Jeff City atmosphere. His twisted ideas and concepts were the *assumptions* of the prison culture.

---

It would be hard to imagine any instrument that would have been more precisely designed to twist and distort Ray's political ideas than amphetamine — "Speed" to the inmates of Jeff City. Speed is a drug that does not so much alter a man's personality as it does exaggerate what is already there, and the one thing Ray's personality did not need was exaggeration.

When a man's on Speed, everything seems to become much more clear to him, every idea and every object. This illuminated present becomes mixed with "sudden intuitive and mostly incorrect abstractions and insights." He gets to feel he is clever. A surge of "invigorating aggressiveness" comes over him. Everything seems to fall into a pattern, but a false one. The man who gets into Speed finds himself constantly adding up all his past and present, looking for significance, striving to find *universal* meaning in his life.

Then, shoulder-to-shoulder with those feelings, those "crystal clear" insights, comes another set of feelings — fear, suspicion, awareness, a feeling of being watched, from someone who is behind you or at the side of you. "Under the effect of the drug," says another medical expert, "the user has an intense fascination with all his thoughts and activities which extends even to the paranoid fear and anger he almost inevitably experiences."

Doctor John D. Griffith, assistant professor of the Department of Psychiatry at Vanderbilt University, has discovered that small frequent doses of amphetamine "induce a brief psychosis similar to paranoid schizophrenia. They perceived themselves as subject to danger. They read highly personal meanings into objects or situations."

Somebody else has said that amphetamine leads its users into a "mimic schizophrenia." All of these effects of amphetamine are multiplied when the drug is *injected.* Amphetamine is one of the few drugs that moves people to action on their own hallucinations.

You begin to be obsessed with the idea that you have *"a specific immediate task,"* says one study.

---

I had asked Curtis when I talked with him in Dalton about Ray's use of drugs, a reminder to me that the English police had found a syringe in Ray's London hotel room. I knew Curtis was a user. Curtis said:

"Ray used to drink on just about every job he did, and then he discovered amphetamines, that it makes your mind sharp. He started using Bennies [Benzadrine] at Leavenworth. When he was under drugs, he just acted as calm and clean and cool as you please.

"I never saw him take an overdose. He was on the stuff some way back in the Jackson County jail [in Kansas City]. He's used it fifteen years I know of at least. He never took hard stuff that I know of. There wasn't much hard stuff in Jeff City, but he wouldn't have taken it anyway I don't think. You could tell when he was really on the stuff. He dropped down in his weight when he was using. He drank a lot of mineral oil to put oil back in his body."

Ray shot the stuff with a needle. "That gives you a faster

reading," Curtis said. "He wasn't the kind of fella to talk much. But if he was high he would talk, and I've seen him *top stage*, as high as you can get.

"He would lay down in his cell and he would think. He would say how it made his mind clear up. He would go all the way back until he was six or seven years old. Or, he might go over a job and see the mistakes he had made in that job.

————————

Just as he had back in Ewing when he was a young boy, Jimmy began to follow the news on the cellblock TV and with a transistor radio in his cell. In technology, if not in ideology, he had come a long way since that crystal set in preacher Graves's classroom. His hope that politics was a way to set right what he thought was wrong with the world rose again, out of the ashes of his disillusion with Germany, nazism and Hitler. Jerry thinks he noticed a point at which Jimmy's political hopes and dreams were rekindled: with the nomination of Barry Goldwater for the presidency in 1964. With that, according to Jerry, Jimmy saw a chance for a "conservative" government in the United States, and he began to read and study intensively to re-educate himself politically.

Ray himself has written: "I read most all kinds of books & newspapers & magazines such as *True, Argosy*, and James Bond books. But I think I read more law books than anything else since you half to do a lot of your own legal work in prison." But that is not quite candid. He read other things, other political things. He got his later alias (Eric Starvo Galt, Ray's mispelling of Stavro) from two books he is known to have read. The "Galt" he got from *Atlas Shrugged* by Ayn Rand, whose novels tend to be tracts for her extreme right-wing political philosophy. That book opens with the sentence, "Who is John Galt?" The other part of Ray's alias seems to have come from *On Her Majesty's Secret Service*, a James Bond book — "a most diabolical plot for murder on a mass scale" — one of whose characters was named Ernst Stavro Blofeld.

When I visited Jeff City, I was told that Ray's library records had been destroyed. On a tour of the prison, I went into the library, asked again there, was told there were no records, walked through the stacks, noticed a convict library aide trying to catch my eye, and as I passed him, he said: "Politics and travel, that's what Ray read."

Ray was designing his own political cosmos. It might have the catchwords or the raiment of some other political philosophy, but to Ray his philosophy was always a personal one. If it seems *absurd*, that this convicted habitual criminal was working away there in the grim old prison on the Missouri River to find a meaning in American life, that is no more absurd than the fact of Lee Oswald reading Marx in the public library in New Orleans; or than Sirhan scribbling his confused thoughts about Arab nationalism in a crude notebook while working as an exercise boy at a California racetrack, or than Brimmer, who carried his mishmash of weird political concepts in his head on his way to and from a sexual massage parlor in New York City.

---

In 1963 and 1964, Martin Luther King was on TV almost every day, talking defiantly about how black people were going to get their rights, insisting that they would accept with nonviolence all the terrible violence that white people were inflicting on them until the day of victory arrived, until they did overcome.

Ray watched it all avidly on the cellblock TV at Jeff City. He reacted as if King's remarks were directed at him personally. He boiled when King came on the tube. He began to call him Martin "Lucifer" King and Martin Luther "Coon." It got so that the very sight of King would *galvanize* Ray.

"Somebody's gotta get him," Ray would say, his face drawn with tension, his fists clenched. "Somebody's gotta get him."

There were those slogans, "K . . . K!" understood to mean either "Kill King!" or "Kill Kennedy!" which bespoke the murderous racial passions that were flowing through the prison in the early 1960's. But in 1963, the talk got a little more specific.

"We first started talking about killing King in 1963," says Raymond Curtis. "It began partly because some ol' boy from Arkansas came in the prison there and was supposed to have said that he knew a bunch of Mississippi businessmen who were willing to pay a hundred-thousand-dollar bounty for King's head. It's possible that the boys added to the amount as they went along. They added to everything in Jeff City."

When President Kennedy was assassinated in Dallas, Ray was visibly upset. "He stood up and got angry," Curtis remembers. "He said he had two plots to kill Kennedy himself. He said, 'Oswald didn't do it!' But then a couple of days later, Ray was telling me how Oswald goofed. He said Oswald had done the job and had paid with a bullet. Well, I just thought, this is the way people talk in the penitentiary."

In that atmosphere, inside Jeff City, it got so that talk about killing King seemed perfectly ordinary, something rather plausible, not at all unreasonable, certainly possible. Ray and Curtis would sit around, often high on Speed, while Ray would spin out the details of how he would do the job on King. Ray was a man who liked details; he had spent time in Leavenworth going over "mistakes" he had made on his other jobs. He would sit on his bunk, his head thrown back, as Curtis remembers the scene, spinning out critiques of Lee Oswald's "job," of the mistakes Oswald made.

"Ray said he would have the place all set up, all lined up, then he would get his money, his papers. It was his idea to get plumb out of the country. He said if he killed King he would have a chartered plane to get him out. We talked about a lot of different countries where he would go. We used to send off and get atlases, books that give you the population, what they raise. We used to talk about New Zealand because it was founded by convicts. There are two places you can go in Mexico that don't have extradition. We talked about them, and about some of those other countries down there. We found out a fellow could go to Guatemala or Costa Rica and be pretty well fixed.

"Ray even used to have ideas like how he would put tinfoil in his hubcaps so he couldn't be tracked by radar."

There is no sign that he ever believed the rumor about the Mississippi businessmen, not that particular rumor. But the idea did grow that perhaps there was a constituency, that there were people who would come to his support if he did kill King. That was a better way to look at it, for Ray. He was not the kind of fellow to take anybody from the outside in with him on his Big Job. If there was a bounty for King (and he had passed the stage of caring whether there was or not), he would wait until *after* the job was done to collect it.

As King and his people moved on through the streets of one southern city after another, refusing to be stopped by bombs, burnings or beatings, the job fixed itself more and more in Ray's mind as his personal mission, as something that *he* must do, for nobody else seemed capable of putting a stop to King.

There had been the time when Ray had thought there might be a bounty on King's head, and he said, in front of Curtis, about King:

"You are my big one and one day I will collect all that money on your ass nigger for you are my retirement plan."

But as the months passed, Ray seemed to have given up caring about money, if he ever did consider it seriously, for he got so he would say, about King:

"If I ever get to the streets I am going to *kill* him."

# Chapter 20

By the beginning of 1966, James Earl Ray's situation was this. He was in a murderous rage at Martin Luther King and had by then constructed for himself a political ideology that gave him a justification, a logic, a context in which to make sense of his murderous intention. What's more, he had accumulated a considerable stash of money for himself outside the prison.

Having reached an accommodation between his anger and his ideals, he could no longer bear to be locked up.

On the night of March 10, 1966, James Earl Ray tried to escape.

---

Considering how terrible prisons are, it might seem strange prisoners don't spend more time trying to break out. But escapes are fairly rare, especially in the big penitentiaries. There are several reasons why. One is that most of the people in prison don't seem really to want out, or don't want to take the risk of being caught. If they are caught they lose their "good time," must do their whole sentence, and if they get into a fight with a guard while trying to escape, they get time added to their sentence. About 90 percent of the people in prison have pleaded guilty. Many are repeaters. They want to do their time as quickly and as quietly as possible. A penologist once asked a cross section of inmates in a large penitentiary to rank rule infractions by the seriousness with which they, the inmates, viewed the infractions. They ranked escape as number two out of more than twenty, put it ahead of forcible sodomy, for example. In Jeff City, there are only about six or eight escape attempts a year, and these are usually made by men with hopelessly long sentences for whom there is nothing to lose if they do get caught.

But Ray was willing to take the risk. He had taken it once, in that St. Louis courthouse, and lost, and the judge had socked it to Ray with a long sentence. He had taken it again, on the night of November 19, 1961, several months after he had gone into Jeff City. But that time he was caught in the attempt. He failed to get across the wall when a crude ladder he had made fell apart under his weight. That time he wasn't tried in court, but received punishment from the warden of six months in The Hole, or The Basement, the Jeff City isolation ward where prisoners were given only one square meal every three days.

Ray did not attempt to escape again for five years, until March 10, 1966, when, as he himself has related: "One night when the cell house went to the show I took some wire cutters I had come by cut the screen out of the back windows. I took a long iron pole which was used to open windows fastened a hook on it went through the hole onto a tunnel which connects all the cell houses. I crawled up the tunnel until I got to the security chief office crawled over it hooked the pole on the administration building roof. It was raining lightly that night and the pole had got wet. When I got about to the top my hand sliped off and I fell on my arm resulting in it getting num. I then hid a small building near by which houses a generator. I came out the next night but they had a guard in the security office & he caught me. When I fell off of the building my shoes come of. I had 4 10 dollar bills in one shoe & 4 1s in the other."

What he did not mention was that he also had with him, according to the prison record, "one bag of assorted pills." He knew he needed that help.

Ray was out of his cell twenty-seven hours, and Warden Swenson brought charges against him. This meant a court case, and Ray asked for a court-appointed lawyer who immediately, at Ray's direction, asked for a mental examination. This was granted by the Jefferson City Circuit Court. On September 8, 1966, Ray was transferred to the state hospital in Fulton, Missouri, twenty-three miles from Jeff City. He was there thirty-nine days, until October 17.

Ray has since then tried to convince people that he conned himself into the hospital, just to get out of prison. His words:

"I tried to get to Fulton State Hosp. without sucess. After I had attempted to excape and was put in isolation I made another attempt which was sucessful. Another prisoner told me what to say to have a mental examination. They were

1. Say you had amnesia
2. Had compulsiveness
3. Heard voices
4. See things

"Under Missouri law if your att. request a mental examination the court must grant an examination I forget what I told the judge No. 1 or No. 2. But I got the examination."

When Ray got to the hospital, he told doctors his story, that he could not remember trying to escape and that he heard voices at night. But he soon discovered the danger of relying on information from the prison grapevine. The treatment for amnesia at Fulton was electric shock, and he was terrified, and so, the next day, Jimmy told the doctors another story. He *did* remember the escape; his real trouble had been confusion. He was not given shock, and on October 24, 1966, the Fulton staff made this report on Ray:

He is oriented for time, place and person. His memory is unimpaired for both recent and remote events. He is coherent, alert, relevant, and there are no hallucinations or delusions. He appeared to be somewhat tense and anxious and at times showed some mild depression but not of psychotic proportions. He has a good verbal assessment of reality but in the past he has used poor judgment. He has an IQ of 105 which places him within the average range of intellectual functioning. Tests showed no evidence of a psychosis.

This patient has been observed, studied and tested. No symtoms or signs indicating a mental disease or defect could be found. Although he showed signs of anxiety and depression, these could not be considered of psychotic proportions.

DIAGNOSIS: Sociopathic Personality, Antisocial Type with anxiety and depressive features.

This medical finding on Ray was written at the time when murdering Martin Luther King was a predominant thought in Ray's mind. Thus the report raises a question with a significance beyond its and Ray's: can assassins be spotted in advance, even by people qualified to perceive and diagnose mental diseases? The simple answer is that assassins cannot be spotted in advance, not as assassins, or not unless they do something so overt as to write a threatening letter to the person they mean to kill, and by no means does every assassin do that.

The rule about psychiatry is that qualified psychiatrists can, and often very quickly, discover and correctly estimate the nature and depth of mental disturbances. But they cannot predict the specific kinds of symptomatic behavior that will follow from these disturbances. The symptomatic course of organic disease is often well known, and the options are well defined and limited. But the course of a mental disturbance, its ups and downs — its timing — and its symptomatic by-products, cannot be limited or precisely predicted.

Even so, when the technical language in the Fulton report is de-coded, the report depicts a human being with very serious problems. By saying that Ray was not "psychotic," the report is only saying that Ray was not outright crazy, as the layman thinks of crazy. If he had been crazy, he would not have been capable of killing King. In saying that Ray was a "sociopathic personality," the report was saying that he was sick in his relationships with society; that described Ray exactly. And to say that he was anxious and depressed suggests that Ray's illness was acute.

The purpose of the Fulton examination must be kept in

mind. "We were asked only to determine if he was mentally capable of standing trial," says Dr. Donald B. Peterson, who was superintendent at Fulton when Ray was there. That is, they were deciding whether Ray was capable of standing trial for the charge that would be brought against him for trying to escape. They obviously were also looking at Ray to see if he would create more difficulties inside Jeff City than he would in a state mental institution. Was he too unstable to live the life of a prisoner?

Thus they were in reality faced with the very real and cruel limitations of state mental institutions. If in prisons there is no rehabilitation, in mental hospitals there is more often than not little or no therapy. Both are devoted to custodial care. It might be said with hindsight that almost any amount of money it took to "cure" James Earl Ray would have been well spent. The social chaos that resulted from King's death brought property damage in the uncounted millions of dollars. The state of Missouri could have built a new mental hospital and financed its operation for a decade for what Ray's act was to cost.

There are experts who believe that the psychiatrist cannot usefully decide what the Fulton doctors did decide — whether a man is mentally competent to stand trial. There are deep differences in outlook between law and psychiatry, and some authorities believe the gap is unbridgeable, and that "psychiatrists should get out of the business of being the janitors of the legal system." That is the opinion of Dr. Alan Stone, a psychiatrist who teaches at Harvard Law School.

"Essentially, we are talking about two different systems of belief," says Dr. Stone, "one in the social sciences and one in the law — built on mutually contradictory assumptions. Law rests its case on theories of moral causation and the concept of volition. Man in the eyes of the law is rational and he makes conscious choices. This notion of free will, however, is antithetical to the theory of contemporary social sciences — economics, sociology, behaviorism, or psychoanalysis. Where a court may only be willing to ask if a defendant *meant* to commit an act and *understood* that such an act was against the law, the psychiatrist sees the act as the product of a far more complex series of influences."

Ray himself later added a comment on his stay at Fulton. He read some years later a newspaper article which said that he had told one of the Fulton doctors that he planned to do something violent. This brought on a stern letter from Ray (the jailhouse lawyer) who wrote:

"If you would get a copy of the Missouri law covering mental illness you would find that any conversation between patient and doctor is confidential. I read the law many times, it went on the books in 1963."

And he could not resist making an allegation against Fulton. "Also while I was their was a lot of beating," he went on, "and some former employes or inmates would probably teisty to this, Fulton is a small town about 9000 & it would be to mush trouble to find someone."

Ray was in the courts, in litigation, awaiting a trial, a moment of joy and challenge for him. Despite the Fulton report which cleared the way for Ray's trial on the escape charge, Ray had a chance, under a new Missouri prison regulation, to apply for a mental examination by an independent psychiatrist, and he took that opportunity. Before his application was acted upon, however, Ray's case came up for routine hearing by the Missouri state board of pardon and parole. The board assigned its psychiatric consultant, Dr. Henry V. Guhlman, Jr., to interview Ray, and he did so on December 13, 1966. Dr. Guhlman made this report:

Board of Probation and Parole
Box 267
Jefferson City, Missouri

Re: Ray, James Earl
#00416-J

Gentlemen:

This 38 year old white male was seen for psychiatric evaluation on December 13, 1966.

Ray is an interesting and rather complicated individual. He reports that within the last year, he has had considerable difficulties from a physical point of view, involving a number of somatic complaints such as pain in the "solar plexes," tachycardia and "intracranial tension." When we commented that these were rather large words, he reported that he had been reading up in the medical literature. He then stated that he thought at times that he had cancer or heart trouble but that he no longer feels this way. On certain days, he has rather severe head pains but this is only intermittent. He is now on librium and works intermittently on a construction job.

This man's basic problem revolves around what appears to be an increasingly severe obsessive compulsive trend. He states that at the age of ten, he awoke one night and thought he had lost his eye sight. He became quite fearful. These various fears confront him from time to time and in a typical obsessive compulsive way, he feels that he must do certain things in order to undo what he feels is going to occur and might result in harm to him. For instance, he describes a feeling of fear which can be alleviated if he takes his glass of water which he is drinking and sets it on the table and moving it back and forth several times. He also describes at length some rather marked obsessive compulsive features but is reluctant to go into them in detail. He is of the opinion that his escape attempt was the result of undue anxiety and tension with the need to actually do something.

He is fearful that this might lead into more serious difficulties.

At the present time, there is no evidence of delusions, hallucinations, or paranoid ideas. He is not psychotic but severely neurotic. Within the last year or so, there is evidence that he had become overly concerned about his physical health and some of his obsessive compulsive concerns have moved in this direction.

At the present time it is doubtful that he is in a position to be considered for parole. It is felt that he is in need of psychiatric help. He is becoming increasingly concerned about himself.

> Sincerely yours,
> Henry V. Guhlman, Jr., M.D.
> Psychiatric Consultant

Ray was in Fulton for thirty-nine days, and Dr. Guhlman saw him for only a few hours, but the difference in perception of James Earl Ray is wide. Of course, Guhlman's task was different; he was to decide whether it was wise to turn Ray loose on the streets.

Aside from the matter of psychological definitions, of what is an "obsessive personality," Dr. Guhlman's language is clear enough. Ray was "severely neurotic," was having severe head pains, was in need of psychiatric help. Ray's escape attempt was not just an attempt to get out. It was the result of anxiety and tension "with the need to actually do something," and Ray himself was afraid "this might lead into more serious difficulties."

Guhlman did what he could. He recommended against parole, the parole was refused, and James Earl Ray was returned to prison to fester.

# Chapter 21

Ray never did get better. He never did calm down at Jeff City. That Librium Dr. Guhlman put him on did not help tranquilize James Earl Ray in the sixth year of his incarceration at the Missouri state penitentiary. People around him in prison were beginning to notice the change that was taking place in Ray. Jerry Ray became aware on his visits that Jimmy was getting "nervous." Miles, the convict who ran the libraries for Ray, could barely get a word out of him: "He got so there at the end he wouldn't talk to *nobody.*" What was happening to him became apparent in little ways. He had told Dr. Guhlman that he was afraid of what he might do, and what he did not tell Guhlman was that the idea of killing Martin Luther King had become a fierce, angry resolve.

After he was returned to Jeff City, Ray was not so aimless

about where he would go when he made his next attempt to escape. He began to talk to his brother Jack, when Jack came to visit him, about Ian Smith, about Rhodesia, about going *there* when he escaped. His ideas had come together, the idea of killing King, the idea of working for a new political structure in America, were one. The two ideas that had been separately forming and re-forming themselves in his reveries had come together in his head. The idea of killing King had been given new layers of meaning for Ray by the realization that by killing King he could become himself an actor in the turbulent ideological drama of his times, the drama he had heretofore only watched on the cellblock TV. He saw how King's assassination could serve a larger political purpose, how he could alter (or so he thought) the balance of political power by a single act performed by *him*. And he saw at the end of the road a hero's sanctuary, if he turned out to need a sanctuary, in several places, one of which was Rhodesia.

It had all come to have an appealing harmony to Ray — Ayn Rand, Goldwater, the rise of a new American conservative movement which would be abetted by him, by what he would do himself, by his killing the man he had begun to refer to as "Big Nigger."

But wasn't this just another twisted dream cooked up by a stir-crazy con? Wasn't this a piece of audacity so zany it mocked itself, especially when it was conceived by a man who was locked solidly behind bars and would almost certainly be for another fourteen years? Who was this little fella, this two-bit criminal — this little bungler — to sit in his cell and decide he would wipe out the life of the man thousands of other people had obviously hated? Martin Luther

King had walked through the streets of the South for nearly a decade, presenting his body to his enemies since the Montgomery bus boycott of 1955, and not one person had ever fired a shot at him.

Who was this ignominious little person to dare embody within himself the passions of hundreds, thousands of others, and set his mind to do the deed none of them had dared to do?

What set *him* apart?

The decision itself.

By its very nature it set James Earl Ray apart. He was going to kill Martin Luther King because King *stood for something* to him. It takes an exceptional person to kill a symbol. It is true that Ray felt deeply about black people, but so did others who did not kill King. What's more, King had never presented to Ray the direct threat he had to hundreds of thousands of others. King had never come into Ray's hometown and raised up the blacks in demonstrations. Ray had no property or possessions threatened by the changes King was struggling to bring about. Besides, Ray had never met King or seen him in person, and almost all homicides are committed by people who know well, or are kin to, the people they murder. It is worth remembering that Ray had had few direct contacts with black people in his whole lifetime.*

---

* In its investigation of the Martin Luther King assassination, the F.B.I. is reported to have had more than 3,000 agents working, and it is taken for granted that the investigation was one of the most thorough jobs of criminal detection ever undertaken. It is known that the F.B.I. questioned almost everyone James Earl Ray knew about Ray's racial beliefs and attitudes. Their findings boiled down to very little. The man who was to have prosecuted the case against Ray in Memphis told me: "We had almost nothing on his racial views we could go into court with, maybe one thing about a fight he had in a bar, and I didn't think that was very strong." If Ray had

It is obvious then that the relationship that Ray saw as existing between himself and Martin Luther King was all inside Ray's head. The crime of assassination, when it is done by one person, grows out of a relationship between the assassin and the assassinee that exists solely within the mind of the assassin. This is what makes it so difficult to comprehend the "why" of assassinations; more often than not the assassin does not seem to have any reason for his act. There is seldom a motive in the usual criminal sense, and the reason is that the raw material out of which the assassin has constructed his motive is hidden deep within the recesses of his psyche, in his unconscious, so that he himself does not understand the reason — the reason he has murdered where other people have not.

In fact, in the assassin's mind, the relationship between the assassin and his victim *is* close. It is passionate, loaded with feeling, and those passions have found their genesis in the qualities he has attributed to the other person. You don't need to know another person to feel passionately about him or her. Love at first sight is a common experience. So is puppy love. And the qualities we attribute to the loved ones are obviously in our minds for we don't really know the other person. The qualities a man like Ray attributed to Martin Luther King are not in the reality of King but in Ray's construction of that reality. The materials for that construction grow out of Ray's emotional preparation for the

---

been tried in court, the prosecution would have done little or nothing to try to establish a *motive* for the assassination; they would have been content to let the facts of physical evidence speak for their case that Ray was guilty. That would have satisfied the requirement of the law for a conviction if the jury had agreed with them. You don't have to prove a man's motive if you've got the goods on him.

perception of the other person, and James Earl Ray's life was a preparation for the act of King's assassination. In this sense there was a conspiracy, a conspiracy of the influences on Ray as an individual to lead him to make his decision; in this sense his decision to kill King was an over-determined act.

We all know that there is an unconscious life. We know that our mind goes on working when we are not conscious, because we all dream, day and night. However insubstantial they are, these dreams, these fantasies, these reveries are the substance of the unconscious and the gateway into it.

James Earl Ray did have fantasies. He had them in Jeff City, and they were not quite the usual criminal daydreams. One of his most persistent daydreams was so unexpected that Curtis, to whom he often talked about it, remembers it vividly.

Ray's dream was to start an orphan asylum. "When I pull a job," Ray used to tell Curtis, "I'm gonna take that money and start an orphans' home. If people didn't want their kids, I'll take them, just go pick them up myself and take them to this orphans' home in the country. I'm going to pick the doctors and the nurses myself. I won't let anybody else do *that*. Don't worry, I'll keep the place going! I'll do a job or two now and then."

This was a curious dream for a man who seemed not to have any close relationships at all, a loner. And yet there was more evidence that the plight of children, neglected children, struck some profound chord in him.

Once Curtis and Ray were watching a documentary on India on the cellblock TV. Some bloated-bellied, starving children were shown. "That's a disgrace," Ray said angrily, "with all the money there is in the world."

Oddly, Ray's sympathy did not extend to adults. He seemed to hate them as much as he sympathized with children. When starving Indian *adults* appeared on the TV tube, Ray said: "I don't give a damn about those niggers." Only when the news program showed a crippled man fleeing on crutches from a burning Vietnamese building, Ray spat out: "Why, that sorry son-of-a-bitch! All *he* wants is sympathy." To a radio item about a man who had been burned to death, Ray said: "He got what *he* deserved."

There were the fantasies about children, about adults, and then there were fantasies of violence — of violence as an end in itself. Ray used to talk admiringly about a man he called "Kirk Ponger," who was, Ray believed, "the top torture man in the Communist Party." Ray would describe about how Ponger would "take a man's nuts and hold them right up to electricity." At other times, he would brag about what he would do if he were surrounded by cops, when and if he did his next job.

"If the cops had me pinned down," Ray said, "I'd pretend to give up. I'd throw my gun down. Then when they stepped up to take me, I'd take *them* with me. I'd do it with maybe two ounces, maybe four ounces of nitroglycerin."

What do these reveries mean, what do they reveal about Ray and his inner life, his unconscious, and do they tell about the motives that led to his conscious acts? His concern for children and his hatred of adults, the way that either seemed to set off explosions of feeling in him, show that his passions came from his own childhood, more exactly from his infant experiences. It's perfectly plausible when you think about it why the first relationship one has in life is so important. The nourishment you get from your mother is your first exchange with another human being. As the months pass, if all goes well, you are less and less dependent on a direct physical contact with your mother, and eventually, if your emotions develop as they should, you are able to sustain the pleasure and reassurance you felt when you were with your mother, when she is no longer around. The feelings you have learned from her are now a part of *you;* you have "internalized" them.

But if your mother hasn't met the needs of her infant, if she is erratic or barren of tenderness, the result is devastating for you. You haven't seen any consistent cause-and-effect pattern in your emotional world. You learn that you cannot trust your mother, and you conclude that you cannot trust anyone, or life itself.

As an infant, James Earl Ray suffered from this loss. One clue that he did is the fact that from the earliest time anybody seems to remember him, he had an uncontrollable temper, quick flashes of anger, rage beyond any explicable provocation. Another clue is his reaction to the TV movie on India. To Ray there are no "good" adults; "adult" stands for people who don't take care of children. The intensity of his rage directed at these adults who stand to him for parents has its explanation in the fact that Ray was deprived of parental love and affection at the moment when he was utterly dependent on his parents, on adults, for warmth.

To Ray all children are people who have not received their due, who have been treated unjustly; infancy and childhood stand to him as periods of unhappiness. His daydream of starting an orphan asylum proves that he felt unloved and unwanted in some way that was important to him.

It all goes back to Ceal (for whom we cannot have enough

compassion): a woman who, as the lives of her children prove, had little to give them; married to Speedy, a man who gave her and the children nothing. It was not the economic poverty of Ray's infancy and childhood that seared his psyche; it was the poverty of warmth, of affection, that created within him his murderous feeling of deprivation.

But why did Martin Luther King magnetize and become the focal object of these emotions?

Martin Luther King stirred Ray's feelings by being a figure who offered love and warmth to thousands of people. King reminded Ray in a pointedly bitter way of how *he* had not been taken care of. In this sense, King became, in the symbolic functions of the mind, the mother Ray had not had; King performed the functions that Ceal did not.

What made King an even more highly charged figure was that he made up for the vacancies of Speedy, too. King was not effeminate. He may have had the loving capacities of a mother, but he had also combined the love and strong dependable affections of a father. Ray's focus on King points to Speedy's failure just as much as it points to Ceal's. In the symbolic sense, Ray's decision to murder King was a parent-i-cide, a revenge for the withholding, unloving aspects of *both* his actual parents.

The degree of feeling Ray brought to King as a symbol showed in his violent reveries. It showed in his fictional enactment of his capture, of how he would kill the cops and himself, too. It is an axiom of behavior that every murder is a suicide, and every suicide is a murder. If he took King's life, he would, in an emotionally real sense, be taking his own. The depth of his passion can be measured by the price he was willing to pay.

No matter how abstract these concepts seem, King was murdered out of their force and intensity, out of their emotional *actuality*. They are as real as the fact that King is dead today when he might, but for them, be alive.

---

Don't we need to know more? Is it enough to say what has been said in the foregoing pages? Don't we need a clinical description? Was Ray neurotic? Was he obsessive compulsive? Was he paranoid? Was he manic depressive? Was he schizophrenic? Was he a sociopath? A psychopath? The truth is that he possessed some of the symptoms of all of these diagnostic descriptions. Ray's behavior was across the border into the field of abnormal psychology; no doubt about that. But to be "abnormal" is only to exaggerate normal behavior. That is why, when we read case histories, say in a book on psychology, we always see something of ourselves.

Besides, the clinical terms are not all that exact. They describe, at best, loose constellations of behavior. They overlap. The experts themselves do not agree always on the definitions. That is why psychiatrists so often run into trouble in the courtroom; their labels are not precise enough to withstand hostile cross-examination.

It would be possible to take all the phenomena of Ray's behavior, and break them down, event by event, act by act, into compartments, drop some into Obsessive, some into Compulsive, some Paranoid, and some Schizophrenic. But what we would have when we finished would be a file not a person.

---

A truck from the Renz honor prison farm backed up to the platform on Sunday morning, April 23, 1967. Because it was Sunday, the truck was driven by a relief man. He did not notice that something was a little unusual that day. One of the boxes in which the bread was shipped was already sitting on the lip of the platform. The usual practice was to wheel the boxes out when the truck arrived. Each box held sixty loaves; they were four feet long, three feet wide, and three feet deep. The truck was covered, but open at the back.

There was a reason that box was out there ahead of time. The people who had put it there wanted to make sure that it got into the load that day. It contained a special cargo, human cargo, the living body of James Earl Ray. Its presence there meant that someone had helped Ray, taken a risk in helping him, had certainly been well paid.

Ray had made detailed plans for his escape, some of them with his brother Jack who had visited him just the day before, on Saturday, when they set up a rendezvous.

Ray had access to the bakery. He worked there, was that day, Sunday, on the 11 A.M. to 7 P.M. shift. He ate breakfast at 8 A.M. He carried a sack with him which did not attract attention because bakery workers were allowed to shower and shave in a bathroom there. In that sack, however, Ray had twenty candy bars, a comb, a razor and blades, a broken piece of mirror, and a transistor radio.

"I ate a good breakfast of about six eggs," Ray has written, in describing his escape, "since I knew this might be my last meal for a while. Then I went to the break room where I had hidden a white shirt and a pair of standard green prison pants [which he had dyed black] and a green shirt on top of them. I transferred the items in the sack to my pockets, then stuffed the sack under my shirts. I went down the elevator to the ground floor . . ." where someone loaded him into one of the boxes, covered him with loaves of fresh bread and rolled him out onto the platform.

The truck came on schedule, Ray's box was rolled into it, and when the order for Renz was filled, it drove out through the Jeff City walls. Somewhere out there, Ray unloaded himself, his radio (and $300 in stash he didn't mention in his own account), and hit the road, a free man.

# Chapter 22

In 1927, a gangland war was being fought in the streets of Chicago over control of the Union Siciliane. Joseph Aiello, a black-browed figure who was king of the city's bootleg industry, had made an alliance with the O'Banionites, led by Bugs Moran, and was challenging Al Capone's leadership of Chicago's underworld. Aiello imported five gunmen from New York to wipe out Capone's people but the outsiders lasted only a few days in the Windy City. Aiello then imported Angelo Lo Mantio, a Milwaukee torpedo, who set up an ambush for Capone himself. It was known that Capone liked to stop by a cigar store at 311 South Clark Street to chat with its owner, Hinky Dink Kenna. Mantio rented Room 302 in the Hotel Atlantic across the street from Hinky Dink's and clamped high-powered rifles to the windows in expectation of sighting in on Scarface. But, as it happened, Mantio was caught first in a police net, and Capone became the city's Number One underworld chief.

Forty years later, in 1967, another event of some historical consequence took place at this site. By then the Atlantic, an old graystone building with 450 rooms, had gone badly to seed. It had once served train passengers who arrived in Chicago at the La Salle Street station. But when people stopped riding the railroads, the hotel lost its clientele and, for that matter, the southside section of Chicago in which it was located turned into a skid row of short-order beaneries, porno bookstores, and a disreputable floating sidewalk population. The people who stayed in the Atlantic were "transients" and "show people." In fact prostitutes were working out of the place. It wouldn't have been at all surprising to see Sam Spade or Lew Archer emerge from one of the hotel's three dingy old elevators. Or, for that matter, James Earl Ray.

On the afternoon of April 24, 1967, two men approached the desk of the Atlantic, and registered. One *was* James Earl Ray and the other was his brother Jack. Before nightfall the two were joined by Jerry. They had business to discuss.

The three Ray brothers are not exactly outgoing, warm, affectionate men, but their mood that night was one that was for them almost jubilation. The three of them had not been together for nearly twenty years. It was not that they had all been in jail all that time, but it was that there had never been a moment in that twenty years when all of them were *out* at the same time. They were genuinely glad to see each other, and they put pleasure before business. As soon as they were all settled in their rooms, they went next door to the bar of the Hotel Victoria to hang a few on, and to catch up.

Jack's news was that he was trying to go straight — or at least he was operating a pub in St. Louis. It was called The Grapevine, the prison jargon word for the convicts' underground communication system. Actually, Jack was not eligible to get the license for the place, not with his prison record, and their sister Carol, now Mrs. Albert Pepper, living respectably in St. Louis, had got the license in her name. But Jack lived over the place and ran it.

Jerry had come to terms with his life. For many years now he had stuck to his resolution to stay out of jail, even if it meant working as a busboy in a suburban Chicago country club, where he "lived in." A few drinks in a neighborhood bar would put him in a good mood, when he would, as he always had, turn into a clown, a prankster. In the glow of his resolution to stay "outside" he had even married, had a child, but by 1967 his wife had gone off to Tennessee with the child and Jerry was trying to get a divorce from her. This divorce had become a preoccupation with Jerry; anything that got on his mind became a preoccupation; he could not, or perhaps did not, try to hold too many things in it at one time.

As they talked in the Victoria bar, Jimmy grew tense with excitement. It was the first time he had been in a bar in seven years. The very strangeness, the noises, the pace and unregulated movements of the people in the bar, all the life around him seemed to be anarchic and chaotic after the minutely regimented life of Jeff City. Jerry began to talk, trying to put Jimmy at his ease. Jerry talked about old times, times when they had all been more or less together as young boys in Quincy, times when they had robbed vending machines.

Jerry put Jimmy and Jack in stitches with his stories about how he used to roll drunks in Washington Park. Walter Rife's name came up. Jimmy liked him. They told stories about him, and had a few laughs. At the moment, Rife was out, and running a restaurant at the Virginia Hotel in Quincy, an honest business with a somewhat disreputable clientele. It was something like The Grapevine, straight, but not so straight as to be out of touch with what was, well, crooked. The flood of reminiscence was loose, and went on late into the night.

Finally, when they rose to go to bed, each of them got a girl. They were not men who liked to be in too close proximity with other people. Their years in prison had made them consider privacy a luxury, and they had taken separate rooms. "The main reason we took separate rooms," says Jerry, as if his reason were self-explanatory, "is that Jimmy had been in a long time." Jerry likes girls, and he remembers his mate for that night. "Her name was Co-Co," he says.

---

The next morning the brothers got down to business. The subject was, what was Jimmy going to do now? And how could they help him?

Jack had already helped Jimmy to escape. When Jimmy had kited a letter out to Jack asking him to come visit in Jeff City, Jack had gone; they arranged a rendezvous, and Jimmy escaped the next day. Never mind that there had been a foul-up, a misunderstanding about the exact place of the rendezvous, it had all worked out, and Jack had eventually found Jimmy, they had driven to Chicago together. That was a sacrifice on Jack's part; if he, an ex-convict, had been caught helping another convict escape, it would have gone hard for Jack. He would have done flat time.

And both Jerry and Jack were ready to take other risks to help Jimmy get on his feet again. They listened to him, waited to see what his ideas were. "Don't worry," Jimmy started, "I haven't been wasting my time in Jeff City." He did not need to tell them that. They didn't believe that Jimmy had been wasting time, not Jimmy. "You know Jimmy," says Jerry with the awe with which he almost always talks about his older brother. "He's *serious*. He's a businessman."

"I'm not going to do anything right away," he went on. "I'm gonna rest up for a while. I'm gonna look for a job and get straightened out."

And after he did get straightened out, he was going to be cautious. It would go hard for him if he ever got back in. He owed Missouri thirteen years, even if they didn't lay any additional time on him, and they were certain to do that since his escape was his third attempt. If he was caught again, he could say good-bye to any meaningful free life. He would be an old man when he got out. He told Jerry and Jack that he "didn't want to put a gun on anybody," he didn't "want to get the heat back on me." He wanted to stay out, he was determined to stay out for a while, he told them.

"Jimmy came out of Jeff City thinking he had graduated from this robbery stuff," says Jerry. "He didn't want to go back to that stuff.

"What we talked about was mainly legal stuff."

But what *legal stuff* did Jimmy know, or, for that matter, did Jerry and Jack know? Their view of the law, of legality, was warped out of all recognition by their long history of disobedience and contempt for it. All three of them had long since lost touch with the straight world and its values. What was "legal" to them was quite a different thing from what might be legal to an ordinary man or woman.

In fact, *nothing* they talked about was *legal*. It appeared that their definition of what was legal was — any job where you don't have to use a pistol.

Jerry had got a glimpse of the life of glamour and the celebrities who lived it while working in the country clubs. He suggested that Jimmy, and perhaps all of them, do a kidnapping. At first, Jimmy didn't go for that. He said flatly that he wouldn't have any part of it unless they all three went in it together.

But kidnapping had its pluses, to them. They could make a lot of money quickly; they would not need to shoot anybody; the victim would probably cooperate. It seemed "legal" by their standards.

"And one of us would have to get out of the country with the money," Jimmy said. He told them that they should all three have passports. The easiest place to get one, he told them, was Canada. He had studied it in Jeff City. He mentioned that he would like to go, if he were going to be the one to leave the country, to Rhodesia.

But Jerry said he wasn't going to leave the country. He told Jimmy he didn't "want to get mixed up in any passport stuff." Jack nodded his agreement to that.

"It began to look like getting out of the country was the biggest thing on Jimmy's mind," recalls Jerry.

Jerry had some names for them of people he believed could be kidnapped, and for whom there would be a big reward. He cited then-Governor Otto Kerner and another man whose name was a household word in Chicago: Jack Brickhouse, a sports broadcaster for WGN-TV.

They talked about those names, and the talk was conducted in a fuzz of unreality. They never got down to it.

In fact, Jimmy seemed to have something else in the back of his mind.

They turned to something else "legal." Jerry doesn't remember who brought it up, but it was something some of the members of the family did know about, a craft in which they had some experience and savvy. This was the pornographic picture business, not then sanctioned, as it was later, by a Supreme Court decision. It was against the law, and in 1963 some of the family had been investigated by U.S. Post Office postal inspectors. The postal investigation had shown that a "J. Ray," who gave his address as 1913 Hickory Street (the address of Mom Maher's boardinghouse), was running a business in porno. It turned out that J. Ray was Jack Ray, and that he had been helped in the business by his brother Franklin "Buzzy" Ray and a girl friend of Buzzy's who posed for the photos. Shortly after this Buzzy met a tragic death when he missed the Quincy bridge and drove his car into a slough of the Mississippi where he and his girl friend were drowned. After Buzzy's death, the postal inspectors dropped the investigation, which led the brothers to think that porno was a very low-risk business.

Porno seemed the very thing for Jimmy to go into now.

"Porno was the main topic we discussed," said Jerry. "There was less chance of getting caught if you did it right. Also, Jimmy thought there would be more money in it than anything else. He thought he could turn that porno into a big thing. We discussed where to run them ads, either in underground newspapers or scandal sheets. We were going to advertise for models. A woman knows if she answers one of those papers that you want everything.

"Customers have different things they like. To do business you've got to have everything, every kind of thing going on, Black and White, head jobs, whipping, queers, lesbians, somebody beating somebody, everything."

They got down to the mechanics of porno.

Jack warned that you couldn't answer the letters in longhand because that might give you away: you would have to have a typewriter to correspond with the people who answered your ads. That was an item of expense. Then there would be cameras. Then you would have to pay the girls.

As the talk went on, Jimmy got more and more interested.

"I read in prison," Jimmy chipped in, "how guys get rich off it. I'd get Mexican girls to make pictures. They'll do anything for almost nothing." He had been in Mexico on a spree after his first Kroger robbery in July, 1959.

"The thing you've got to be careful about," said Jack, "is not get any fingerprints on the pictures, on your envelope, or on your letter. You've got to wipe them good."

———

The porno business looked good. They reached a consensus of grunts and monosyllabic words of agreement on it.

But long before that agreement was reached, it had begun to be apparent that Jimmy had something more on his mind than had yet been discussed. He had something on his mind he had not yet told them about. Jerry knew Jimmy well enough to sense that.

They were about to get down to a reckoning of the money that was coming to Jimmy, when he suddenly said:

"I'm gonna kill that nigger King. That's something that's been on my mind. That's something I've been working on."

Well! Jimmy had not been wasting his time in Jeff City.

Actually, neither Jerry nor Jack was that much surprised. It was just like Jimmy to get an idea like that, so big, so grandiose. As far as the notion itself, they could not have agreed more, at least as far as hating black people, hating "liberals," Jews, but neither of them would have ever conceived of killing King. For their separate personal reasons, they would not have killed King.

Jerry had his divorce on his mind. Besides, it was too big a job for him, too big and too dangerous. He was determined to stay out of prison if he could manage it at all.

He told Jimmy flatly then and there that he would help him where he could, but he did not want to be in on that job. He wanted to stick with Jimmy. He felt he understood Jimmy better than Jack did. He could grasp, or at least accept, the contradictions in Jimmy.

Jerry even understood, grasped, Jimmy's idealism. "He felt everybody had *responsibilities*. Jimmy felt if you don't do your duty, it's not worth living."

Beyond that, Jerry understood something of Jimmy's psychology. "Why, it didn't surprise me at all that Jimmy was going to try to do two or three things at once, things that didn't seem to go together. I knew that when he got back out on the street again he would be having several things on his mind all at the same time."

Jack as always in the family was the ultimate realist. His reaction to Jimmy's news was one of unqualified pragmatism:

"That's *crazy!* You can count me out of *that* deal. There ain't no money in killin' a nigger. I'm going back to St. Louis."

And he did, shortly after that.

"Jack was sore if that was what was up," explains Jerry. "He had taken a risk going down there helping Jimmy get out of Jeff City. Then ending up in a deal where there wasn't any money."

Jerry was more or less glad to hear Jack say what he said. "Jimmy and Jack was too hot-tempered to ever work together on a job. Sometimes Jimmy would write Jack a sarcastic letter, and Jack would *blow up.* I'll tell you it would have been a bull of a fight if those two had ever gone up against each other!

"As for me, Jimmy knew I never would get mad at him no matter what he did or said. I just would say to myself, 'That's Jimmy.'"

----

Next, Jerry and Jack made an accounting to Jimmy of the money he had been sending out to them. Jerry says that they handed over to Jimmy that day in Chicago his accumulated earnings.

Jerry handed Jimmy eight $100 bills.

Jack handed over $3,800 in bills.

That made a total of $4,600.

Jimmy had carried out $300 with him when he escaped.

That brought the total up to $4,900.

Jerry says that the money he handled was mailed by a prison guard at Jeff City who sent the money in plain envelopes to him at Box 22, Wheeling, Illinois. He says he actually received $1,000, but paid $200 of that to a Jefferson City lawyer who represented Jimmy on an appeal. He says that Jack had a "contact" through whom he received the money from Jimmy. This suggests that it might have been done in a roundabout way, with the payoff coming from somebody already outside prison.

"Jimmy first began to send money out in 1963. At first it was about $500 a year, but he stepped it up as time passed and his contacts in Jeff City got better."

Jerry says that he held $1,500 for Jimmy, in case of an emergency.

That brings the total to $6,400.

With some earnings Jimmy was to make later, the total sum of money available to him rises to about $7,000. That is just about the amount of money he was to spend between that day in Chicago and the day he was captured at Heathrow airport in London.

A detailed breakdown of Ray's known expenses during the period he was free, with reasonable estimates for the expenses not specifically known, comes to just under $6,800.

I have talked with three different wardens at Jeff City and custodial officers who served at the prison during the time Ray was there. With one or two exceptions, all agree that drugs were sold in Jeff City at that time, and that it was possible for Ray to make an arrangement to get money out of the prison through a guard.

There is very little question but that either Jerry or Jack or both of them handled some of his money for him, although it is probable that they did not know until their meeting in Chicago what he meant to do with it.

These references suggest that Jerry and Jack did not turn

over all the money that day at the Hotel Atlantic. Jerry may have held for Jimmy more than the $1,500 he acknowledges having held. He may have supplied money to his brother during the year his brother was free, and the evidence suggests that he did. Jerry and Jimmy were in frequent touch with each other during the year of Jimmy's freedom.

It is possible that some of this money passed at some stage through one or more bank accounts. On September 2, 1970, I interviewed Philip Canale, who was then attorney general in Memphis and had been in charge of the Ray case ever since Ray was brought to Memphis from London. I asked Canale then if it was possible Ray had made money while he was a prisoner in Jeff City. Canale's reply was: "Sure. Ray sent about $7,000 out of prison. The money was banked by Carol Pepper, Ray's sister. A few days after Ray escaped from Jeff City she withdrew the money from the bank."

In 1975, I talked with Robert K. Dwyer about the Carol Pepper bank account. Dwyer was the assistant attorney general under Canale who would have prosecuted the case in the courtroom if there had been a trial, and he was the attorney who represented the state of Tennessee in the proceedings when Ray pleaded guilty in Memphis.

"It was our belief that this bank account was the source of at least some of Ray's money," Dwyer told me. "It was our intention to introduce this bank account and to question James Earl Ray about it."

Other evidence that Carol handled the money comes from Jack (John Larry) Ray. He reportedly told two F.B.I. agents who interviewed him on May 15, 1968, that: "Carol handled the money. If I want money, or if Jimmy wants money, we would go to Carol. Carol deposits the money."

---

In November, 1967, Carol Pepper applied for a liquor license (granted November 29, 1967, by the Missouri liquor control board) for a business to be called "Jack's Place," at 1928 Arsenal Place, St. Louis. In fact, the "Jack" turned out to be her brother Jack (John Larry) Ray, who operated the place (sometimes called The Grapevine), and lived over it.

It is getting somewhat ahead of the chronological story, but fits here as part of the story of Ray's finances, to relate other episodes. Later, when Ray was in Los Angeles in 1968, he told Rita Stein, a woman he had become close to, that he was "waiting for more money from my brother." When Ray was captured in London in June, 1968, there was still apparently money available to him, money of his own, from and through these family arrangements. He told a London lawyer that if the lawyer needed money to get in touch "with my brother Jerry." In a letter to his lawyer, Arthur Hanes, written from London in 1968, Ray told Hanes that he was instructing his brother to send Hanes a retainer. He gave Hanes the address and phone number of Carol Pepper in Maplewood, Missouri.

———

But before he was captured in London, Ray was broke, something he is not likely to have been if he was, as he has sometimes insisted, an agent of a foreign government. The facts seem to be that he had got beyond the limits where Jerry could send him money, or beyond the point where Jimmy wanted money sent to him. At any rate, he was down to his last $20, he told someone later. On June 4, four days before he was captured, he robbed the Fulham Branch of the Trustees Savings Bank in London, and took away about a hundred English pounds, or the equivalent of $240. At the time of his arrest, he had $123.54.

Yet another piece of evidence (never disclosed before this writing) exists that Ray was broke even after he was returned to Memphis and facing trial. Jerry Ray was out searching for money for James Earl Ray's defense before he stood trial. Shortly after Jimmy was captured, in 1968, Jerry made an appointment in New Orleans with Kent Courtney, a dedicated anti-Communist who had often accused not only Martin Luther King but also Nelson Rockefeller of being a Communist. Courtney was national chairman of the Conservative Society of America, for a period had his own newspaper, the *Louisiana Eagle,* and has recently been broadcasting over KWDH in Shreveport, Louisiana.

When I reached Courtney at a phone number in Alexandria, Louisiana, on June 16, 1972, and asked him if he had met with Jerry Ray, he answered:

"Yes, sir! I met him in a park in New Orleans. I had a policeman sitting right there with us. You never know how the Communist conspiracy might work. That's not all. I had another detective hidden in the bushes taking pictures.

"Jerry Ray called me up and said he wanted to see me. He said his brother had read my newspaper when he was in jail in Jefferson City, Missouri. But he wasn't on my subscription list. I checked it.

"At first I couldn't figure out what Jerry wanted. It sounded to me like it was all marshmallows. He didn't like that other man being present. Finally he asked me if I would help with a lawyer for Jimmy. Well, I wanted to see Ray get help on his trial. I wanted a trial just to see what would boil up out of it. But I wouldn't have anything to do with

Stoner. I told Jerry I wouldn't help as long as Stoner was in the case."

Courtney says he never heard from Jerry again. Jerry confirms the meeting and Courtney's version of what happened. "He wanted me to pose for a picture with him and I wouldn't do it," says Jerry.

The "Stoner" Courtney refers to was one of Ray's attorneys. He is J. B. Stoner, leader of the National States Rights Party of Marietta, Georgia, which is forthrightly anti-Negro and which has a Nazi swastika on the masthead of its publication, *The Thunderbolt*.

If James Earl Ray was paid by a foreign government, or by anyone, it is very unlikely that Jerry, who had become his ambassador and public relations man, would have had to be going to Courtney for financial or legal help.

---

A couple of days after the Hotel Atlantic meeting, James Earl Ray took a twelve-dollar-a-week basement room at 2731 North Sheffield Avenue on the northside of Chicago and in accordance with his strategy of lying low, getting used to life in the Free World, took a dishwashing job at the Indian Trail Restaurant in suburban Winnetka. He kept his nose clean, worked hard, even got a promotion.

He spent his lunch hour avidly reading the day's newspapers which he brought to work with him, and he would certainly have read then that the U.S. Supreme Court on June 12, 1967, upheld the 1963 conviction of Martin Luther King for defying an Alabama state court injunction, and the report that King meant to go to jail in Birmingham the next month and serve his sentence.

Ray did some going back and forth to Quincy, and to see Jack, and for several visits to Ted Crowley's bar in Quincy where, Jerry says, Jimmy made the contacts to get a pistol. I have spent an evening with Jerry and Jack at Crowley's bar where I was hospitably treated by Crowley and his customers. It is a dark, quiet, timeless place, distinguished by the fact that Ted has refused ever since to take down the Christmas decorations which he had hung a decade before. They have somehow curiously blended into the decor and do not seem at all out of place. When I left the place with Jerry, he explained: "Most of those fellas in Ted's have done time, most of them have been down at Menard."

Jimmy spent several evenings with Jerry, sometimes at the Northbrook Tavern, sometimes at the Cypress Tavern, both hangouts of Jerry's.

Ray quit his job at the Indian Trail on June 24. He asked that his final check be sent to Jerry. He had received eight weekly paychecks from May 7 to June 25, 1967. His taxable earnings were $813.66, with $112.60 withheld for federal income tax and $36.72 for social security. His take-home pay was $664.34. That would have given him a total of nearly $5,600.00.

Ray's next business was in Canada, and on July 16, 1967, he crossed the border driving a 1962 Plymouth for which he had paid $200.

———

This is the time James Earl Ray was supposed to have come in contact with "Raoul," an agent of a foreign government. The story about Raoul was related by Ray to William Bradford Huie, a writer who had entered into a contract with Ray under which Huie paid Ray for his "story." Huie was not able to interview Ray face-to-face. Ray sent a tale about Raoul out from his cell in Memphis through his lawyers at the time, Arthur Hanes and Arthur Hanes, Jr., of Birmingham. Huie was writing the story concurrently with his receipt of these handwritten notes from Ray, and publishing it in *Look* magazine.

It was a series of three articles. They appeared on: November 12, 1968, November 26, 1968, and April 15, 1969. In his third article Huie concluded that there was no such person as Raoul and reversed his position.

Up through 1975, the only physical evidence there has ever been of Raoul is in James Earl Ray's handwriting on the pages of a legal pad now yellowing in the files of Hanes's Birmingham office.

The question of whether or not there was a Raoul was asked of Percy Foreman, one of Ray's lawyers, when he was giving a deposition under oath about his handling of the Ray case. Foreman swore:

"Ray bragged about the fool he was making out of Huie. Ray told me he invented Raoul for Huie. He said there wasn't any Raoul."

I once asked Jerry about Raoul.

"That's just bullshit stuff Jimmy made up for Huie," he answered with a hearty laugh.

But Raoul was an alter ego for James Earl Ray. It was no trouble at all for a man like Ray to slip over into the identity of another person. He had used aliases many times before. So had his family; their identity as a family had always been shaky and uncertain. What's more, a man like Ray often reaches the point where, deep down, he is not sure *he* exists.

And when the real James Earl Ray was, in a sense, non-existent, it was that much simpler for him to create a "real" person and the more delightful to wave that person in front of others, entice them to enter into his fantasy, and force them to take seriously the historical, albeit fictitious, character he had created.

"Raoul" was many of the things James Earl Ray had never succeeded in being, a successful big-time criminal with international connections and influence with powerful figures in the straight world; Raoul was a man who could pay others to do the dirty work for him.

Even the word "Raoul" is not without its significant overtones. Indeed words that are chosen for purposes like this are never idly chosen, never without their own meaning. "Raoul" was not only glamorous and foreign-sounding, but it was also only another variation of Ray — Ray-oul, a perfect choice for an idealized self, a fine mask to wear to cover the inadequate identity of a real self.

Of course Raoul is nothing but a phantom. Not even Ray himself ever gave Raoul a last name, never even bothered to claim that anyone had ever seen Raoul and himself together. Of course not: they are the same person.

---

There *was* a kind of conspiracy in the assassination of Martin Luther King. The meeting between the brothers at the Atlantic meant something to them, that they were all more or less willing to support Jimmy, if not join with him, in his act, knowing, understanding, sensing that he was going to avenge them all.

It was a conspiracy of the spirit, the bitter spirit that was their common heritage.

On Wednesday, December 10, 1975, I called Jerry Ray at Carol's house in St. Louis where he had gone for the Christmas holidays. Carol answered. "You want Jerry?" she asked, and laughed. There hadn't been anything to laugh about that I could see, not up to that point, although there was often something to laugh about when I talked with Jerry.

Suddenly the phone trembled in my ear with a sharp blast of sound. I could barely hear Jerry's voice.

"Georgie boy. Georgie boy. That you?"

"Cut that thing down, Jerry," I yelled, "I can't *hear* you."

He left the phone, and cut the volume. Suddenly, with a shock, I knew what I was hearing.

It was a tape recording of the voice of Martin Luther King, delivering his valedictory address in Memphis.

"Yes, I've been to the mountaintop," King was crying out, there out of the earpiece of my phone.

"Jerry . . ." I said, so stunned, saddened, that I could not say anything else.

"Why, Georgie boy," Jerry laughed loudly. "That's your friend. Sure, he's *right here*. He's not *dead*. Come on out and meet him."

I did not know what to say, exactly.

"I'll call you another time," I said, and started to hang up the phone.

"Don't hang up. Don't hang up, Georgie boy. He's right here. He's not *dead*."

But I did hang up then.

# Chapter 23

Now Jimmy knew what he wanted to do. It was only a question of working out the details.

During the day of July 16, 1967, he crossed the border into Canada in his 1962 red Plymouth. He spent the night somewhere nearby in Canada, exactly where nobody knows except him. By the next night he had reached Montreal where he stayed at the Bourgade Motel. He signed the register there as "John L. Rayns." That signature was the last vestige of the old James Earl Ray. That was to be the last time in many months that anyone (outside his family) was to know him by anything that linked him to his real name and his real past.

The next day, July 18, he took an apartment in Montreal at 2589 Notre Dame Avenue East, agreeing to pay $75 a month for six months. The place was called the Har-K Apartments.

The name he signed to the Har-K lease was "Eric Starvo Galt." With that new name, ringing with its aristocratic sound and having its origin in his political attitudes, there emerged the new James Earl Ray — the new Jimmy who was really the original Jimmy, the Jimmy his family had pinned their hopes on, the smart Jimmy, the ambitious Jimmy, the Jimmy who was going to *be somebody*.

The Eric moniker was not the only new thing. His head was full of schemes and stratagems, and his mood was one of self-assurance when it was not one of contemptuous cockiness. He was every bit as confident of himself as he had been when he went off to Germany to put new juice into the Nazi party. He had not for nothing spent all those years in prison studying his mistakes. He was absolutely sure now that he would outsmart everyone — cops, detectives, customs men, everybody.

He was going to kill King and *he* was going to get away with it. He was not going to run stupidly through the streets as Oswald had done. He, Ray, was going to know where he was going after he had done the deed. He was going to have an escape plan. And more. He was going to have a plan for a better life, the life he would live after he killed King. He would do something for society, kill King, but he would also do something for himself. He was never again going to be a small-time criminal, crawling in and out of fleabags, getting his ashes hauled by whores. He was determined to wear good clothes, a tie, to be able to go into a decent place and know how to act, not stand out, know how to make the women there like him. He had a list of things he was going to learn, social graces and vocational skills he was going to acquire, at the very same time he was working out his plan to kill — and to escape after killing — King. He did not see anything absurd or contradictory in his plans to learn at the same time how to forge a Canadian passport and how to dance.

These are the kinds of real-life stories the twentieth century is asking us to accept: not, as in Graham Greene, a fictional man with a split lip who was paid by munitions manufacturers to assassinate a liberal cabinet minister at his desk, and who could do it with utter callousness and cool indifference; not a man with a split lip, but a man with split emotions, a passionate political idealist, a man who could kill out of his beliefs, an ideological murderer, and yet one who could be as cool in the planning and execution of his murder, just as calm in the deed, as if he had been paid; a man in real life so sure his murder was the right thing to do that he felt no guilt, that he could put murder in one compartment of his mind, close the door on it, and in another compartment of his mind blithely go about preparing himself for a new life.

His most serious business was to look further into how he could get himself a Canadian passport. He already knew that it was not too hard to forge one. "In prison I studied about how a broker named Burell or Birrell got a Canadian passport and escaped to South America," Ray later wrote. He had undoubtedly read about Lowell Birrell in the February 27, 1962, issue of *Look* magazine, which showed the former New York stockbroker living luxuriously and with immunity from extradition in Brazil. Birrell had entered Brazil carrying a forged Canadian passport.

Ray had written to the Canadian Embassy for information while he was working at the Indian Trail Restaurant, and when he got to Montreal he called a travel agency to "ask what I.D. I needed to get a passport." Having done that, having confirmed that it was possible, he decided that he had done enough. The final work of forging the passport he would leave for a later time.

On this trip he was *laying out* Montreal, familiarizing himself with the cheap bars and hotels he would want to fold himself inconspicuously into when he returned this way — a hunted man. He looked into the idea of escaping from Canada on a ship. He hung around the Neptune Tavern, 121 West Commissioners Street, talked with seamen about how to go about getting a job on a ship, and concluded that it was not easy. He wouldn't have time to stand around a hiring hall waiting for a job call after he had done what he was planning to do.

In another compartment of his mind he was planning his future career. He hadn't been kidding when he told Jerry and Jack that he wanted to find a new profession whose requirements did not include the use of a gun. He was in earnest about the porno business. It was just safe enough, and there was just enough of the old Con in it, of exploiting suckers, to appeal to him. That was what he was up to when, on July 24, he wrote Futura Books at Inglewood, California, asking them to send him three sex manuals they had advertised in an underground newspaper. He wanted to study the poses. He was going to hire models and make his own blue pictures as the raw material of his porno enterprise.

In the ad Ray read, one of the manuals he ordered was described:

"A Sex Manual. Valuable for three reasons. One, it covers the entire subject of sex in marriage. Two, male and female reproductive organs; sex impulse in men vs. women; masturbation in and out of marriage; precoital stimulation; problems of sexuality; frustrated wives with case histories; sex myths; aids to penetration; oral eroticism; enlarging the penis to a maximum; assistance in overcoming premature ejaculation, etc. Original drawings."

Ray placed at least one ad in the Toronto *Flash* for a participant while he was in Canada, he told Jerry. It was his first open move in the porno business. He got one reply: "he was surprised," says Jerry, "she was a nice-looking woman."

Four days later, on July 28, he bought a Canadian money order for $17.50 and used it to make a first payment on a mail order course in locksmithing. He did this, says Jerry, because "Jimmy always was afraid he would lock himself out of a car at the very minute he wanted to use it." Perhaps. Or perhaps he wanted to be able to get into other places to which he had no key. It was a handy skill for a straight life or a crooked life.

He had not neglected during his days in Montreal the contents of yet another compartment of his mind. He was going to upgrade his looks. One of the first things he did in Montreal was get a new wardrobe. On July 19, the day after he got a room, he went into the Tip Top Tailors, at 488 St. Catherine West, a medium-priced clothing store where suits cost between $65 and $110 — better clothes than Ray had ever worn before. He bought himself a new brown suit, a pair of conservative gray slacks, plus a red T-shirt, a yellow T-shirt, yellow swimming trunks, red pajamas, socks, some underwear and a couple of neckties. Two days later, he bought more clothes, conservative clothes, a $150 custom-made business suit which he ordered and was fitted for at the English and Cottonwood, Ltd. He was not in any particular hurry for this suit; he later notified the tailors to mail it to him at an address in Birmingham, Alabama.

Nor was he quite finished turning himself out. He went to the Queen Elizabeth Hotel and got a haircut and a manicure. A manicure? Well, wasn't that what Capone used to do? Wasn't Arnold Rothstein shot in a barber chair while getting a manicure?

An astonishing thing happened to Ray in Canada. He had a romance. He discovered that he was more successful with respectable women than he might have expected to be, considering how little experience he had ever had with them. He found out that they were just as approachable, if not more so, than the professional women he had known. In fact, he was picked up in the Gray Rocks bar by a government employee on vacation from her job in Ottawa.

"Last year, after years of trouble with an aggressive man," this woman told Huie, "I had taken steps to get my divorce. A woman friend and I drove to Gray Rocks for a long weekend. We began the evening in the lounge of the inn. We found it crowded and people were drinking and dancing, and there was this lone man sitting at a table. He was neat and well-dressed and shy. My friend said, 'Let's sit with this man,' and we introduced ourselves and sat down and ordered drinks and began trying to talk."

There were, she said, "aggressive men" all around in the bar that night but Ray was "so unaggressive. He had such a lost-and-lonely manner. You didn't feel sorry for him, but you sort of wanted to help him have fun and not feel so lonely."

She got him on the dance floor, but he was clumsy. She tried to teach him a step, and "he was good-natured about it." They had a good time together. They drank a lot. "As the evening wore on, he seemed to become more confident," she said, "and more protective toward me." She went to Ray's room and stayed the night; and sexually, "I thought he acted perfectly normal."

That was not the end of the affair. The woman came to Montreal with her friend on August 7, the night after they left Gray Rocks. Ray's apartment at the Har-K was small, and "seedy and run-down," she found. Nevertheless she and her friend stayed the night, "the three of us slept across his bed in his one little room." Nor was that the end. Ray kept in touch by phone, calling from Montreal to Ottawa, and on August 18 he went to Ottawa to see her. He stayed at the Town and Country Motel, and they spent that night and the next one together.

He talked with her about "niggers." "You've got to live near niggers to know 'em," he told her. He also mentioned his brother, told her he was going to have to leave Montreal for some business deal the two of them were in together.

Whether Ray at this moment was "normal," "shy," "un-aggressive," are judgments that seem to lie more in the eye of his companion than they do anywhere else. What she thought was lack of aggressiveness was probably only Ray's faceless anonymity. He had always kept his distance from people. He had learned through years of study how to avoid making an imprint of personality. It was not that he was a skilled imposter; he was not. It was not that he had *become* Eric Galt, created a personality to fit that name. Rather it was that his stamp was so faint that he could fit any name or that any name would fit him. He was the kind of person you could look at and not *see*, not remember, carry away of him no impression.

That was not the end of this girl friend of his. He was to be in touch with her once again. It is clear that she made an *imprint* on him. He had not had a relationship like this, acted out in a respectable setting, since that girl friend he had had in Chicago after he came out of the army; an interval of almost twenty years stretched between the two romances, practically his whole adult life. Both of the romances happened at a time in his life when he was confident, hopeful, saw a future for himself. Both of the romances happened at a time when he, at least as he saw it, had some hope of going straight, for that is what he meant to do after he killed King.

Thousands of words have been written speculating about other events that were supposed to have happened to Ray in Canada on this trip, that he met and got directions from "Raoul," that he smuggled drugs across the border, that he held up a supermarket, that he robbed a Montreal whorehouse. No evidence whatever to support any of these fictions has ever been turned up by the Royal Canadian Mounted Police, by the F.B.I., by customs investigators, by narcotics investigators, by local or state police forces. *Ray* is the author of the stories, and he has *admitted* that at least one of them — that he got $1,700 from the whorehouse — was "a little lie." The whorehouse he really robbed, he said some time later, was in Chicago, and he had done the job in 1959, not 1967. It seems unlikely that Ray ever held up any whorehouse. That was the kind of job that would make him enemies in the wrong places, enemies in prison, enemies in the underworld in which he moved. He was too "concrete" to do that.

Anyway, holding up *anything* was the last thing he wanted

to do at this moment. He did not need the money. He told his Gray Rocks girl friend, when she asked him how he stood on money: "Don't worry, there's more where this came from." He was determined to stay low, not become "hot," not use a pistol. That was the logic of his movements in Canada, and if his logic is hard for others to understand, if what he did doesn't seem to "make sense" to ordinary people, well, that isn't what is important. What matters is that what Ray was doing made sense to *him*.

Jerry says: "The whole thing about Raoul and running drugs from Canada was bullshit. He went to Canada the first time to look the place out, how to get out of the country. The reason he broke off with that girl was that he was getting serious. He really liked her. He got afraid and broke off her. That wasn't his aim in life, to stay with a woman. He wanted more than that. He wanted The Big Boy."

James Earl Ray crossed the border back into the United States at Windsor on August 21, his business in Canada done, apparently to his satisfaction.

The two brothers, Jerry and Jimmy, got together on the night of August 22, took a room at a hotel on North Avenue. They were beginning to feel easy with one another. They were getting to know each other after the years they had been separated by prison bars. Jimmy began to discover that he liked telling Jerry about his plans. Jerry agreed with Jimmy's ideas about King. Jerry took Jimmy seriously when Jimmy wanted to be taken seriously, and there was no question at all of Jerry's loyalty, complete trustworthiness. Jerry might be a clown but Jimmy enjoyed it as a change, for his mind was full of so many things that sometimes it seemed as if his head would *burst*. That's what he told Jerry.

Once more, as he had when the three brothers had met a few months before at the Atlantic Hotel, Jimmy asked Jerry to come in with him on the porno business and the rest of his schemes, to come with him to Birmingham, Alabama. But Jerry begged off. Again, he told Jimmy that he had to get his divorce, had to stay on his job, make enough money "to pay some witnesses." But in the back of his mind, what he did not tell Jimmy was that he never again in his life wanted to go back into prison. Jerry was determined to stay on the outside.

Well, anyway, Jimmy liked having someone to talk with, just as he used to talk with Earl. He had not forgotten how good it was to tell Earl what was going on, to report to Earl week by week, even day by day sometimes, as he had often done when he was forging money orders with Rife years ago.

That night of August 22, the two brothers agreed to keep in touch from this point on. They would write each other. They would phone each other. Jerry even promised that he would come to wherever Jimmy was if Jimmy needed him badly enough.

It was a good deal for both of them. Jimmy was pleased to have a confidant, and Jerry was excited, fascinated by the chance to have even a secondhand view of something so big and important, such a completely worthwhile, as Jerry saw it, adventure. It lifted Jerry out of his doldrums, out of the narrow and humiliating confines of his own life. It gave him a sense of purpose.

It took some of the loneliness out of both their lives.

"Jimmy was going to Birmingham to take out citizenship papers in Alabama," says Jerry. "He believed that if he killed King in Alabama, or if he killed him anywhere in the South, it would help him if he showed he was a resident of Alabama.

He was determined to kill King in the South. Of course if he killed King in Alabama, he believed Wallace would eventually pardon him, not at first, but after a few years when things had cooled off."

This was the time when the presidential campaign of Alabama Governor George C. Wallace was beginning to be taken seriously outside the South.

"Jimmy was getting caught up in the Wallace campaign," says Jerry. "He was talking as much that night in Chicago about getting Wallace in as he was about rubbing King out. He had it in his head that it would help Wallace if King wasn't around."

The next morning, Ray was ready to make his move to Birmingham. He gave his red Plymouth to Jerry, who washed it thoroughly that day for he thought it was "hot," and he wanted to make sure there were no fingerprints on it. And the next morning, August 24, James Earl Ray caught the Illinois Central to Birmingham. He spent the first night in a cheap hotel there, the Granada, and on August 26, he found himself lodging at the Economy Grill and Rooms, a large, once-imposing run-down stucco house at 2608 South Highland Avenue in a run-down section of downtown Birmingham, where he could get room and two meals a day for $22.50 a week. He signed himself as Eric S. Galt, said he'd been working at the Ingalls Shipbuilding yards in Pascagoula, Mississippi. An older Greek man named Peter Cherpes ran the place, and he got a good impression of Ray. Ray was a little dressier, a little sharper, than the usual roomer at Economy, whose customers were mainly hard-working men.

And, as always, Ray was "quiet," didn't bother anybody, didn't get in anybody's way, didn't come in drunk, didn't get in arguments. In fact, nobody there at the time remembers getting into any kind of conversation with Ray. He was a "concrete" boarder, just as he had been a concrete prisoner. This was Ray's style which of course became him at this moment because he was an escaped convict. A man on the run from the law may disappear for half a lifetime, and then be caught in some small, accidental mistake if he lets his guard down, if he is not always alert.

Ray had some important things to do in Birmingham. He needed some transportation and equipment, and he needed to establish Eric S. Galt as a legal entity — and it was Ray's plan to combine the two things, to make one thing work for the other. For example, Ray intended to buy a car.

On August 27, William D. Paisley, the sales manager of a Birmingham lumber company, ran a classified ad in the Birmingham *News:*

"Mustang. '66, V-8, auto trans. Radio, W. W. tires, factory warranty. Individual, $1,995. 592–0448."

The next day, August 28, Ray telephoned Paisley, arranged to come see the car at 6 P.M., after Paisley got home from work, and Ray arrived promptly at the Paisley home in a cab. Paisley offered to let Ray test-drive the car, but Ray objected that he didn't have a driver's license. It was a white Mustang with red interior, the sportiest car Ray had ever owned. Paisley drove Ray around the block, and Ray said, with no more ado, "I'll take it off your hands." He then told Paisley that he "did business" at the Birmingham Trust National Bank, and arranged to meet Paisley there the next morning at 10 A.M. when he would, he said, pay Paisley in cash for the car.

Next morning, the two men met downtown. Ray startled

and somewhat alarmed Paisley by counting out $2,000 on the street in front of the bank. Paisley walked into his bank, across the street, cashed the money and brought Ray $5 in change. They walked together to the parking lot where Paisley had left the Mustang, and there Paisley handed over two sets of keys and the car.

On September 6, 1967, Ray persuaded Mr. Cherpes, his landlord, to go with him to the Jefferson County courthouse in Birmingham where Ray applied for a driver's license. It was necessary to have an "accompanying driver" when the application was filed; Cherpes said he was glad to go along because "I thought he was just a good fellow temporarily out of work."

The driver's license was good I.D. for Eric Galt. It is the kind of thing that most people will readily accept as identification. As filled out by Ray, it said that Galt lived at 2608 Highland Avenue South, that Galt was born on July 20, 1931 (Ray made himself a little younger), that he weighed 175 pounds, was five feet eleven inches tall (a little taller). The examiner said that Ray (Galt) "needs training as to posture and attention," but passed Ray with an 86 percent score. Ray's vision was 20/20 in each eye and in both eyes. Ray did not buy new license plates for the Mustang until October 2, but he obviously waited for new Alabama annual plates to go on sale on October 1. But with the plate (its number was Alabama 1-38993) he got his registration certificate for the car. He now had substantial I.D. for Galt — a driver's license, a car registration certificate, a car title, and a bank-box contract.

Ray wasn't kidding about the bank. He had done some business at the Birmingham Trust National Bank. He had rented a safety deposit box, 5517, giving as reference Karl Galt, with a St. Louis address, in the morning of August 28, the day before he bought the Mustang. He did not open the box until that afternoon. The box, and what Ray had in it, is a mystery still. But his first access to it was at 2:32 on the afternoon of the day he rented it. He couldn't have been taking anything out then; he must have been putting something *in*. He has said he put "Rayns I.D." into the box, that is, the identification papers, such as they were, that he had been using since he escaped from Jeff City, what he had used in Chicago and in Canada. But that is not enough of a reason for Ray to have taken the box, risked going into the bank, for every appearance in a public place is some risk to an escaped convict. A bank box would not have been a place that he would have stored drugs; it would have been the last place for that. Ray had no other documents, no will, no deeds to property, no contracts. There is only one thing he could have rented the box for and that was to keep his stash secure. He would have needed it if he had had large sums of money which he did not want to risk carrying on his person or trying to conceal in a rooming house.

On October 1, Ray made another purchase. He answered another ad in the Birmingham *News*. This one was placed by Walter L. Spain, who wanted to sell a revolver. Spain got a call from Ray, Ray came out to Spain's house, asked Spain what he wanted for the revolver, Spain answered sixty-five dollars, and Ray reached in his pocket, pulled out a roll of bills, and paid Spain the sixty-five, pocketed the gun, and left.

Meanwhile Ray had not neglected his other goals, his

future career. On September 1, he mailed an order to the Superior Bulk Film Company, 442 North Wells Street, Chicago, for:

| | |
|---|---|
| 1 Kodak Projector M95Z | 168.00 |
| 1 Kodak Super 8 Camera M8 | 160.00 |
| 1 HPI Combination 8mm. Super Splicer | 4.49 |
| 1 Remote Control 20-foot cable | 4.75 |
| | $337.24 |

Ray asked, in a note on the back of the order, that he be sent manuals on "sound stripers; descriptive circular on LSF automatic cine printer; the price of the Eumig Mark S Sound Projector," and that everything be sent to him special delivery.

On October 5, Ray bought another piece of camera equipment, a Polaroid 220 at $245 from Lollar's Camera Shop in Birmingham.

All this activity and money, more than $600 in purchases, was for the porno business. Taken together, the movie equipment and the manuals he ordered from Superior were "a completely self-sufficient movie-making unit of good quality," according to an expert filmmaker. They made Ray capable of filming a porno movie if he wished to make one. The only thing he lacked was equipment to print movie films, and there was a host of such independent film printing companies in a place like Los Angeles.

Somewhere he must have got advice about what to buy.

He had some technical information. On the same day that he bought his Polaroid, he returned to Superior the movie camera they had sent him on his order. It was not the right one, and he knew that it wouldn't do for him. "The camera you sent has only one film speed and I wanted the Kodak M8 which has four." He expected to need that extra flexibility, the ability to photograph under differing light conditions that different film speeds would give him. What's more, he knew that he might want to photograph himself, for wouldn't it save money if he himself appeared in his porno photos, if he were his own model? That is why he ordered the cable release.

He laid the groundwork for more porno activity in Canada, if and when he should return there, by enrolling from Birmingham in a Canadian lonely hearts club. "The people in these clubs," he later wrote Huie, "are not criminals, but they are not what you would call square." From this, he never got a bite.

He dutifully went right on with his other vocational training, regularly sent in his locksmithing correspondence lessons during the weeks he was in Birmingham. He enrolled in a $10 course in dancing lessons Tuesday nights. He was a silent, "shy" pupil, the instructors remembered. But his shyness here was like his lack of attention when he took his driver's test. It was that he was on guard, shy of contacts in the dancing studio, as he was watching *everything* around him, and not just his driving, when he took his test.

He took care of his person, too, prepared himself for his new life and challenges by having his eyes refracted and glasses made while he was in Birmingham. He was a tidy, prudent fellow, and he spent some of his time with a small sewing kit, mending his socks, stitching up torn places in the crotch of his underwear.

There was only one clue that all was not going well with James Earl and his plans. He found it necessary to go to the doctor for some "anti-depressant" pills. One of the doctors he visited for help was Dr. F. F. Schwartz, who has a clinic at 916 South Twentieth Street in Birmingham where, he says, he treats only "physical diseases," like arthritis. Dr. Schwartz admits that he saw Ray but claims that he cannot reveal what Ray complained of or what treatment he prescribed.

This meant two things. One: if Ray was smuggling dope, in touch with a dope ring as has often been alleged, he would not have needed to walk in off the street to a straight doctor to get pills. Two: he was having trouble with himself. He was not quite so solid a piece of merchandise as he wanted to think. He was having trouble holding himself intact, having trouble keeping himself from fragmenting. For him, by this time, killing King was not a luxury. He needed the mission, he needed the concept of killing King to hold himself together. It gave him the cohesion he was utterly dependent on. It was not just a twisted ideal that led him on. It was a compulsive obsession, and he was having trouble sustaining it over the period of time he had set to accomplish his disparate plans. Killing King was an extremely efficient psychological solution to James Earl Ray's own personal dilemmas; as a solution, it pulled everything together for him. Given the chain of circumstances of his life, killing King had become Ray's destiny. And now he was struggling inside himself to fulfill it.

James Earl Ray was not as "shy," as cool as he seemed.

He was ready to move on by the first week in October. He

was ready for his next step. He left Birmingham on the morning of October 6, 1967, and crossed the border into Mexico on a tourist's permit at Nuevo Laredo on October 7.

---

On Thursday, October 19, 1967, a single man turned up at the desk of the Rio Hotel in Puerto Vallarta, Mexico, registered for a $4.80-a-day room, signed his name "Eric S. Galt," and wrote down his business as "publisher's assistant." As proof of his profession, he carried a portable typewriter.

This was James Earl Ray, ready to go seriously into the pornographic picture business. It was Jimmy, the Raynes boy who was someday going to go straight — going straight in the Raynes perception of what going straight meant, that is, any business in which you don't need a pistol.

He had traded off a TV for the typewriter at a pawnshop just before he crossed the border. Jack, the experienced member of the family in porno, had warned Jimmy when they met at the Atlantic Hotel in Chicago that it was absolutely necessary to conduct correspondence on a typewriter if the business were to look businesslike enough to rope in suckers.

He did not waste any time, unless you count the time he had spent getting to Puerto Vallarta, for Ray had first gone to Acapulco, a place he had visited before. This time he found Acapulco too expensive. "Everybody had their hand out," he said. He seems to have spent a couple of days in Guadalajara, where he claims to have gone to a dentist. It is not impossible that he was seeking more pills for his disturbed inner feelings, not for his teeth. Puerto Vallarta, his next stop, was boosted into a tourist attraction by the fact that Tennessee Williams's *Night of the Iguana* was filmed there with Elizabeth Taylor and Richard Burton. It was not a wholesome movie, and Puerto Vallarta was not developing into a particularly wholesome resort at the time Ray arrived in what had been only a fishing village.

That first evening Ray went into a local joint, a whorehouse and nightclub called the Casa Suzanna, and selected himself a girl. She called herself "La Chilindrina," "The Little Trifle," and Ray told her he was an American writer on vacation whose name was Eric Starvo Galt. If anybody who hadn't actually been a pimp himself knew how to deal with whores, knew that business, knew the codes, knew how a girl operated with her "John," or "trick," understood how she must get her money first, get rid of the guy as quickly as possible, knew all this and much more, it was Ray. He had grown up in those whorehouses in Quincy. He fell in easily and quickly with The Little Trifle and spent the next few nights with her, stayed with her until she went out of town, and then fell in with "Irma," another whore in the Casa Suzanna.

What sex he was getting is another matter. There had been a long hungry spell in prison. Ray had never fallen in with the homosexual world at Jeff City. Someone who knew him there said that Ray's form of sexual satisfaction was "to get his knob polished," a job (fellatio) that was done for money by the water boy who worked his cellblock at Jeff City.

The world of prostitution is changing with changing sexual mores in the straight world. When almost any presentable man with heterosexual intentions can find himself a sexual mate in a "singles" bar, a more exotic custom falls to the whore. She gets the men whose wives won't do the sexual things they want to try, she gets the men who are kinky, who want to spank her, who insist on some form of perverse or abnormal sex. By the 1970's professional whores were telling interviewers that 80 percent of their trade demanded some form of sex from them other than normal intercourse. The "blow job" has become the whore's most efficient method of quickly satisfying her customer, one that gives her more control of the pace of the event. Fellatio has probably become the most common form of purchased orgasm. It would be surprising if Ray had not formed the habit of enjoying it. Both Rife and Jerry Ray say that this is what James Earl Ray enjoyed.

Ray got so he would eat lunch at 3 P.M., usually a hamburger and Pepsi, at the discotheque and go to the beach for a while. Often Irma went with him. One day he stopped the car and got out his Polaroid camera. He asked Irma to pull up her skirts and pose for him. She did. But he didn't like what he got, and tore up the photo. They drove on. Once more he gave her directions on how to pose. But once again he was dissatisfied and once again tore up the photo.

Irma claims that before their romance ended, Ray asked her to marry him, and that she refused. He had begun to drink heavily, so much so that she had occasionally refused to sleep with him. Nobody has as much pride, nobody's feelings can be as easily hurt, as a whore. He told her that he was thinking of settling down in Mexico, that he had looked at a piece of land, that he might swap his Mustang for it. That was a lie — that he would swap his Mustang away for anything. But it is not altogether improbable that he thought of marrying, and perhaps of marrying Irma. They might make a life together, a life and a business, the porno business with him as the manager, promoter, photographer, and her as the model. He liked Mexico. He had been there before. It was one of the options he had seriously considered in Jeff City. There is some evidence that he was considering Mexico even up to the time he killed King. It was only, Jerry Ray has said, when James Earl Ray was driving from Memphis to Atlanta, after he had shot King, that he realized what the public reaction would be, and specifically that the F.B.I. would be called in. It was that news he heard on the Mustang radio that convinced him to make his escape through Canada. He had believed that his act would find wide support in the public.

One night in November he told the girls in the Casa Suzanna, rather dramatically and a little suddenly: "I'm finished with Irma." He moved out of the Hotel Rio and to the Hotel Tropicana, where he soon picked up with "Alicia," a cigarette girl and photographer's aide. The first night he took her home he drank so much he got sick. But he soon had Alicia on the beach in the range finder of his camera. She says they photographed each other. It was with Alicia that he used that cable release, photographed himself with her in some kind of sexual pose.

He got serious with Alicia, too. He gave her $48 with which to rent an apartment for them.

But then, as whores will, she dumped on him. She shoved off to Guadalajara with the $48 and left him a note. She asked him to forgive her. Not that it mattered. He never saw her again. But he was not the kind of fellow to forgive.

There had been one ugly near-thing in Puerto Vallarta, when he was still going around with Irma; it happened at the Casa Suzanna when six men, four black and two white, sat at a table near Ray and Irma. They were American sailors. They got noisy, drunk. Ray got hot.

"I hate niggers," he told Irma, along with many other racial slurs. He jumped up and went over to the table where the sailors were. He said something to one of the black men; Irma did not hear what. He came back to his chair muttering. Suddenly, he left the room, came back a few minutes later. "Feel my pocket," he told her. She felt a pistol. "I'm going to *kill* them," he told her. But he didn't. The black man he had spoken to came over and said something — it must have been conciliatory — to Ray, and he led his companions out of the place. Ray wanted to follow them, but Irma told him it was about the time the police came on their nightly rounds. He kept his seat.

There had been some good times in Mexico, some surcease from the pressure he otherwise almost constantly felt to keep himself emotionally intact, of a piece. But the pressure was still there, the responsibility of bringing off the big assignment he had set for himself, and keeping the rest of his life in some equilibrium.

He complained to Irma practically the whole time he knew her about tiredness, and about having headaches.

A few days after Alicia split, Ray left Mexico, probably around November 16 or 17, 1967. He went from Mexico to Los Angeles, driving the white Mustang, and he turned up in Los Angeles on November 18, 1967.

# Chapter 24

On November 19, 1967, James Earl Ray, using his Eric S. Galt alias, rented Apartment Six at 1535 North Serrano Avenue in Los Angeles.

*Los Angeles?*

Why on earth did Ray go there, so far from "King country"? If he was set on killing King, why didn't he go ahead and do it? Nearly seven months had passed since Ray rode that bread truck through the Jeff City gate to freedom, and King had been an easy target in public a hundred times since then.

What is wrong with those questions is that they assume James Earl Ray was operating on rational lines. James Earl Ray would kill Martin Luther King when he, Ray, was ready, not when Martin Luther King was ready. The murder was still altogether inside Ray's head, as it had been ever since

Jeff City. Ray would kill King when the act became an over-whelming emotional imperative — when things had reached the point when he had to kill King to keep himself intact. To Ray, King was an abstraction, almost an *im*personality. In Ray's mind, King's image was still undeveloped, as if it were a latent image on a piece of chemically sensitive photographic paper. The image was there in complete detail, but it would not take shape, define itself, until it had undergone chemical treatment, until it had been in the developing pan for a while, until it had set in the fixative. It was impossible to predict what set of circumstances would set off these chemical processes in Ray's mind.

There is no doubt but that Ray knew he was a disturbed and anxious person when he arrived in Los Angeles. By this time he was less in control of himself than he had ever been since he escaped from Jeff City. He felt this lack of control, worried about it, tried to do something about it in his way. One aspect of his ambitiousness, his striving to be somebody, was that he wanted to cure himself.

----

Ray first became interested in self-help in Jeff City. Somebody in the commissary there, another convict, had put him on to "self-hypnosis," one of those therapies that lie in the shadowland between ethical medical practice and quackery. Ray carried two or three paperbound books on the subject with him; indeed, they were found in his belongings in a London hotel after his capture.

One of the books that Ray carried with him was *Psycho-cybernetics*, by Dr. Maxwell Maltz, a plastic surgeon who constructed a theory of "self-image" from his experience in changing faces surgically. The book's dust jacket promises: "A new way to GET MORE LIVING OUT OF LIFE," and Dr. Maltz explains his concept this way: "Personality" has "a face." If it "remained scarred, distorted, 'ugly,' or inferior, the person himself acted out this role in his behavior. . . . If this 'face of personality,' could be reconstructed, if old emotional scars could be removed, then the person himself changed."

There is an almost infinitely bitter irony — and social tragedy — in James Earl Ray's poring over this book, reading it time and again, studying for example the chapter, "How to Remove Emotional Scars and Give Yourself 'An Emotional Face-Lift.'" Ray would have read Dr. Maltz's warning against "emotional calluses," have read about those people who "cannot get close to anyone because they will not trust anyone. . . . They always have their defenses up. To prevent further rejection and pain, they attack first." This kind of person, Dr. Maltz said, "has an image of the world in which he lives as a hostile place. . . . Frustration, aggression and loneliness are the price he pays."

The deep problem is "low self-esteem," and the person who has that problem needs to "build it up." "Try *giving* affection, love, approval, acceptance, understanding to other people," Dr. Maltz goes on, but he does not tell his readers exactly how to do that. His one practical, if it is that, suggestion is to "Relax Away Emotional Hurts," as a subchapter heading reads. "Scientific experiments have shown that it is absolutely impossible to feel fear, anger, anxiety or negative emotions of any kind while the muscles of the body are kept perfectly relaxed," Dr. Maltz observes. That was practically a prescription for hypnosis and Ray, with his characteristic ambition, wanted to learn to do hypnosis for himself by himself.

How seriously and literally Ray took Dr. Maltz's teachings is shown by what Ray did a few days after he reached Los Angeles. On November 27, 1967, Ray turned up in the office of Dr. Mark Freeman, a psychologist who practiced at 9952 Santa Monica Boulevard in Beverly Hills. As Dr. Freeman remembers it, Ray told him that he wanted to "overcome his shyness, gain social confidence, and learn self-hypnosis so that he could relax, sleep better, and remember things better."

As he does with most things where he is vulnerable, Ray tends to toss off his efforts to seek help. "I also took a course in hypnosis while in L.A.," he wrote for Huie. "I had read a lot about it in prison on how it was used in dintristry and medicine . . ." But how seriously he took what he was doing at the time is shown by one fact above all: he gave Dr. Freeman his real name, James Earl Ray. He did not do this solely because he thought he might give his real name anyway under hypnosis. It was more subtle than that; it was a plea for help, and help for the real person, not for Eric Galt, nor help for any one of the other identities he tried to create for himself. No, in Los Angeles, when he went to Dr. Freeman, he wanted help for James Earl Ray.

Exactly what help he expected is difficult to say. Did he want the kind of help that he had read about in Dr. Maltz's book? Or did he expect simply to find some peace with himself — "to sleep better," as he told Dr. Freeman? And what did he mean when he told Dr. Freeman that he wanted to "remember things better"?

Whatever it was Ray hoped for, he did find himself in a relationship with Dr. Freeman that seemed to be mutually enjoyable. Dr. Freeman *liked* Ray. "This fellow really wanted to improve his mind," Dr. Freeman, who still practices in Los Angeles, told me. "He had an awe of learning. He had a bent for reading. He didn't fight hypnosis. He learned something.

"You've got to keep in mind that I get a lot of *angry* people around here. A lot of the people who come to me want to teach *me* how to do it. I get a lot of rough stuff around here. I mean psychotic, that stuff. But I couldn't pick up on any of that with Ray. He made a favorable impression on me. He was a good pupil. I'd show him how to go under, and pretty soon he'd be lying on the couch on his back and start talking. I taught him eye fixation, bodily relaxation, how to open himself to suggestion. I gave him lots of positive feelings of confidence."

Ray went to Dr. Freeman five times. That in itself is a tribute to Dr. Freeman, to how comfortable he was able to make Ray, usually a highly suspicious person, feel. The subject matter of Ray's talk proves he had learned to have confidence in Dr. Freeman. In fact, he got around to telling Dr. Freeman about his uncle Earl, one of the most meaningful people in Ray's life. Dr. Freeman also remembers that Ray told him that he, Ray, didn't like blacks. Dr. Freeman doesn't know why Ray didn't come back, and Ray himself has never offered a reason. It may be that Ray didn't return just because the relationship had become too close, that it had opened up avenues of memories and feeling that Ray did not want opened.

Ray told Huie that he went to as many as eight different

psychologists in Los Angeles, but the only other one that Ray is known to have consulted was far less successful with Ray than Dr. Freeman. Weeks later, on January 4, 1968, Ray kept an appointment with Reverend Xavier von Koss, at 16010 Crenshaw Boulevard, Los Angeles. Von Koss thought of himself as "an internationally-recognized authority on hypnosis and self-hypnosis." Von Koss claims to remember Ray well, remembers that Ray did know all the literature of the self-hypnosis field, could talk about the methods, even appeared to be something of a self-taught expert.

But the two of them didn't strike it off. Von Koss tried to tell Ray "that he must work hard, that he must go to night school, that he must construct a settled-down life." But as he lectured Ray in this fashion he could "feel a wall rising between us. I lost him." He concluded that Ray had a "strong subconscious resistance" to him. Ray never went back.

But Ray still needed help. He was no less disturbed. He began to drink too much, and became a habitué of a bar where he drank several vodkas every night. One person who knew Ray in Los Angeles reported that Ray "lived on aspirin when he was here." What is more telling is the observation somewhere made that he was frequently "drowsy." The question of whether Ray used drugs, and which ones and how often, is something that cannot be answered until he himself talks about it. The people who knew him in Mexico, where it was reported that he drank heavily, also said he smoked marijuana. A hypodermic syringe was found in his hotel room in London after his capture, leaving little doubt that he was using drugs then or earlier. And of course Ray not only sold but took drugs in Jeff City. It is certainly a possibility that he was using drugs while in Los Angeles.

Nevertheless, Ray was trying to keep up that incredible program of vocational and social self-improvement that he had launched himself upon in Canada. On December 5, 1967, he put down five $20 bills as a deposit on a $465 rumba course at the National Dance Studios at 2026 Pacific Avenue in Long Beach. The teachers found him "shy" and uncommunicative. "One time I talked to him for an hour and tried to break him down," said one of the instructresses. "Every time the conversation got personal he became quiet. He was a clam." Another noticed that he trembled whenever he held her close. "He was awkward and a poor dancer," she said. But he stuck to the course until February 12, 1968. On January 15, 1968, he signed up for a $220 course at the International School of Bartending, 2125 Sunset Boulevard, which Ray attended until he graduated on March 2.

He went about his pornographic business. He subscribed to a dollar-a-month telephone answering service and placed on February 2 the first of several ads, this one in the "underground" Los Angeles *Free Press:*

"SINGLE MALE. cauc. 36 yrs. 5'11" 70 lbs. Digs Fr. Cult. Desires discreet meeting with passionate married female for mutual enjoyment and/or female for swing session. Apt. furnished. Will ex photo. Write Eric S."

French culture is a euphemism for oral sex. To fulfill possible requests for his photo, he took a dozen pictures of himself with his Polaroid. Around the middle of February, Ray answered an ad by the Swingers Club of Downey, California, asked for the list of six girls they offered for a dollar, and then wrote each of them, enclosing a photo.

He got a nibble and replied:

"Dear Miss: I think I share most of your interests, with emphasis on Fr. Cult. And swing sessions. I've just returned from Mexico after five yrs. and the few females I've met don't go for the swing parties & it takes two to swing. The same routine gets boring, don't you think? Will close till I hear from you. I'll be 36 yrs."

He was willing to go into more exotic variations than "French culture." In February, while busy with his advertisements and his photos, he wrote off for a pair of Japanese handcuffs, presumably for some sado-masochistic porno photos, and he ordered a chemical which turned ordinary plate glass into a two-way mirror, a peep show device. No longer satisfied with the sex manuals he had bought in Canada, he bought yet more of them in Los Angeles.

As far as anyone knows, nothing ever came of Ray's porno activities in Los Angeles. There is no evidence that he ever actually took or sold any pornographic photos there. When the bartending school offered him a job, he turned it down. All of these lessons and advertisements were merely preparation for his future life.

———

The main reason James Earl Ray didn't go ahead and kill King immediately after his stay in Mexico is that he was preoccupied, if not obsessed, with the presidential candidacy of George C. Wallace. It even seems possible that it was to help Wallace that Ray left Mexico when he did. At that moment, in November, 1967, Wallace supporters in California were making a hectic effort to place Wallace's name on the California ballot. This required getting ten thousand signatures on a petition. Ray took an apartment on November 19, the day after he arrived from Mexico, at 1535 North Serrano Avenue, and got a telephone, when phones were not easy to get quickly, by telling the phone company that he was a campaign worker for Wallace.

The deadline for the Wallace petition was January 1, 1968, and by December 15, 1967, Ray was well known at Wallace headquarters in North Hollywood — so well known that some who saw him thought he was an employee of the Wallace campaign. The knowledge of Ray's Wallace work came to light in a roundabout way. After he had been in Los Angeles a while, Ray began to hang out in the Sultan bar next door to the St. Francis Hotel.

There he struck up a friendship with Marie Martin, a cocktail waitress. Marie introduced him to her cousin, Rita Stein, a go-go dancer, and to Rita's brother, Charles Stein, a man with a long and sordid police record for offenses such as pandering.

Rita asked Ray if he would drive to New Orleans and bring her children back to L.A. and take Charlie along. Ray agreed.

At first, Rita had hesitated to introduce her brother to Ray. She was afraid the two of them wouldn't hit it off. She got a picture of Ray, a tight, close-mouthed fellow, and saw how different he was from Charlie, a bearded fellow who ran to fat and believed in such things as flying saucers. But these differences turned out to be superficial, amounted to nothing compared to what the two men shared — their background in crime and in the sleazy world of prostitution.

A controversy has arisen over what Ray was actually up to, why he was willing to make the trip, and whether he might have had other business in New Orleans. There has been speculation that he was hauling drugs from New Orleans to Los Angeles, and that he made several trips. That is possible. It would not have been hard for Ray, with his criminal background, to have made the contacts. But there are reasons why he would not have gone into the drug business even as a deliveryman, the same reasons he did not want to commit robbery, or use his pistol. He did not want to be caught, and the drug underworld is full of informers. Ray wanted to stay free for his own good reasons. The deep net the F.B.I. cast over Ray's movements in New Orleans turned up nothing, and there is no evidence he ever delivered or sold drugs in the months that he was free.

One better reason Ray agreed to make the trip was politics. When he agreed to take his white Mustang across the country, Ray laid a condition on the Steins and Marie Martin: if he went to New Orleans, they would have to go with him to Wallace headquarters and sign the Wallace petition. Well, they didn't give a shit about politics, one way or the other, and they went with Ray and signed the petition. It was then that they noticed that Ray was well known in the North Hollywood office. "I figured Ray was getting paid for votes," said Stein.

Another reason Ray may have agreed to make the New Orleans trip, and it is an emotionally persuasive one, is that he made it simply for the reason Rita had asked him to make it, for the children, to unite them with their mother. That would have been perfectly in keeping with his deepest feelings, fitted with the fantasies he had in Jeff City about children, about running an orphanage, about doing something for children who were separated from their parents. He was going around himself, in that fantasy he used to have in Jeff

City, to pick up the children for that orphanage he dreamed of running someday.

The two men left Los Angeles on December 15 and returned with Rita's children on December 21.

At any rate the historical function of Stein, his sister and Marie Martin is to confirm Ray's deep commitment to Wallace; and Wallace meant a great deal to Ray. Ray had dreamed that there might be other people who felt as he did about black people and about King. He had hoped there were many such people. He had told himself that there were people who would support what he intended to do to King. Wallace's candidacy and Wallace's constituency proved to Ray, as Ray saw it, that Ray had a constituency too.

———

Ray's passion for Wallace nearly got him into bad trouble in Los Angeles. He got in a scrape, and the wonder is that somebody didn't call the cops. In December Ray began to drink at a place called the Rabbit's Foot Club, 5623 Hollywood Boulevard. He parked his white Mustang with its Alabama license plate outside until people in the bar began to think he was flaunting what they assumed was his home state. Inside the bar he "preached Wallace for President" in a running argument with Jim Morison, the bartender. One night in late December, just as the deadline for signatures on the Wallace petition was nearing and tension must have been high in Ray's mind, he got into an argument at the Rabbit's Foot that turned into a brawl. Ray wrote about it for Huie:

... On this particular nite they was someone sitting next to me who talked about 30 minutes without stopping about the state of the world. Their was also a young girl sitting on the other side of me. I mite of told the guy who was talking to me where I was from as I think he ask me, or she mite have seen my car with the Alabama license on it. Anyhow when the conversationlist left she started by asking me how come they deny colors their rights in Alabama. I think I ask her if she had ever been there or something like that and walked out. Their was two guys next to her and when I went out they must of followed me.... Anyhow the big one grab me from behind and pulled my coat over my arms (I had a suit on) the shorter one started hitting and asking for my money. He pulled my watch off I jerked away (as I was scared police would show up) but he held on to my coat and guess he still has it. I ran across the street to the car but couldn't get in as the keys were in my coat. I had a 38 under the seat so maybe it was just as well.

Ray's work for the Wallace campaign in California sharpened his political sensibilities. At some point (the evidence suggests that it was late December) there begins to be a relationship not only between what Wallace did and Ray did but also between what Wallace did, Martin Luther King did, and Ray did. When Ray had been in Birmingham, according to Jerry, he had Wallace in the front of his mind. Wallace was still his main political interest through his early weeks in Los Angeles. In late December Ray began to take steps that showed he was again focusing on King. He came to believe that killing King would help Wallace to become President. He did not do anything precipitately. The image of King was emerging again slowly.

One day in late December he called the local office of the John Birch Society, the conservative political organization. He told them he wanted to know whom to write about emigrating to Rhodesia. The Birch Society gave Ray the address of the American South African Council in Washington, D.C. Ray wrote the Council on December 28, 1967:

Dear Sir: I recently read an article in the L.A. *Times* on your council. . . . My reason for writing is that I am considering immigrating to Rhodesia. However, there are a couple of legal questions involved.

1. The U.S. Government will not issue a passport for travel to Rhodesia.

2. Would their be any way to enter Rhodesia legally (from the Rhodesian Government point of view?)

I would appreciate any information you could give me on the above subject or any other information on Rhodesia.

> Sincerely,
> ERIC S. GALT

The Council wrote back to Ray that it did not handle such matters, but a Rhodesian government representative agreed that it might have been difficult for the United States to extradite Ray if he had reached that country. "I thought I could get to Africa and serve two or three years in one of those mercenary armies, and those people wouldn't send me back," Ray later told one of his attorneys.

The event that seems to have caused Ray to take the step about Rhodesia was an announcement by Martin Luther King on December 4 that he and his organization, the Southern Christian Leadership Conference, were going to stage a Poor People's March on Washington on April 20, 1968. King in 1967 was still a heroic, God-like, deeply revered man among black people, but his influence as a tactical leader of the racial movement had actually been declining since 1964.

The racial movement that grew out of the Montgomery

bus boycott of 1955 and the first sit-ins in Greensboro, North Carolina, in 1960, was never an army of squads, platoons, companies, or battalions. There were four organizations of black people that mattered — the Southern Christian Leadership Conference, the Student Non-violent Coordinating Committee, CORE, and the National Association for the Advancement of Colored People, but of them only the NAACP had a significant membership base. The others were only cadres, in some instances (as with SNCC) a dozen or two students.

The struggle between these organizations during the late 1950's and the early 1960's was not so much a struggle for control as it was for the right to set the *tempo* and *direction* of the movement.

The peak of King's influence came with the great street demonstrations in Birmingham in 1963, when the black people marched bravely against high-pressure fire hoses so strong that the torrents tore the bark from trees in the city parks. It was the climax of the social movement to which Congress responded — almost had to respond — by passing the 1964 Civil Rights Act. The triumph of the movement, as some of its leaders saw the possibility, was to be the conquest of the state of Mississippi in the summer of 1964. King had more or less stayed out of Mississippi, and that racial frontier was to be penetrated by a guerrilla army of white college students recruited from across the nation. The leadership was to come from the young, militant, and (more than King) ideological SNCC cadre. It was not an unalloyed success, that 1964 summer. At the end of it the SNCC group drew up and issued a "position paper," in which SNCC concluded that its members could never again work in tandem with whites. This was the beginning of Black Power. By 1965 Stokely Carmichael took over the leadership of SNCC, beginning that fall his speeches to black college students advocating and insisting on separatism and a greater militancy. His appeal was more successful than anyone had expected, and from that moment on King was no longer The Point of the racial movement. Black Power quickly became black anger; nonviolence was no longer an acceptable tactic for young black Americans. They were determined never again to present their bodies passively to white men. King never regained the unchallenged leadership of the racial movement, but he made several attempts. The Poor People's March of 1968 was to be one of them.

---

The effort by King to revitalize himself as a black leader ironically led Ray to take up again his plans for murder. On February 12 King announced that in order to organize the Poor People's March in Alabama, he was himself going to Birmingham and Selma.

From this point on, cause and effect between Ray's movements and King's movements is clear.

On February 13, the day after King said he was going to Alabama, James Earl Ray took his car to a Los Angeles service station to have it serviced.

The next day, February 14, Ray swapped his console TV (on the back of which he had written "Martin Luther Coon") for Rita Stein's portable TV.

On February 19 Ray called a Los Angeles surgeon to make a date to get his nose bobbed. He had always thought his nose his most prominent identifying feature. The surgeon,

Dr. Russell C. Hadley, 7080 Hollywood Boulevard, gave Ray an appointment for an operation that is noted in Dr. Hadley's records as "reduction of prominent nasal tip." On March 5 the operation was done under a local anesthetic in Dr. Hadley's office.

Ray wanted his nose bobbed to help his disguise because, he said, he expected to be on the F.B.I.'s Top Ten Wanted list soon.

Ray returned on March 7 to have a nasal pack removed and on March 11 to have the sutures taken out. "Healing well," noted Dr. Hadley, and he asked Ray to return in six weeks. However, six weeks later Ray was not in a situation where he could return to Los Angeles.

Ray had even tried to outsmart Dr. Hadley. "After he had finished," wrote Ray, "I went back to the hotel room and while the nose was still numb I removed the tape and pushed the nose to the other side and down to change the way the doctor had shaped it in case he remembered me. . . ."

---

On March 16 Martin Luther King came to Los Angeles. During the day he held a press conference at the Disneyland Hotel at Anaheim, and that night he spoke to the California Democratic Council's state convention. King talked politics, talked tough politics. He called on the convention to defeat President Lyndon Johnson, said he thought Senator Eugene McCarthy, whom the convention had just endorsed, was a good man, and also praised Bobby Kennedy. "We must end the war in Vietnam," King said. "I must say, I'm very disappointed in Mr. Johnson, and I think a change is absolutely necessary." He talked about his "spring demonstrations" in

Washington and promised that he might lead demonstrations at the national Democratic convention in Chicago.

Excerpts from King's talk — King's image — were carried that night in Los Angeles on all three of its network affiliate TV stations. Ray, an inveterate watcher of TV news, is almost certain to have seen on his home screen the face that had galvanized him when he'd seen it on the cellblock TV at Jeff City. He must have been acutely aware of King's proximity.

The next morning Ray left Los Angeles — but not before he had dropped off a change-of-address card at the post office. He asked that his mail be sent to Atlanta. Ray was on his way to stalk and kill a man, but he still didn't want to miss the last of his correspondence lessons in locksmithing.

# Chapter 25

Now that James Earl Ray had settled it in his mind that he was going to kill Martin Luther King, he felt better, more pulled together, sharper, more focused, better able to *concentrate* on the tasks at hand.

These were tactical. He had in front of him the planning of a small military operation. He had to decide where he was going to kill King and how. Ray was determined to make a clean getaway. That meant laying out an area, making sure he had an escape route. He had to buy a gun. It would have to be accurate at long distance if he was to have time to get away from the scene, and it would have to be deadly, powerful; he might have time for only one shot. He would need a base from which to conduct his one-man operation, and he chose it even before he left Los Angeles. He left as his forwarding address: General Delivery, Atlanta, Georgia. That was where King lived, had his office, his church.

But Ray did not drive directly there from Los Angeles. He went 180 miles out of his way to drop off some clothes for Rita Stein's children in New Orleans. Murder was on his mind, but he still had time to do something for a child.

While Ray was in New Orleans, the newspapers there announced that King was going to be in Selma, Alabama, on March 22; he was recruiting in Alabama for the Poor People's March. On March 22, Ray appeared in Selma, took a room at the Flamingo Motel, near the famous Edmund Pettus Bridge where civil rights marchers had been brutally beaten by Alabama state police in 1965. But King was delayed in the small Alabama town of Camden, where he spent the night.

Ray did not wait. He drove on to Atlanta on the twenty-third where he registered at one of those seedy rooming houses that were his normal habitat. This one was at 113 Fourteenth Street North East, near the intersection of Peachtree and Fourteenth, the Times Square of a run-down section of Atlanta that was both "combat zone" and hippie community, a mixture of cheap bars and "head shops." Jimmy Garner, owner of the rooming house, gave Ray Room No. 2 on the ground floor, and Ray paid him $10.50, a week's rent. Ray moved in his portable TV, and stocked himself for light housekeeping with a box of Nabisco crackers, a can of Carnation milk, a jar of instant coffee, sugar, an electric cup to heat water, a bottle of French salad dressing, a package of frozen lima beans and a tin of ground pepper.

Ray spent four days in Atlanta. He fixed the locations of the Southern Christian Leadership Conference (King's office), the Ebenezer Baptist Church (King's church), and King's home. He circled these sites on a map of Atlanta which he left behind in the rooming house (and from which the F.B.I. would obtain some clear fingerprints of their suspect). Ray circled one other site on the map, a housing project near the Georgia state capitol building, across town from the rooming house. He selected this as the place to leave behind his white Mustang when the time came. The parking lot of Capitol Homes was a place where his car would not be immediately noticed by police.

He had now answered the question, Where? That had taken four days.

———

On March 27, Ray was in Birmingham, Alabama, 150 miles from Atlanta, shopping for his murder weapon — Birmingham for the same reason he had gone there in the first place to get his car, his driver's license, his "I.D.," because he believed that if he were a "citizen" of Alabama, George Wallace would somehow help him out. Already he had some idea of what he wanted when he turned up at the Gun Rack in Birmingham and asked the clerk, Clyde Manasco, to see a Remington .243 caliber rifle. Ray asked so many questions about the rifle that Manasco's boss, Quentin Davis, stepped in to help. Ray wanted to know about trajectory: How much would a bullet drop in a hundred yards, in two hundred yards?

Ray asked about telescopic sights, and knew the brand names of some of them. Davis offered at one point to hand Ray a rifle, but Ray shunned it, not eager to place his fingerprints on the weapon. Davis tried to press Ray to buy a Remington 30.06 ("thirty-ought-six"). Ray hesitated, then replied: "No, it's too expensive." As Ray got ready to leave, Davis gave him some literature on weapons, including a ballistics chart and a booklet on Redfield scopes.

Two days later Ray appeared at the Long-Lewis hardware store in Bessemer, a working-class suburb of Birmingham, and asked John Kopp, a salesman, for information about high-powered rifles. Kopp offered to show Ray a 30.30 ("thirty-thirty") but Ray said he wanted something more powerful than that. Once again Ray asked about trajectories and asked how long it would take to get a sight mounted. As he left the store he glanced up at a mounted moose head. "I once tried to bring down a moose but I missed," Ray told Kopp. But to Kopp, Ray did not look like a man who had ever been in open country.

At 2 P.M. that afternoon (March 29), Ray turned up at the Aeromarine Supply Company, a large sporting goods complex opposite the Birmingham airport. Aeromarine has one of the largest selections of rifles, pistols and ammunition in the South.

Ray was waited on by Hugh Baker. By this time, Ray seemed to know more about the kind of lethal merchandise he wanted. He asked Baker to see a Remington Gamemaster .243 caliber, looked at it, and asked to see one or two others, then decided on the .243 and asked Baker for a scope to fit it. Baker showed him a Redfield 2 x 7 power variable scope. Ray asked what the total price would be, for scope and rifle, Baker figured it out, Ray said he'd take them, and Baker at once went to work attaching the scope to the rifle. While all this was going on, a bystander in the store asked Ray where he was going to use such a powerful weapon. Oh, he was going hunting with his brother in Wisconsin, Ray answered. The bystander smelled alcohol on Ray's breath.

When the scope was fitted, Ray selected some cartridges, signed the name Harvey Lowmyer on the sales slip, gave his address as 1807 South Eleventh Street, Birmingham, paid his bill and left with his purchases under his arm.

But at about five that afternoon Ray called to say he wanted to exchange the .243. His brother had told him he needed a heavier gun. Wood, son of the owner, answered, and told Ray he would have to come in the next morning. Saturday morning, March 30, Ray arrived at Aeromarine at nine, and selected a Remington Gamemaster 760 30.06 caliber rifle. It was Saturday, Wood was busy, and he told Ray he couldn't change the sight that minute, to come back at three in the afternoon when he would be sure to have it done. Ray returned at three, bought new ammunition, took the new rifle. Wood asked him why he changed. That first rifle will kill anything in Alabama, Wood said. "I'm going to hunt in Wisconsin," Ray replied.

The pains Ray took in studying weapons, sights and ammunition paid off — at least for his purposes. He ended up with what was very nearly ideal armament for an assassin.

As for the scope, the Redfield 2 x 7 had "a wide power range to handle almost every hunting situation," the company says, "wide enough field of view for woods or tracking moving animals, good compromise power for varminting." Its lenses are treated in a magnesium fluoride film which gives greater visibility *at late dusk*.

The Gamemaster comes already drilled and tapped for

scope mounts, and Wood set it for Ray at its maximum magnification, 7-power. This means that the object viewed through the scope would appear to be seven times closer than it was to the naked eye. The scope made the distance Ray fired when he used the weapon in Memphis appear to be *less than thirty feet away.*

As for the rifle, the Gamemaster 760 is "the fastest hand-operated big game rifle made," Remington claims. It is a pump action rifle. Ray could fire a second shot without having to take his eye from the sight or his finger from the trigger. The Gamemaster "actually aides the shooter in staying on-target during second- and third-shot situations. The shooter pumps the fore-end straight back in a fast, comfortable move. His finger stays on the trigger as he works the pump action for additional shots." It is powerful, the only pump action rifle available for the heavy 30.06 ammo Ray bought; it is able to handle that size ammunition because it has a "super-strong artillery-type bolt."

As for the ammunition, the bullets Ray finally bought weighed twice as much as those he had selected at Aeromarine the day before. They travel 2,670 feet per second at 100 yards and drop less than .01 inch in that distance. Their knock-down power is *2,370 foot-pounds at 100 yards.*

At sixty-eight yards, the distance the bullet traveled that killed King, it would have killed him if it had hit him *anywhere* in the head, the chest or the stomach, and if it had hit him in the thigh or groin King would almost certainly have died from shock and loss of blood.

On that Saturday afternoon, Ray's bill at Aeromarine came to $265.85. He paid and left.

While Ray was buying his rifle, Martin Luther King was in Memphis leading — or trying to lead — a strike of municipal garbage workers, most of whom were black.

For some reason that was probably only accidental, Memphis had avoided longer than most southern cities its confrontation with the rising black racial movement. Memphis is a large city, a very large one by southern standards, actually has more people within its city limits than New Orleans or Atlanta. It was, in 1968, very much Old South — not just the marketing center for west Tennessee, northern Mississippi and eastern Arkansas, but also the spiritual and cultural capital of the Mississippi Delta. In the cities of the South during the 1950's and 1960's, racial change was like death — nobody ever expected it to happen to *him*. When the confrontation came to Memphis, it was just as if there had not already been the riots in Little Rock, in Birmingham, in Jackson and Greenwood, Mississippi, in Albany, Georgia, in Danville, Virginia, and in both Knoxville and Chattanooga, Tennessee.

"Why, they're still playing Mah-Jongg in Memphis," one of its expatriate sons told me at the time of the garbage strike.

When the garbage men walked out on February 12, 1968, the mayor and city leaders of Memphis made little if any attempt to deal realistically with the workers' demands. It became apparent that the strike was going to turn into the racial confrontation Memphis had so long avoided. The city has one of the highest percentages of black population of any city in the South, more than 40 percent, and the black community of Memphis was obviously placing its sympathy with the strikers.

A group of Black leaders, most of them preachers, turned to King for help, and he went to Memphis on March 18, fresh from the talk in Los Angeles that had triggered Ray.

King spoke that night in Memphis to an enthusiastic crowd. He was pleased with his reception. It seemed to be like the old times of 1963 and 1964, and he agreed to return to the city on March 22 to lead a march. But a freak snowstorm on the twenty-second caused the march to be called off. It was rescheduled for March 28.

There was something frighteningly *wrong* about the demonstration on March 28. It got out of hand. It turned into a small riot. King and his men lost control of what went on. They could not handle some of the young Memphis blacks, particularly a group called The Invaders. There was violence and looting. King was despondent that night, and he made arrangements to meet the next day in his motel room with the leaders of The Invaders. They met at 3:00 P.M.

The Invaders were tough, angry, militant, looking for trouble. Indeed, they asked King for money, insisted in a rather ugly way that they had a right to some of the money King had raised for his SCLC. But King balked. He wanted them to promise not to loot, to be nonviolent. But at that The Invaders balked. It was a standoff. It was *King's* confrontation, probably one of the most disheartening moments in his career as a Black leader. Even more despondent than he had been earlier in the day, King flew back to Atlanta late in the afternoon — about the time that Ray was telling the people at Aeromarine that he wanted that bigger, more powerful rifle.

The next day, Saturday, March 30, King and his associates met at SCLC headquarters in Atlanta to consider whether King would return to Memphis, whether he should continue to identify himself with the garbage strike. On Monday, April 1, King announced that he was going to return to Memphis, and he did so on Wednesday, April 3, arriving in Memphis at 10:33 A.M.

He went directly to the Lorraine Motel.

King was not feeling well. He was still deeply depressed about the Memphis situation. He was supposed to speak that night at a rally, at the Mason Temple, but he sent Ralph Abernathy, his lieutenant. The rally did not go well. Abernathy called from the hall to ask King to come and King reluctantly went.

At first, as he began to talk, King spoke directly to the twelve hundred people in the Mason Temple. He had done this a hundred times or more — raised up the hopes and the courage of people, brought them to the point where they would go out on the street with him. "Yes," he said with the warm assurance that was so characteristic of him. "Yes, there's going to be a march. I'm going to lead the march on Monday."

But having said that, having done his duty to the moment and its local imperatives, his mood changed. His voice became a song of lamentation, elegiac. He recalled how a "demented woman" in Harlem had tried to and had almost succeeded in taking his life in 1958. She had stabbed him in the chest. The tip of the knife came so close to his aorta that the doctors had told him that "if I had sneezed I would have been a dead man."

As he went on, his voice began to cry out over the heads of

the people in the Mason Temple, as if he had assembled in his mind's eye every face he had ever spoken to, a vast, limitless sea of faces — his people.

"I don't know what will happen now," he said, almost sobbing. "Like anybody I would like to live a long life. But I'm not concerned about that now. I'm not fearing any man. I have been to the mountain top. Mine eyes have seen the glory . . ."

King was not the only new arrival in Memphis. At the very moment King was speaking at the Mason Temple, a man who signed the register as "Eric S. Galt" took Room 34 at the New Rebel Motel at 3466 Lamar Avenue.

This was James Earl Ray. He had come to Memphis to murder King.

After he had bought his rifle in Birmingham, Ray had returned to Atlanta. Early on Monday morning, April 1, he had taken his dirty clothes to the Piedmont Laundry at 1168 Peachtree Street. He was remembered there because he gave detailed instructions about how his laundry should be done.

April 1 was the same day King publicly announced he was going back to Memphis on April third. Sometime, within a few hours after that announcement, Ray made his decision to be in Memphis when King got there.

"Jimmy didn't know he was going to Memphis until a couple of days before," Jerry Ray told me. "When he got there, it just clicked for him."

Ray drove to Memphis in the white Mustang. He stopped along the route at a place that seems from his description to have been Corinth, Mississippi, the site of the Civil War

Battle of Shiloh. Somewhere near Corinth, he drove off the highway to a secluded spot and test-fired his rifle. He had to do this to align the sight. Even though the people at Aeromarine had set the Redfield sight, it was still necessary to fire the rifle to make sure it had no idiosyncrasies, and that if it did these were corrected by making adjustments to the sight.

He seems to have spent the night of April 2 in a motel in northern Mississippi, near Memphis. Ray has said that he did that. It is probable, logical, that he spent the day of April 3 laying out the Lorraine Motel and the neighborhood around it, for that is the day King registered at the Lorraine.

Any difficulty Ray may have had in fixing the exact spot where King was to be found in Memphis was settled when, on the nightly news broadcasts of April third, Memphis TV stations carried a picture of King standing on the second-story balcony of the Lorraine in front of his room. The number "306" was plain. The next morning's *Commercial Appeal,* a copy of which was later found in Ray's belongings, also carried a photo of King on the Lorraine balcony.

---

In the twelve months since his escape from Jeff City, Jimmy had been in regular touch with Jerry. He had called Jerry as often as three or four times a month, says Jerry. It was almost the only contact James Earl Ray had with anyone who knew his real identity. He liked to talk with Jerry. He still kidded Jerry, just as he had done ever since they were boys in Ewing.

And now he made one last call from Memphis. It seems to have been on the morning of April 4. Jerry was in Chicago, working at a suburban country club as a night watchman. It was in the morning, Jerry's off-time, that Jimmy phoned.

"I don't know where he was in Memphis when he called," says Jerry. "I don't think it was on the road. There wasn't any sound of cars. It wasn't a tavern, no sound of voices, just his voice and my voice. I guess he talked about two minutes. He always kept it under that three-minute limit, I know that.

"Usually when he called, he talked, I talked. But not this time! If I tried to tell him anything, he wouldn't let me. He wasn't wanting any jokes or small talk that day. He was excited and all worked up. What he said was:

" 'Jerry, tomorrow it will all be over. I might not see you and Jack for a while. But don't worry about me. I'll be all right! Big Nigger has had it!' "

The night of April 3, the night clerk at the Rebel Motel noticed that the lights were on in Room 34 at 10:00 P.M. They were still on when he checked at midnight. They were still on when he checked at four in the morning.

---

The balcony of King's room looked out across a lot strewn with trash and garbage and up to the back of a row of old two-story brick buildings that faced Main Street. They made up the 400 block, a point where Main Street turned from its downtown respectability to seedy cafes, and flea-bitten rooming houses and small stores. One of the commercial establishments was a jukebox repair store, Canipe Amusement Company. Above Canipe's, on the second floor, at 422½ Main Street, Mrs. Bessie Brewer ran a rooming house. The windows of Mrs. Brewer's rooms looked down on the Lorraine.

At about 3:15 P.M. on Thursday afternoon, April 4, a man who called himself John Willard (and who was James Earl Ray) appeared at the top of the stairs where Mrs. Brewer had her office and said he wanted a room. Mrs. Brewer had her hair in curlers that afternoon. Everything is relative, and by Mrs. Brewer's standards Ray was well dressed. He wore a dark suit with a tie. A dirty T-shirt and a pair of greasy pants was the accepted costume in that rooming house, which was largely patronized by "transient" men, men just one stage above being derelict.

The usual outlook of landladies like Mrs. Brewer is one of cynicism and suspicion. She wondered about his being so well-off and what he was doing in her place at all.

She questioned him: "For the night?" No, he said, for the week. She showed him Room 8, at $10.50 a week her most expensive room. It was a kitchenette apartment with a stove and a refrigerator. He turned it down. She showed him 5-B, and he glanced around the room. There was no reason really for him to have looked at all. He had seen a thousand such rooms. A handle fashioned out of a metal coat hanger served for a doorknob. The inevitable unshaded light bulb, with a dirty string pull cord, hung from the ceiling. The "dresser" was a tired and rickety piece of Grand Rapids borax. The brown metal bedsprings sagged under a soiled, lumpy mattress. The "curtain" on the room's one window was limp, greasy and sooty, the window shade torn and frayed. The linoleum floor was cracked, turned up at the corners.

The place smelled with that heavy pungent odor common to every flophouse, jail and low rooming house in America, what is delicately called "pine" disinfectant.

While Ray was standing in the hall, Charlie Stephens, a

man with the reputation of being a lush, came out of his room next door, 6-B, spoke to Mrs. Brewer — and got a look at Ray. With only a glance at the room, Ray told Mrs. Brewer that he would take it. Having made sure that it had a view of the Lorraine Motel (unlike the first room she had shown him), Ray was satisfied. They went back then to Mrs. Brewer's office where Ray pulled out a crisp $20 bill and paid for the room. When he got his change, he left. It was only after he was gone that Mrs. Brewer realized that he had no luggage.

As Ray came out of Mrs. Brewer's office he bumped into "Uncle" Bertie Reeves, an old hotel clerk who had in his day seen every piece of shady business there was to see. He took a look at Ray as Ray went down the steps and out of the place.

Ray's white Mustang was parked on Main Street, and from there he drove directly to the York Arms Company. Ray told the clerk, Ralph Carpenter, that he wanted to buy a pair of field glasses. Carpenter offered Ray binoculars that cost $200.00, then a pair that cost $90.00, and when Ray started to walk out, Carpenter called him back and offered him a pair of $40.00 Bushnell binoculars. Ray bought them. The bill came to $41.55. Ray paid slowly, first two twenties, then a one, two quarters, and finally five pennies. He drove directly back to the rooming house, parked in front of Canipe's Amusement Company.

It was now about 4:45 P.M.

But he didn't get out. He just sat there. Mrs. Elizabeth Copeland who worked across the street at Seabrook Paint and Wallpaper Company noticed the car, mistook Ray's Mustang for a white Falcon owned by Charles Hurley, the husband of one of her co-workers. She told Mrs. Peggy Jane Hurley that Charles had come for her, and Peggy Jane went to the window. She said, No, that isn't Charlie's car. And she took a look at Ray. The bookkeeper, Mrs. Frances Thompson, was waiting for her daughter to pick her up. She went to the window and saw that it wasn't her daughter. She noticed Ray in the car.

Ray did not stir until five, when he got out of the car, went to the back, opened the trunk. He lifted out a bundle wrapped in a green and yellow bedspread, put the bundle under his arm, closed the trunk, and walked to the door of the rooming house and went inside.

---

On that Thursday morning, King had had another tense and unresolved meeting with The Invaders. It was another bad day for King, at least until the late afternoon when all of his own veteran staff began to gather around him at the Lorraine, where they also were staying. They had proven their courage against physical danger on the streets of dozens of southern cities and they were bound together by the hazards, the high hopes and the zeal they had so long shared.

Late that afternoon, they were all primping to go with King (or "Doc," or "Martin" — as most of them called him) to a soul food dinner. Their host was to be the Reverend Samuel B. ("Billy") Kyles, a local minister.

Abernathy was in King's room with him, while the Reverend Mr. Kyles came and went, urging them to hurry, insisting that the dinner was at 5:00 P.M., and that Mrs. Kyles expected them to be on time. King was a meticulous dresser, almost always appearing in a pressed black suit with narrow lapels, a white-on-white shirt, and a conservative narrow tie. He took his time shaving and dressing. He fussed with his shirt. The one he had chosen was too small. He couldn't button the collar. He had gained some weight.

As the men moved around the motel, they joked, and the party grew. They clustered around a Cadillac limousine which had been loaned to King by a funeral home for his stay in Memphis. The Breadbasket Band, a soul music group, had come from Chicago to play for King's rallies in Memphis. Could they come to Billy Kyles's for dinner? No, there were too many guests already.

King, now satisfied with his appearance, came out on the balcony. One of the men standing by the Cadillac yelled up: "Doc, this is Ben Branch who plays in our band."

"How are you, Ben?" replied King.

Branch waved up to King, who was leaning over the balcony, looking down at the men lounging easily around the Cadillac.

King remembered Branch. He called out in that melodious and emotionally-charged voice of his:

"Ben, I want you to sing for me tonight. I want you to sing 'Precious Lord.'"

That was the last sentence Martin Luther King ever spoke.

---

Ray may have bought the cheapest pair of binoculars from Carpenter, but they were precisely what he wanted. The Bushnells were 7-power — exactly the same power as his Redfield sight, would give him exactly the same image. King would appear to be thirty feet away. Now, with the binoculars, Ray went directly to 5-B, put his bundle down on the bed, unwound the bedspread from around the carton that held his rifle. He went to the window, pulled a chair over to it, looped the curtain back against the mantel, raised the shade, opened his binoculars, and sat down to watch. He focused across the garbage-strewn lot, down on the Lorraine, on King's room. The tableau of the waiting Cadillac, the men around it, the door to Room 306 was clear with that heightened clarity a lens, by its selectivity, seems to give an object. But the door stayed closed. Behind it, King was dressing.

There was an even more direct view of the Lorraine from the rooming house bathroom and Ray decided to have a look from there. The walls at Mrs. Brewer's were paper thin, and Charlie Stephens, next door in 6-B, the room between 5-B and the bathroom, heard Ray moving about, heard Ray go to the bathroom, return to his room, and return once again to the bathroom.

About 5:40 Willie Anschutz, another of Mrs. Brewer's roomers, tried to use the bathroom, found it locked, went away, came back, found it still locked, put his head in Charlie Stephens's room and complained. Stephens told Anschutz that the fellow in 5-B was in there.

It was probably on his second trip to the bathroom that Ray took his Gamemaster. He was going to make his shot from the bathroom. He raised the small window as far as he could, and knocked out the rusty screen. It fell two stories to the ground.

He rested the rifle on the windowsill and aimed it.

To do so meant that he had to stand in the bathtub, lean one arm against the wall. There was something inglorious in that, and something fatefully typical of Ray and his crimes. He was going to carry out the most important single act of his life and he had to do it with his feet in the old, stained, rooming house tub.

He watched through his binoculars until King came out on the balcony, until he was sure it was King. He aimed carefully and, at 6:01 P.M., he fired a single shot which hit Martin Luther King in his right jaw, shattering that side of his face, and which went on into his body to lodge in his vertebrae. King fell back on the balcony, mortally wounded.

Instantly, those people in the Lorraine courtyard pointed directly at the window where Ray had been.

Ray quickly went to his room, picked up the carton and the bedspread, wrapped the rifle in them, started down the hall. Willie Anschutz, bound again for the toilet, met Ray.

"Hey," he said, "that sounded like a shot!"

"It was," Ray calmly answered and went on along the hall, down the stairs and out the door.

Ray ran out the door carrying his bundle. At that moment something seemed to have flustered him. As he passed Canipe's window, which is set back from the sidewalk, he suddenly dropped his bundle, the rifle, the bedspread, there in the window's inset.

He got quickly into the Mustang and drove away at high speed, tires squealing.

He barely got away. Without telling King, Memphis police had put a security guard around the Lorraine. Cops had been stationed at a firehouse only a few steps away from the rooming house door. These policemen had fanned out along Main Street and, within minutes, one of them came upon Ray's rifle. Within fifteen minutes, the Memphis police radio broadcast a description of Ray and of the white Mustang.

But by that time, according to Ray's account, he was outside the city limits, driving south, in the gathering dusk, into Mississippi. He drove all night, east through Alabama, into Georgia.

---

He listened intently to his car radio as he drove. He was astonished at what he heard. The news broadcasts made it sound as if the killing of King was a national disaster.

"Jimmy didn't *dream* there'd be that much heat on him," says Jerry Ray. "It seemed like even before he got out of Memphis, he heard the F.B.I. was in it. The way Jimmy had it figured, Hoover would stay out of it. He figured Hoover hated King, that Hoover didn't want King to come to Washington on that march, and that Hoover wouldn't care if Jimmy did cut King off. Jimmy's thinking was that if King went to Washington he would get some strong laws passed. Even though Jimmy does break laws all the time, *he* goes by the law book. If King got the law changed, well Jimmy thought that would be serious.

"As for Memphis, Jimmy had it figured before he ever went there, that things wouldn't go too tough for him there. He thought the Memphis police were up in arms about King, and that the whole town was against King.

"Why, he even thought at one time he might be able to keep his car. He thought he might be able to go to Atlanta, pick up his stuff, and go to Mexico."

Ray may have been surprised that the F.B.I. was "in it," as Jerry said, but he did not panic. All his thoughts were already too deeply embedded in his own distortions. James Earl Ray sincerely believed that someday, sooner or later, he would not only be exonerated from his crime but that he would also be praised for it, that someday he would be able to identify himself, or allow himself to be identified as — well, it didn't matter how that happened, he wanted to be *known* as the man who killed Martin Luther Coon.

He drove directly to Capitol Homes, that fourth place he had circled on his map of Atlanta.

At about 8:00 A.M. on April 5, after a night of driving, Ray pulled into the project's paved parking lot. He got out of the car and walked away, but not without having been noticed by a housewife who had just got her children off to school.

Just as if he was not at that very minute the most widely and desperately hunted man in the world, he went confidently about his ordinary business. He felt intact at last. He had never quite felt so much *himself*, the self he thought he really was. All the threads of his life had at last been pulled together by his profound deed — the family's hopes that Jimmy was going to amount to something, that Jimmy was going to make up somehow for all their misery, atone for it and avenge it, his pro-German friend's hopes for him, Mabel Fuller's hopes for him, Ceal's and even Speedy's, and even those of Virgil Graves. He had been true to his own dreams, and to his almost obsessive conviction that he was a figure of destiny and, as he saw it, an American hero.

From Capitol Homes he went straight across downtown

Atlanta, back to Peachtree Street, where he had left his dirty clothes at the Piedmont Laundry. At about 8:30 A.M., he handed over his ticket and collected his bundle.

Sometime during the morning, it seems to have been his last act in Atlanta, he took the pains to mail off the final lesson in his correspondence course in locksmithing.

He had not forgotten his dreams that he would live a better life, that he would use his lessons, that he would somewhere soon be mixing drinks at a bar, talking and laughing with easy charm to his customers, winning over classy women, and lightly dancing the nights away.

At 11:30 A.M., he boarded a bus to go north, to Canada.

# Acknowledgments

First to my wife, Priscilla Johnson McMillan, without whom this book would not exist. Her unflagging and discriminating encouragement made the crucial difference.

Next to the band of helpers who have worked for me over six years, who came as typists or researchers and stayed to nag me, shore me up and make me feel I had to finish: Miamah Braddox, Louise Cole, Donna Everett, Katrin Fletter, Brad Leithauser, Laughlin McDonald, Margie Riesenbeck, Kitty Terjen, Beth Vogdes, Betty Vorenberg, Carol Watson, and May Louise Zumwalt.

I have been the beneficiary of generous help from many members of the psychiatric community, but several took special pains to bridge the gap between their world and mine. They are Doctors Jeffrey Andresen, William Binstock, Gordon Harper, John D. Griffith, Ross Grumet, Daniel Levinson,

John Mack, Bennett Simon and Alan Stone. Professor Bruce Mazlish, a psychobiographer, made several useful suggestions.

The members of the Group for Applied Psychoanalysis read the early chapters of the book and devoted one of their meetings to a discussion of them. As a result, I think I was able to avoid some errors of interpretation.

A group of psychiatrists at the National Institute of Mental Health took part in setting up a program for the computer of the National Medical Library out of which I received a bibliography of some five hundred articles and books that were pertinent to my subject.

Two people helped me understand some aspects of poverty. They are Professor Lee Rainwater of Harvard and Dr. Lola Ireland of the U. S. Department of Health, Education and Welfare. John Boone, former Massachusetts Commissioner of Corrections, went with me to the Missouri State Penitentiary at Jefferson City and saw many things that I missed. Professor Lloyd Ohlin, a criminologist at the Harvard Law School, read and made helpful comments on my chapters about Jefferson City. Charles Matthews, Director, Center for the Study of Crime, Delinquency and Corrections, certified me to the Illinois prison system where I got much useful help.

William Bradford Huie, the author of a book on the King assassination, generously made all his research material available to me. Henry Haile, former Assistant Attorney General of Tennessee, helped me check many facts of evidence. Percy Foreman, one of James Earl Ray's attorneys, introduced me to the Ray family. Superintendent Clinton Chafin of the Atlanta Police Department is an old and valued friend who has helped me with many other projects and was cheerfully ready to help again with this one. Leslie Dunbar of the Field Foundation opened several doors for me.

I don't know exactly how to express my gratitude to members of the Ray family for their help — to Mrs. Carol Ray Pepper, to John Larry Ray, to Jerry Ray, and to Jerry Raynes, their father. They told me their life stories and took what I have always thought to be a genuine interest in my book although they were torn between their loyalties to their brother and their hope that I would be the one to hold the mirror in which they could see themselves with more charity than society had ever seen them. Perhaps I have done so. They may not want my thanks, but they have them anyway.

G.M.
Frogmore
South Carolina
May, 1976

# Index

315